THE WARS OF MYRON KING

THE WARS OF MYRON KING

A B-17 Pilot Faces WWII and U.S.-Soviet Intrigue

James Lee McDonough

The University of Tennessee Press ★ Knoxville

The paper in this book meets the requirements of American National Standards
Institute / National Information Standards Organization specification Z39.48-1992
(Permanence of Paper). It contains 30 percent post-consumer waste and is certified by
the Forest Stewardship Council.

Library of Congress Cataloging-in-Publication Data

McDonough, James L., 1934–
The wars of Myron King: a B-17 pilot faces WWII and U.S.-Soviet intrigue / James Lee
McDonough. — 1st ed.
     p. cm.
Includes bibliographical references and index.
ISBN-13: 978-1-57233-675-9 (hardcover)
ISBN-10: 1-57233-675-7 (hardcover)
  1. King, Myron Lyzon, 1921–
  2. Bomber pilots—United States—Biography.
  3. United States. Army Air Forces. Bomb Squadron, 614th.
  4. World War, 1939–1945—Germany—Berlin.
  5. World War, 1939–1945—Aerial operations, American.
  6. World War, 1939-1945—Regimental histories—United States.
  7. King, Myron Lyzon, 1921—Trials, litigation, etc.
  8. Courts-martial and courts of inquiry—Russia (Federation)—
     Moscow—History—20th century.
  9. United States—Foreign relations—Soviet Union.
  10. Soviet Union—Foreign relations—United States.
  I. Title.
D790.263614th .M33 2009
940.54'4973092—dc22
[B]   2009015036

To Myron Lyzon King and his B-17 crew: William J. Sweeney III,
Richard I. Lowe, George E. Atkinson, Patsy DeVito, Ernest S. Pavlas,
Robert E. Pyne, Philip A. Reinoehl, and K. Hampton Speelman

Contents

Illustrations

Figures

Maps

Preface

IN 1944 AND 1945, WHEN I WAS TEN YEARS OLD, THE MARVELOUS AIR-craft of World War II fascinated me, whether Allied or Axis planes. I built models of several of those airplanes. One of my favorites was the four-motor Boeing B-17 Flying Fortress. My interest in the planes of that vast conflict remained with me as I grew older, fueling a lifelong, ever-broadening study of the war that culminated when, for a number of years, I taught a course in the history of World War II at Auburn University.

All of this helped prepare me to write about the experiences of Myron Lyzon King. While I was building models of war planes, and generally "playing war" with some of my boyhood friends in 1944–45, Myron King and his B-17 crew were involved in the real thing, first training in the United States and then flying combat missions over Germany. King and his crew served with the 614th Squadron, 401st Bomb Group, 94th Combat Wing, First Air Division, of the Eighth Air Force. They participated in an air war like no other before or since. Nor, in terms of a maximum development of propeller bombers and fighters, will there ever again be such bloody campaigning in the air.

For that matter, they were involved in a war like no other. Never before in history has a conflict been waged on such a destructive scale or on such a global scale. For millions of people worldwide, there never was a war so totally and intensely consuming. Those who compare the present situation to World War II obviously possess little knowledge of the conflict that raged in the late 1930s and the first half of the 1940s. Myron King's experiences in that unparalleled struggle were both fascinating and unique. And they were significant, particularly the events in Soviet territory. These proved not only adventurous but disturbing— disturbing relative to the Soviets, but perhaps equally disturbing relative to the Americans. It is a privilege and a pleasure for me to recount Myron's intriguing story. I hope that I have done it justice.

James Lee McDonough
October 2008

Acknowledgments

SEVERAL PEOPLE ASSISTED ME WITH THE PREPARATION OF THIS BOOK. First, I must acknowledge the invaluable contribution of Myron Lyzon King. Myron generously met with me many times, recounting his pilot training and combat experiences, as well as his unique adventure in Poland and Russia. Myron also assisted my research both by providing a copy of the transcript of his trial by court-martial and by permitting me to borrow several books that proved useful in developing his story. Without Myron's help this book would not have been written.

Two other members of the King crew rendered important assistance to my research. Navigator Richard I. Lowe and ball-turret gunner Richard A. Reinoehl wrote letters responding to my questions and contributing their memories of various events. Reinoehl, fortunately, kept an "Overseas Diary," which I found very useful. The diary enabled me to pinpoint several facts and occurrences, as well as occasionally providing human-interest comments for the narrative. I am grateful for the input of both men.

Also, I must thank George Menzel, a bombardier who served with the 401st Bomb Group. In the early 1990s, Menzel wrote a book about the B-17 Flying Fortress, known as "Maiden U.S.A.," and the crews who flew her—which included the King Crew. Menzel graciously shared some of his research materials with me. Most significantly, he sent me a copy of the petition for a new trial of King, prepared by Lieutenant Colonel John A. Doolan, United States Air Force, which analyzed the proceedings at the King court-martial, pointing out the numerous errors made during that trial and clearly, convincingly demonstrating the gross miscarriage of justice. Menzel also sent a copy of the various cables exchanged between U.S. military personnel at Moscow and Poltava relating to the King court-martial. Important, too, Menzel shared a letter by Leon Dolin, now deceased, who was King's assistant defense counsel at the court-martial; in that letter Dolin described, at some length, the bizarre circumstances of the trial as he recalled them years later.

⊅ I appreciate also the assistance of Myron's wife, Eleanor, and their son, Ron. Deserving recognition as well are Dr. Walter E. Brown and Dr. Vivian Rogers-Price of the Mighty Eighth Air Force Museum, Pooler, Georgia, and Ms. Marcie Green at the Historical Records Division, Maxwell Air Force Base, Montgomery, Alabama. The readers for the University of Tennessee Press caught some errors of fact that I made in an earlier version of the manuscript. Also, I wish to acknowledge the good work of Scot Danforth, director of the University of Tennessee Press; Gene Adair, manuscript editor at the press; and all other UTP staff members who assisted with publication. I am grateful to my wife, Nancy, and our daughters, Dr. Carla McDonough and Dr. Sharon McDonough, who read large portions of the book in manuscript form and shared with me their impressions of the work. To all who labored on the production of this book in any manner, I wish to convey a sincerely felt "thank you." I hope that any mistakes are few and trivial. Obviously, any errors are solely my responsibility.

Finally, as anyone with a little age on him or her and who has thought about the accuracy of memory, is aware, people do not always recall events correctly when they describe them years later. While I cannot guarantee that everything Myron King told me is unquestionably true, I do have good reason to believe that the story he recounted is substantially accurate. First, I could compare what he said years afterward with his trial testimony in 1945. Also, the trial testimony of three crew members who were with King in 1945 assisted me further in testing the truth of his account. In some instances, what King told George Menzel in an interview in the early 1990s could be assessed by what he told me in 2006 and 2007. Phil Reinoehl's diary at times provided still another check. Three letters written by Richard Lowe confirmed some of the incidents that King related. And, of course, there are significant books and records about the operations and missions of the Eighth Air Force. Perhaps I should also add that I first met King soon after he came home from the war and heard him then describe, in general outline, his experience in Poland and Russia. All in all, I am convinced that his memory of those stirring events remained basically sound and consistent through the years.

Prologue

THE AIRFIELD LAY ABOUT SEVENTY MILES NORTH AND SLIGHTLY WEST of London. Designated Station 128, in the parlance of the United States Army Air Forces, the base was located between the villages of Deenethorpe and Upper Benefield, Northamptonshire. Familiarly known to the airmen as Deenethorpe, it was home to the four-motor Boeing B-17 Flying Fortresses of the 401st Bombardment Group, U.S. Eighth Air Force. Dawn would not be graying the east for another three hours or more, but the area already pulsated with activity, as hundreds of men and machines had come alive despite the early morning darkness. The date was Saturday, February 3, 1945.[1]

Several years had come and gone since the pompous Hermann Göring—flying ace of World War I, recipient of the Blue Max, head of the German Luftwaffe, and a man of "monstrous" girth (to borrow Sumner Welles's term), with an ego of like proportion—uttered his euphoric boast (and anti-Semitic slur) that, if an enemy bomber ever penetrated the Fatherland, "My name is not Hermann Göring. You may call me Meier!" Quite some time had passed, too, since the blustering Reichsmarschall's condescending, dismissive proclamation that the entrance of the United States into the war "would have little effect."[2]

Hundreds of missions had since been flown by the Allies, and thousands of heavy bombers had toured the Fatherland, striking the German Reich again and again. Yet, February 3, 1945, would be a special day. The Eighth Air Force was going to "Big B," as the airmen commonly referred to Berlin. From the onset of the war, bombing the German capital symbolized the ultimate objective for many an airman, both American and British. Not only were the bombers going to "Big B," but they were going in massive force. The mission would be an awesome display of U.S. air power, sending a thousand heavy bombers and a total strength, including the fighter escorts, of more than two thousand Eighth Air Force planes over the capital of the Reich. The air leader of the Eighth for the historic strike would be the able and experienced Colonel Lewis E. Lyle, commander of the 379th Bomb Group.

Never before had the Eighth hit Berlin with such strength. Additionally, the timing, thought some, could not be better. A wrathful Red Army lay within thirty-five to fifty miles of Berlin, and its blood-soaked advance, ranging over a wide swath of the eastern Reich, had packed the capital with large numbers of refugees, mostly women, children, and the elderly. They had fled before the path of the revenge-seeking Russians as they pillaged, raped, and murdered their way westward. A major air raid under such conditions, targeting the German War Ministries that were concentrated in the central city, as well as military installations, would create even more problems than usual for the German authorities in Berlin. And, obviously, it would kill a huge number of civilians. In Nazi-occupied Europe, General Carl A. "Tooey" Spaatz later wrote, "We never had as our target . . . anything except a military target—except Berlin."

This is not to say that Spaatz favored the mission. An advocate of precision bombing, with oil targets as his primary concern, Spaatz thought that striking the center of Berlin was of little value. Other brass at High Wycombe (the Eighth Air Force headquarters on the outskirts of London) agreed. Above all, General James H. Doolittle, commander of the Eighth Air Force, was against the raid. Significant military targets in Berlin were few, and Doolittle, on principle, did not believe in targeting civilians. Besides, terror bombing did not break German morale, which Doolittle considered the British night attacks to have proven.

But orders had come from higher up. Specifically, General George C. Marshall, the army chief of staff, was ready to try anything that might shorten the war in Europe. Worried about growing American war weariness, he wanted to get on with the struggle against Japan, the conclusion of which seemed far away. Generals Dwight Eisenhower and Omar Bradley also favored any measure that might possibly lessen the losses of U.S. ground forces in Europe. This was particularly true after the surprise German counteroffensive of mid-December 1944. While Eisenhower declared that he had always favored "precision targets" for U.S. air power, he then stated that he was open to "anything that gives real promise to ending the war quickly." And so the controversial Operation Thunderclap, as the February 3 attack on Berlin was known, had been approved and ordered by the highest American military authorities.[3]

Group briefing for the 401st took place at 0300 hours, at which time the crews had already been awake an hour and a half, with some men feeling they had hardly slept at all. They had washed, dressed, shaved (generally the men thought shaving advisable to minimize the discomfort in an oxygen mask), and breakfasted on fruit juice, cereal, eggs, or pancakes, with toast and coffee. "If they gave you eggs you *knew* you were about to go a long way," remembered one of the pilots. Briefing for the mission then followed, held in the customary large Nissen building, at one end of which a huge map of western Europe, concealed behind a curtain, awaited unveiling. As if in a movie—only this was for real—an instant of drama occurred as the group commander entered the building, strode between the rows of seated men to the front, and drew back the curtain.[4]

There, marked with colored ribbons and pins, lay the mission route, the rendezvous points for the escort fighter planes, and the target for that day, February 3: Berlin! Reactions, expressions, and comments varied, but one opinion was universal. Nobody thought this mission would classify as a "milk run," the common description for an easy assignment when little enemy opposition was anticipated. "Big B" meant a deep penetration into Germany, entailing nine or ten hours of flying time. It meant encountering enemy fighters, even if the Luftwaffe had been greatly reduced in strength from the earlier days. Probably, Messerschmitt 109s (ME 109s) and Focke-Wulf 190s (FW 190s), the small, single-engine, fast, and heavily armed aircraft that had long been the staple of German defense, would be trying to break through the shield of American fighters; certainly they would be seeking out any crippled, straggling bombers. Perhaps also Messerschmitt 262s (ME 262s), the Luftwaffe's new twin-engine jet fighter, faster by far than any fighter flown by the United States or Great Britain, would be prowling the skies in search of easy prey. And "Big B" meant heavy antiaircraft fire (or "flak," as it was commonly known, short for *Fliegerabwehrkanonen*, antiaircraft artillery), which, since the protective cover of long-range fighter escorts had become the norm, typically constituted the greatest menace the big bombers faced.[5]

The briefing lasted about thirty to forty minutes, revealing—and what an attention-grabber it was—that this mission would attempt to strike the Reich capital with more bombers than ever before in a single mission. Engines were to be started at 0630 hours; taxiing would begin at 0645, with the first bomber taking off at 0700. The briefing included approximate target time, bombing altitude, route from the Initial Point (IP, from which the bomb run began) to the Mean Point of Impact (MPI, the actual target for the bombs), predicted flak activity, and the weather forecast of heavy clouds over the continent but clearing at the target. Also, the group received warning that they would be flying within thirty-five to sixty miles of the Russian lines advancing on Berlin. Possibly Russian aircraft (fighters) would appear near the target area. If accosted by a Soviet plane, the bomber commander should "drop feet [wheels] and flaps," fire the red flare gun, and follow the Russian. This was not a particularly appealing thought, constituting yet another unpleasant scenario possibly awaiting some unfortunate crew. Then there were words of encouragement and the opportunity for questions. Meanwhile, as the flight crews were briefed, the ground personnel, already hard at work for some time in the cold, dark morning (the base was blacked out in case the Luftwaffe should surprise with a night attack), continued their task of preflighting the planes.[6]

Ordnance and armament men were hauling and loading the twelve five-hundred-pound bombs carried by each Fortress and supplying the .50-caliber machine gun ammunition for every aircraft, although the guns would not be loaded, as a precaution against accidental firing, until the bombers were airborne. Flak protective suits and steel helmets were also delivered for each crew. And all around the field, crew chiefs and assistant crew chiefs of every plane were busy checking out the engines. Their toughest work, physically, was hand-pulling the heavy propeller blades to turn the motors, thus removing oil build-up in the cylinders.[7]

Then, one by one the motors were started, run up, and held at full power. The mechanics looked for any indication of a possible malfunction as they monitored the oil pressure, turbo-supercharger, and magneto. With the performance pronounced satisfactory, the engines were shut down to await the gas truck's visit, when fuel tanks would be topped up to the full load of over twenty-eight hundred gallons of high-octane gasoline. The mechanics also checked out electrical and hydraulic functions and inspected the tires, flaps, ailerons, elevators, rudder, and trim tabs—actually, everything that could be examined while the plane was parked. Ground personnel strove to complete all preflight operations before the air crew showed up to man the particular Fortress designated to them for the mission. Little wonder that crew chiefs, who always maintained the same aircraft regardless of who flew it, thought of that bomber as "their" plane.[8]

★ ★ ★

The time was between 0500 and 0530 when First Lieutenant Myron L. King, pilot, and his crew, part of the 614th Squadron of the 401st Bomb Group, arrived in the big truck at the hardstand, a concrete circular pad where the plane assigned to them for the mission was parked. Crews typically were expected to be at their bomber at least an hour before engines were started. Thus the pilot had time to fill out the required forms and, together with the crew chief, walk around the aircraft for a last-minute inspection. Gunners could carefully examine their weapons again and clean them once more, if necessary, before installation. Everyone had ample time to see that all was in order to carry out his assigned duty. And usually, for those who smoked (although King did not), there was time for another cigarette or two before climbing aboard the plane.[9]

Once more the King Crew would be flying aircraft number 44-6508, a silver B-17G—a Fortress model readily identifiable by the chin turret, which housed two forward-firing .50-caliber machine guns. Bearing the name "Maiden U.S.A.," she was a plane whose large, framed, graceful portrait in flight has for many years adorned one of the walls at the United States Air Force Museum in Dayton, Ohio. The Maiden would be flying her thirty-fifth mission on this day. Myron King and his crew, with twenty missions to their credit, were beginning to think of the Maiden as "their" plane (although it is highly doubtful that the crew chief would have approved of such a claim), having flown her twice as many times as any other B-17—a total of six missions with the Maiden, five of them coming since the first of the year. Whenever the Maiden was ready to go, King now flew her, and on February 3, she appeared to be performing perfectly.[10]

Unlike some missions, there was no delay that Saturday morning. Promptly at 0630 hours, the green flare went up from flying control, the signal to start engines. First into action always was the motor driving the electrical generators, its Curtis-Wright Cyclone power plant cranking the big, five-hundred-pound, three-bladed Hamilton Standard prop, which coughed, caught, and then, with a blast of smoke from the exhaust, began spinning too rapidly for the eye to follow. Soon all four motors were roaring, as King and his copilot, William J. Sweeney III, ran them up, repeating the checks earlier carried out by the crew chief.[11]

What a show it was: the planes beginning to taxi as scheduled, fifteen minutes after the start-up of engines, the pilots of each bomber waiting to turn in behind the aircraft they had been instructed to follow. The 614th Squadron was putting up nine planes, while all four squadrons of the 401st would marshal a total of thirty-nine bombers and one monitor. It was quite a scene: forty planes with 160 open-exhaust engines, each developing twelve hundred horsepower and every one of them sounding, thundering at once. Takeoff would be from runway 23, a six-thousand-foot stretch of eight-inch-thick concrete. Its length offered the fully loaded bombers more time to stay on the ground, more time to increase speed before liftoff, than either of the other runways, which were eighteen hundred feet shorter.[12]

At 0700 hours, right on time, the green light signaling "go" to the lead aircraft flashed from the checkered flying control van, drawn up on the left side of the runway head. With all throttles advanced to maximum power, the first plane roared down the runway. Within about thirty seconds, the aircraft next in line released brakes, beginning its full-power takeoff roll. Myron King, not surprisingly, does not recall just where he was positioned in the takeoff sequence that morning. The important thing, when he released brakes with all motors revved to a shattering roar and headed down the runway, was to keep the main gear on the ground (with only the tail wheel coming up) until near the end of the runway. Only then, having built to a maximum speed of 110 to 120 miles per hour, did he take off, drawing the Maiden smoothly away from the earth. Its undercarriage retracting, the thirty-thousand-ton plane sustained a strong, shallow climb out from the base. King and crew were on their way to Berlin for the second time, the first time with the Maiden.[13]

"After take off each bomber normally kept a straight course for at least two minutes," wrote Roger A. Freeman, preeminent historian of the Eighth Air Force, "and then proceeded to the group assembly area, climbing at a predetermined rate—usually 300 feet per minute at 150 mph Indicated Air Speed (IAS)." Assembling and maneuvering a formation of heavy bombers was anything but easy. It proved extremely difficult when a huge number of planes, as on this day, were involved. Exact headings, speeds, and timed legs to fly had to be observed—and all the more carefully in bad weather conditions, which occurred much of the time. Midair collisions posed a constant risk in a dark, clouded, early-morning sky. And even though weather at takeoff was excellent for a change, the sky was still dark. One airman recalled a midair collision, recording that he watched "two burning aircraft as they fell, one in a flat spin, into a smoldering wreckage on the English countryside."[14]

Myron King, who had great respect for his copilot, said William J. Sweeney was "very good at formation flying." This gave King a measure of comfort during the maneuvering that often took place in the clouds or, as on February 3, in the dawn's first light. Having gained assembly altitude and once over the familiar Cottesmore Buncher (a radio tower broadcasting a coded signal), the bombers first formed elements of three as they flew left-hand orbits, with trailing aircraft turning inside their leader to catch up. In like manner each three-plane element turned inside the leading trio to gain their assigned place and so constructed squadron formations. Then squadrons rose to circle into group and wing formations, at last heading eastward for the channel crossing and the European continent.[15]

The 614th Squadron was flying the high element in the high formation, with King and crew in position as the left wing of the three-plane right echelon. This placed King almost directly behind the lead airplane of the squadron's lead trio, while flying about four hundred to five hundred feet higher than the leader. (The low squadron would fly about four hundred to five hundred feet below the lead, and off to the left; such staggering of altitudes was designed to strengthen the defensive firepower of the combat box, keep bomb patterns tight while avoiding dropping them on other bombers, and make German antiaircraft fire less effective.)[16]

Once headed eastward and out over the channel, the gunners test-fired their weapons while the clouds ahead gradually became heavier, making the weather prognosticators' assurance of cloudy conditions over the continent seem more likely. Maybe Berlin, too, would be covered up, which, of course, would lessen the chances of accurate flak. Soon the escort fighters, hundreds of them, appeared: P-47s, P-38s, and most notably, the P-51s. King said the fighters "just made a big circle. It was like flying through a huge tunnel, all those fighters to the outside of you, ready to take on any German planes that came up. You were 'as snug as a bug in a rug' in that circle. The Germans didn't want to come near those fighters."[17]

An airman in another 614th B-17 thought "a super colossal show was on." He wrote that more than a thousand heavy bombers were "creating a bomber stream that stretched continuously from the Dutch coast all the way to the target, Berlin, the capital of Hitler's Third Reich." That night, when safely back at Deenethorpe, George Menzel wrote home to his family that the event was "the most thrilling thing I have ever participated in." Colonel Lew Lyle, air leader of the mission and thus the first to bomb Berlin, declared that he was one-fourth of the distance back to England before he passed "the tail-end of the great procession of outward-bound bombers."[18]

★ ★ ★

Coming up on the IP for the run to the target, King and crew were flying at the assigned bombing altitude, more than five miles up, experiencing a strong tail wind of seventy-five-plus miles per hour and a typical temperature of around forty-five degrees below zero. In accordance with the forecast, the weather over Berlin had cleared, distinctly revealing the primary targets for the leading aircraft: the German War Ministries, the Tempelhof marshaling yards, and the munitions factories. (General Doolittle, although he had been instructed to aim for the city center, nevertheless had altered the targets to better fit his ideas of how strategic bombing should be conducted.) With cloud cover gone, antiaircraft fire, later officially described as "moderate to intense, accurate for altitude and deflection," seemed to be everywhere. Twenty-four bombers were lost on this mission and most of them to flak, which one bombardier, Alvie Smith of the 401st Group, remembered as "very intense, particularly for ten minutes during and after the bomb run."[19]

Banking left and northward for the forty- to forty-five-mile bomb run, King observed that the target area, despite the clear sky, already had disappeared from sight, obscured by flames and heavy smoke from the tons of exploding bombs unloaded by the planes flying ahead of him. During the bomb run the Maiden's flight path had to remain straight and level, of course, as King and crew watched the flak bursts all around them—flak so thick a man sometimes smelled it through his oxygen mask, concussions so violent that the plane shuddered and men's bodies shook. Survival depended inordinately on good luck, and doubtless the crew was hoping their good fortune would hold one more time.[20]

It did not. King and Sweeney both realized they were about to be hit. Perhaps others of the crew did also, depending upon the direction in which they chanced to be looking at that dire instant. "It happened shortly after we dropped the bombs," recalled King. The Germans were firing 155mm shells, he said, and they were "exploding at our exact altitude." These particular shells were readily identified "because they go off in big white clouds," King explained. "The 105mm explosions are gray and the 88s are black," he continued. "The 155mm explosions go off four in a row and in a straight line (whump, whump, whump, whump). Like plotting a course, when you see the first and second shells explode, then you know where the third and fourth explosions are coming." King had seen number one go off, and two go off, and "I knew the third would get us."[21]

Fortunately the third explosion barely missed being a direct hit, in which case the plane likely would have broken into two pieces with the gas tanks instantly burning or exploding. As it was, King said, "when that thing went off, I thought the whole plane would disintegrate." The shell had exploded on the port side, close to the nose and the number-two engine. The impact, continued King, "went north and south, with metal ripping through the wing and the oil cooler of the number-two motor."

The number-two engine "ran away like crazy" and, if not stopped, "would tear up the airplane." King instantly reached up and pushed the feather button to cut that engine. Nothing happened. Again he pushed it, and still again. He then told Sweeney, "You try it." The co-pilot made several attempts, also unsuccessfully, before King resumed the effort. Moments seemed to drag by—"Five to ten minutes," thought King, "with that thing going crazy." He said, "I felt like giving up, and I was letting off on the button when I heard it growl. I pushed back in on that button and, at last, that propeller's blades turned into the wind and stopped."[22]

No sooner had number two been feathered than King and Sweeney realized the number-four engine (right outboard) was running away also, "which we could not even hear before, because of the noise from number two." Flak had also struck "east and west," penetrating through the nose of the plane, creasing and bloodying navigator Richard I. Lowe's neck near the bottom of an ear. It had cut his throat mike off but luckily missed a vital point by an inch or so. Fortunately, too, King was able to feather the number-four engine without any difficulty.[23]

Then came decision time. If King headed back to England with two motors gone, while bucking a head wind of seventy-five to one hundred miles per hour, the Maiden would not be able to keep up with the rest of the bombers, even if its fuel proved sufficient for the trek. German fighters always kept alert for crippled bombers that were unable to keep pace with their formation. The enemy knew a straggler represented a likely and relatively easy "kill," especially if no American fighter escort was present to shepherd the big plane home. Protective fighter cover all the way back was not a certainty; and if a third motor should fail—always a possibility—the plane would have no hope, while facing such strong winds, of making it across the channel, whatever the circumstances otherwise. Thus, turning toward England had to be considered a long shot.

The possibility of flying across the North Sea and putting down in Sweden crossed King's mind. But not for long. If he should be forced to ditch in the North Sea, King knew, as certainly did all the crew, that a man could not hope to survive long in that extremely cold water. Perhaps, if the sea were not too rough, they might belly in without any man being seriously injured. Maybe they might successfully extricate themselves from the aircraft before it sank, inflate a life raft, and scramble safely aboard. And if they did, what then? King had never learned how to swim. (Incidentally, his mother's two brothers had drowned in the Hudson River, one trying to save the other.) Naturally, King wanted Sweeney's advice. "What shall we do?" he asked. Without hesitation or qualification, the copilot answered: "Don't go back. Head for the Russian lines." Pilot and copilot were in agreement.

Another B-17 pilot, Lieutenant Verner F. Daley, who had also lost two motors to flak, did opt to try for Sweden. His plane was a bit special, having been "christened" some months back by Princess Elizabeth and named "Rose of York" in her honor. The "Rose of York" was flying its sixty-third mission with a senior BBC reporter on board. His name was Guy Byan, and for some time he had sought permission to fly with an American crew on a bombing mission. Last seen over the North Sea, neither the plane nor anyone on board was ever heard from again.[24]

King made the best decision. He turned eastward and headed for Russian-controlled territory. Before takeoff, he had been provided with coordinates for an emergency Russian landing field, if necessary. The wind would be behind him. Russian lines were not far away and the Maiden, at high altitude, could glide thirty miles should the other engines fail.

American fighter planes at once spotted the crippled bomber as she turned away from the formation, flying eastward once more. King said four P-51 Mustangs quickly came up alongside as an escort and accompanied him as far as their fuel would allow. When they had to leave, the fighters came in close, one at a time, waggled their wings and waved good bye. Sixty-one years later, King remembered, "I can still see them now . . . waving. . . ." And he added, "When that last one left us, I really felt alone."[25]

1 ★ A Passion for Flying

"THAT AIRPLANE WAS THE MOST DANGEROUS AIRPLANE I HAVE EVER flown." Thus commented Jimmy Doolittle more than fifty years after he won the 1932 Thompson Trophy and set a new land plane speed record while flying the red and white Gee Bee Sportster, symbolically adorned with 7-11 dice painted on the side of the fuselage. Extraordinarily hot to handle, the plane had an appearance that for many aviation enthusiasts proved unforgettable. The Gee Bee featured a big Pratt & Whitney 750-horsepower Wasp engine, encased in a short but huge barrel of a fuselage with a relatively small wing and a tiny fin and rudder in the back. Doolittle said that he flew it because he thought the Gee Bee would be the fastest aircraft in the race. His fearless flying success (previously he had won the Schneider Cup floatplane race) established Doolittle as an aviator second only to Charles Lindbergh in fame. Also, the Thompson triumph established the volatile Gee Bee as the most notable of all American racing planes up to that time.[1]

Myron Lyzon King was about six weeks shy of his eleventh birthday when Doolittle won the Thompson Trophy. Doolittle's exhilarating victory in the Gee Bee inspired young King to build a model of the famous plane—and look forward to the day, hopefully not too distant, when he himself would learn to fly. King grew up during an enchanting era that appropriately has been hailed as the Golden Age of Aviation: from about 1920 through the 1930s. That period was a colorful, spectacular, but dangerous time for aviators—an era of widespread daring, far-reaching achievement, and unwavering faith and optimism in the future of humans as masters of the skies. The year 1932, in addition to Doolittle's triumph, had already seen Amelia Earhart (in a day when women were not supposed to do things like flying) become the first woman—and only the second person—to span the Atlantic Ocean solo. She and her single-engine Lockheed Vega touched down in Ireland on May 20, exactly five years after "Lucky Lindy's" famed groundbreaking achievement. Like Lindbergh, too, Earhart afterward enjoyed a New York ticker-tape celebrity parade.[2]

Within three months of Earhart's feat, Louise Thaden, in tandem with Frances Marsalis, took off from Long Island, New York, only about sixty-five miles from King's boyhood home, and remained aloft—while refueling time and again in the air and changing oil every twelve hours—for a record 196 hours (eight days). Thaden, who had already won the first National Women's Air Derby—a race from Santa Monica, California, to Cleveland, Ohio, which some wags dubbed the "Powder Puff Derby"—soon became even more famous as "the gal who beat the guys." In 1936 she flew a Beech Staggerwing C-17R to victory in the prestigious Bendix Transcontinental Air Race, an event previously won exclusively by men. (Some considered it THE premier air challenge of the day—in America, at least.)[3]

It was a time—that Golden Age of Aviation—unlike any other. A host of brave men and a few equally brave, adventurous, determined women, all of whom, regardless of sex, had been possessed by a passion for flying, reveled in the exotic young days of aviation. What red-blooded boy of the 1930s would not have been caught up and captivated by the seemingly constant and ubiquitous achievements of "those daring young men [and women] in their flying machines"? So it was with Myron King.

Born October 22, 1921, at Hampton Bays, Long Island, New York, King grew up as a resident of the Good Ground neighborhood in the heart of the fashionable Hamptons. Myron's father, Walter King, had become internationally known as a designer and milliner of ladies' hats. After studying at a New York decorating school, the elder King (having saved eighty dollars, according to the family story) purchased a ticket to Paris and entered some of his hats in a major show. Not only were his hats well received, but additional good fortune followed when word got back to New York that the American ambassador to France had commented to this effect: "Why, King's hats are better than any others in the show."

Walter King knew, of course, that wealthy New York families favored hats from Paris. While enjoying the sights offered throughout that "City of Light," his eyes chanced somewhere to fall upon the name "Lyzon." Liking both the look and the sound of the word, he decided to call his business, soon set up in the Hamptons, Lyzon. It became a favorite of fashionable ladies—the Rockefeller women, the Vanderbilts, Mrs. Henry Ford and her daughters-in-law, Mrs. Al Smith, and so on—of New York and elsewhere. Hats by Lyzon appeared on the cover of *Vogue* and in the pages of *Harper's Bazaar*. And when Myron King, shortly after World War II, established an art gallery in Nashville, he likewise named his business Lyzon.[4]

Hampton Bays in the 1930s proved an excellent site for observing all manner of aircraft. King said Amelia Earhart passed over Hampton Bays en route to Newfoundland, from which she launched her Atlantic solo flight. King's father told him that Charles Lindbergh (Myron being only five years old at the time), after taking off from Roosevelt Field, Long Island, in his Ryan-built "Spirit of St. Louis," flew over their home as he winged toward Paris. When one of the giant dirigibles of the late twenties and thirties would fly the Atlantic, it followed the coast line of Long Island. King said his teachers at Hampton Bays Grammar School would dismiss class, allowing the children to go outside and watch the magnificent airship pass by. It was one of the young boy's earliest and most vivid memories of air travel. In his mid-teens, when the illustrious but ill-fated *Hindenburg* was flying, King took a 16mm movie of the great German ship as she droned along the shore line.[5]

With a touch of amusement, King recalled Douglas "Wrong Way" Corrigan, who in 1938 flew solo from New York to Ireland, in a 1929 Curtiss Robin, after being denied permission to make the flight. Corrigan claimed a compass error caused him to fly east rather than west to California, his supposed destination. While King did not actually see Corrigan's plane, he was well aware of the highly publicized incident.

There was a very memorable aircraft sighting by King about 1939 or 1940. He watched, as it flew low over Hampton Bays, a large, majestic German seaplane that was beginning to make Atlantic crossings seem almost routine. Easily identifiable by a distinctive inverted gull wing and high tail marked by twin fins and rudders, the Blohm und Voss HA 139 was operated by Deutsche Lufthansa and powered by four six-hundred-horsepower Junkers Jumo diesel engines. A heavy trail of smoke poured back from each diesel, and King gazed in fascination until the German craft disappeared in the distance.

The 1930s indeed witnessed a plethora of exciting, marvelous aircraft. Howard Hughes produced his rakish, record-setting, racing plane. He also flew a Lockheed Model 14 Super Electra to a 1938 round-the-world time of three days, nineteen hours, and fourteen minutes. Walter Beech encored his fast, beautiful Staggerwing (some versions of which, flown "balls to the wall," as Beech liked to express it, could hit 250 miles per hour, a speed superior to most, if not all, U.S. fighter planes of 1934–35) by introducing a completely new airplane. The 1937 Beech Model 18-A was a twin-engine, low-wing design, with twin fins and rudders, all-metal executive transport, or small airliner, capable of taking off and landing on short grass airfields when necessary. Elegant, sleek, and dependable, the "Twin Beech" pushed Beechcraft planes to the forefront of the competition.

Lockheed Aircraft also enjoyed a major presence in the skies with its swift, single-engine, highly recognizable Model 9 Orion. Other notable Lockheed planes were the Vega (well known because the famous pilots Wiley Post and Amelia Earhart flew it) and the twin-engine Model 10E Electra, flown by Earhart on her fatal round-the-world venture, when she probably veered off course and ran out of fuel over the Pacific. The Wedell-Williams Gilmore Red Lion Racer of the mid-thirties made an unforgettable impression. So, too, did the Boeing P-26A "Peashooter," the U.S. Army's first monoplane fighter and first all-metal warplane. And in 1938 the Bendix race winner again was a woman, Jacqueline Cochran. She flew Russian Long Island immigrant Alexander de Seversky's powerful, single-engine, all-metal, low-wing, military-type P-35, the forerunner of the outstanding P-47 Thunderbolt fighter of World War II. All these and more were aircraft known by Myron King in his late elementary and high school years.[6]

★ ★ ★

King was not just a New Yorker. His mother came from Chattanooga, Tennessee. The family, generally speaking, spent spring and summer in the Hamptons and fall and winter in Chattanooga, living near the base of Lookout Mountain in the St. Elmo neighborhood. And it was in Chattanooga that Myron took his initial ride in an airplane. Views of Chattanooga, from any of the surrounding ridges and mountains, are imposing after dark when lights are on all over the city, around Moccasin Bend of the Tennessee River, and also dotting the enveloping heights of Signal Mountain, Raccoon Mountain, Missionary Ridge, and Lookout Mountain. The murky outline of the slope and northern point of Lookout, site of the famed "Battle Above the Clouds" during the Civil War, looms particularly massive and majestic on the horizon. At night the serene panorama suggests a tastefully composed work of art. After nightfall one Christmas Eve, pilot W. L. Hill took Myron up in a plane for the first time, affording them a view of the Christmas lights of Chattanooga and Lookout Mountain. It was quite a treat and one the boy never forgot.[7]

Of necessity, moving back and forth between New York and Tennessee every year, King became adept at school transfers. While in the seventh or eighth grade, he started a model airplane club in Chattanooga, once building a rubber-band-powered model that could fly for an impressive number of minutes. He and the club were thrilled to have their picture and an article about them appear in a Chattanooga newspaper.

It was also in Chattanooga that King met Leroy P. Sullivan, a young fellow whom he came to consider his best friend and with whom he went to school from the first grade through high school: "We walked to school together; rode the bus together; spent a great deal of time with each other." King said he felt closer to "Sully" than to either of his brothers, which is hardly surprising in view of Sullivan's interest in flying and the military. As King recalled, it was at Chattanooga City High, where he and Sullivan were in the same class, that Sullivan rose to colonel (top man) in the high school ROTC.

Afterward, when the war started, Sullivan was attending the University of Chattanooga, but the U.S. Army Air Corps required two years of college work for one to qualify for pilot training. Rather than wait, since he did not have two years of college, Sullivan headed for Canada, where there was no such hindrance, and joined the Royal Canadian Air Force. Before long he was flying a fighter plane—the famed Hawker Hurricane—in the European war.[8]

King, meanwhile, continued with his college work in Nashville at David Lipscomb College, then a two-year institution, and worked part-time at Vultee Aircraft plant, which was located beside Nashville's Berry Field, the city airport. All through high school King had frequented the woodworking shop (which he said was of quite good quality) at Chattanooga City High. Consequently, he felt well prepared for the tasks assigned to him at the Vultee plant, which mainly involved making patterns. Among his various endeavors, King worked on the Vultee Vengeance and the Vultee Valiant, the latter a plane he flew when training as an aviation cadet.[9]

While in Nashville, he courted Eleanor Goodpasture, a tall, attractive young woman whom he had met while still in high school and whom he eventually married. It was also in Nashville in 1942, not long after the Japanese attack on Pearl Harbor, that King enlisted as an aviation cadet. He recalled that he was walking across the campus at Lipscomb on Sunday afternoon, December 7, 1941, when he heard the news of the attack that plunged the nation into war. A friend called out: "Did you hear the news? The Japs have bombed Pearl Harbor." King said that his first thought was, "Where in the world is Pearl Harbor?" Many an American wondered the same thing. During the time that the young man waited on his call to active duty, which came in 1943, he got in some more college, attending the University of Chattanooga for a semester. Turning twenty-one years old on October 22, 1942, King stood five feet, eight inches tall. He had become a slim but strong, good-looking young fellow, finally about to realize his dream of becoming a pilot.[10]

★ ★ ★

As Myron King grew to maturity, passing through his high school and college years, another coming-of-age story simultaneously unfolded. A saga quite different in nature from that of King, its development nevertheless eventually crossed paths with the young man (as well as thousands of other young men) and forever impacted his life. On July 28, 1935, a Boeing aircraft, designated Model 299, flew for the first time. Said to have been called a "flying fortress" by an enthusiastic Seattle newspaper reporter when the new plane was rolled out of the hangar for initial public view, the four-engine bomber's design owed much to several of the company's earlier aircraft. In particular, its forebears included the Model 200 Monomail of 1930, a single-engine, low-wing craft with retractable gear, sometimes hailed as "the first modern air transport"; the sleek, twin-engine B-9 bomber of 1931; the twin-engine 247 transport, a commercial craft intended to carry ten passengers; and the Model 300, a four-motor transport project, which later would fly as the Boeing 307 Stratoliner.[11]

In August 1935, the big (103-foot-plus wing span) Model 299 flew the twenty-one hundred miles from Seattle to Wright Field in Dayton, Ohio, nonstop, in a record-breaking nine hours at the then-amazing average speed of 233 miles per hour. In competition at Wright Field, the new Boeing "Fortress" proved far superior to the twin-engine Martin and Douglas bombers and surpassed all of the army's requirements for speed, climb, and range. Shortly before testing ended, however, the Model 299 crashed and burned on takeoff. Even though pilot error—a failure to unlock the tail surfaces before takeoff—was determined to be the cause, this disaster proved a serious setback to the plane's development.[12]

Those who favored smaller twin-engine bombers, along with skeptics who proclaimed the Model 299 "too much airplane for one man to handle" (or even two men, for that matter), grew more bold in their objections to Boeing's new bomber. Also, some individuals who stood to gain financially by the development of warplanes other than those built by Boeing may well have blended their dissenting voices with the rising negative chorus. Consequently, instead of making an anticipated order for sixty-five bombers, the Army Air Corps only wanted a service test order of thirteen following the 299's crash. And perhaps Boeing was fortunate to get even that.[13]

The Boeing bomber's potential, however, for all who possessed unfettered eyes to see, was undeniable. Boeing made various improvements that included, most notably, equipping the craft with more powerful engines; improving the landing gear; fitting rubber deicer boots to the wing's leading edge; equipping the plane with self-sealing fuel tanks and cowl flaps for controlling engine temperature, as well as covering the flaps with aluminum rather than fabric; and devising a checklist for pilot and copilot to prepare the plane for takeoff, flight, and before and after landing. Boeing also began studying the possibility of using turbo-superchargers for high-altitude performance.[14]

For more than three years the plane was flown extensively without any serious accident, during which time it gained an enviable reputation for being ruggedly built and safe to operate. In fact, during World War II the B-17, as it soon came to be known, would enjoy the lowest accident rate of any American military aircraft. In 1938 six B-17s made a goodwill trip to South America, visiting Peru and Argentina; this was soon followed by another group of seven flying to Brazil. The "Flying Fortress" was clearly emerging as America's most recognizable and successful front-line, long-range bomber.[15]

Yet, the Boeing company, at one time, was nearly ready to give up on the B-17, for there seemed to be no financial future in building the plane. The Air Corps balked at the original contract price, and Boeing was losing money even at that price. Fortunately for the United States, Boeing believed so strongly in the future of the plane that the company persevered, continuing to improve and strengthen the craft. Otherwise, the heavy-bomber program well might have failed at the worst possible time—just before World War II. And so the B-17 lived; and, in the final analysis, Boeing made a great deal of money, producing a total of 12,731 of the big bombers.[16]

★ ★ ★

During the warm but pleasant summer days of 1939—those last short days before Adolf Hitler's *Wehrmacht* invaded Poland and plunged Europe, and eventually the world, into war; those innocent days when an era was ending, when concerned minds inevitably gravitated to European tensions and the possibility of armed conflict, yet took comfort in the thought that surely war would not come, that somebody would back down, that important people would compromise, that leaders would act rationally, that somehow the sanguinary nightmare of the Great War would not be revisited—the king and queen of England came to the United States. In Washington, D.C., as the royal couple rode with President and Mrs. Roosevelt in a glittering procession of cars toward the White House, a flight of ten B-17 Flying Fortress bombers roared over the route in salute. For nations on the brink of war it was a fitting symbol.[17]

2 ★ And Then There Was a War On

MYRON KING WENT THROUGH TEN WEEKS OF PRIMARY FLIGHT TRAIN-
ing near Union City, Tennessee, a small town located in the northwest
corner of the state and so named for the junction of the Nashville &
Northwestern Railroad with the Mobile & Ohio line. He soloed in a Ryan
PT-22 (Primary Trainer–22), a single-engine, low-wing, open-cockpit,
two-seat all-metal craft that was the Air Corps's first monoplane trainer.
Not a few pilots, all over the country, lost their lives during flight training.
King experienced a "close call" a week or so after soloing. Having just
taken off and climbing, he was approximately a hundred feet in the air,
obviously a crucial point, when the engine started sputtering. Instantly—
"and if I had stopped to think," he said, "I wouldn't have made it"—
he switched the fuel selector to the opposite tank. "The engine caught
immediately and I flew on," he recalled. The gauge on the first tank had
stuck on "full," but in reality that tank must have been nearly empty when
King began his takeoff roll. He had been fortunate indeed. He also said
that he had made a practice of thinking about what he would do in such
dangerous situations in order not to waste any precious seconds.[1]

It was not long afterward that the young man learned of the death
of his close friend Leroy Sullivan. "Sully," after flying a Hurricane in
North Africa for much of his combat career, had more recently been
piloting a Hawker Typhoon. He died when the Typhoon's engine failed
shortly after taking off from a base in East Anglia, the plane crashing

and becoming instantly engulfed in flames. Understandably, King was quite upset. He wanted to fly to Chattanooga and visit Sullivan's widowed mother. His request to fly was denied, so he got on a train instead and rode to Chattanooga to see her. Although he carried no authorization for the trip, no military authority ever questioned him. "I don't think any M.P. would have stopped me anyway," he said. "Not if I told him what I was doing." Some days later a letter from Sullivan arrived in the mail, written the night before he died and telling King about flying the powerful Typhoon.[2]

Next for King, having mastered the PT-22, came basic flight school (another ten weeks) near Searcy, Arkansas. This involved flying the Vultee BT-13, also a low-wing but a bigger, faster plane than the Ryan. Vultee liked to name their aircraft with inspiring variations of words beginning with a "V." They called the BT-13 the "Valiant." But pilots soon named it the Vultee "Vibrator." Since nearly everything in the plane rattled and vibrated—the canopy, the instrument panel, the rudder pedals, and doubtless unseen parts as well, all of which were really troubling if one thought about it much—no moniker could have been more applicable. The plane introduced the young pilot to more complexity, a variable pitch prop, and other modern equipment. The gear, however, did not retract. Myron probably spent more time in the Vultee than he would have preferred, learning acrobatics and how to fly cross-country, at night, and in formation.[3]

One thing King did like, though, was the opportunity for an occasional "buzz" job. "Buzzing" was perhaps every pilot's favorite thing to do: they would swoop in low over a house, a business, a road, or a car. Give it a buzz, they thought, and create some excitement for the folks on the ground, as well as fun for the pilot. People on the ground, some of them, enjoyed seeing a plane fly right over their heads—but not everyone. Dick Bong, who became America's top ace of World War II, shooting down forty Japanese planes while flying the P-38 Lightning in the Pacific, got into trouble once while training at Hamilton Field, California. He flew so low over a lawn that his prop wash blew clothes off the line, and the irate housewife complained about the antic. Fortunately, Bong was about to go overseas, and the matter proved of no consequence.[4]

Myron King's favorite buzz job while flying the Vultee "Vibrator" occurred at Searcy. In fact, he enjoyed it so much that he did it again and again. His girlfriend from Nashville, Eleanor Goodpasture, was then in school at Harding College. Harding was located on the outskirts of Searcy, a very small town in the early 1940s with farm fields all around. The Church of Christ–associated college had a daily, mid-morning chapel service, and King managed to time his flights perfectly. He approached the campus at low level, with the motor roaring as loudly as possible—and anyone who ever heard a Vultee "Vibrator" in action knows it could make a mighty noise—and buzzed the students as they gathered for chapel.

Undoubtedly, judging from the manner in which King recounted the flights, the young pilot thoroughly enjoyed the stir his antics created on campus. "I never would have buzzed the town like that," he said, "because I would have been in trouble; but Harding was outside the town in farm country." As for Eleanor, she said that "all the kids at Harding," which was a small school, knew who was flying that plane. "He came over at least a half-dozen, maybe a dozen times," she recalled. "Sometimes when I heard that plane coming, and always during chapel, I wished I could hide."[5]

And then came ten weeks of advanced flight school at Blytheville, Arkansas. King had been selected for multiengine specialization, which suited him just fine, because he liked the idea of flying a big airplane. His twin-engine training took place in a Beechcraft AT-10 Wichita, powered by Lycoming R-680, 295-horsepower motors. Regardless of which training phase might be involved, or with which aircraft one might be engaged, danger always lurked near at hand, threatening to claim the lives of young pilots and sometimes in a totally unexpected manner.

Among King's many memories of flying, none is more vivid, he said, than an incident at Blytheville. A large number of planes were airborne when fast-approaching severe weather led the base to recall all aircraft at once. Following another plane on final approach, as he had been instructed to do, King was to land short, with the lead craft landing long—that is, much farther up the runway. However, the plane in front landed short, forcing King to land even shorter and brake very hard. "I came within a few feet of a collision," he said. "I may have forgotten a lot, but I remember that day vividly."

On another morning at Blytheville, a mechanic was running up the motors on an AT-10 but had failed to secure the brakes. The plane jumped the chocks and ran wild into a briefing hut, ripping it apart. Only minutes before, King and a number of other men had been inside the building that the AT-10 devastated. Clearly, they had dodged the proverbial bullet.

The AT-10 Wichita, in the judgment of most pilots, was not a memorable airplane, as it was planned and manufactured strictly for training purposes. Constructed primarily of wood and fabric, the AT-10 was designed to save metal for aircraft intended for combat. "Most pilots couldn't wait to get away from it," wrote authors Warren Bodie and Jeffrey Ethell, "and into combat aircraft." Myron King, like many who flew the AT-10, did not regard it with any particular fondness. But it served its purpose: transition from single- to twin-engine flight and training in long, cross-country navigation. It was quite a contrast, though, when King finally advanced to the big, graceful, and powerful B-17 at Columbus, Ohio.[6]

The B-17Gs that King learned to fly at Lockbourne Field, today's Rickenbacker International Airport, were far superior to that original Boeing Model 299 of the mid-thirties. "These were the Flying Fortresses of wartime newspaper headlines," wrote historian Edward Jablonski, "possibly the most celebrated, best known and widely publicized aircraft of World War II." The B-17G, in addition to the previously noted improvements over that first fortress, was also larger than the 299. The fuselage measured about 6 feet longer, for a total of nearly 75 feet. The wing span remained the same at 103 feet, 9 inches; but the elevator stretched another 10 feet. The vertical tail was much larger than that of the 299; this attention-grabbing, swooping fin, when coupled with the increased elevator span, contributed to greater flight stability. The big tail, which led airmen to fondly dub the fortress "the big-ass bird," also provided accommodation for a gunner and two .50-caliber machine guns, something no one had been concerned about when the first fortress had flown.[7]

Compared to the B-17G, the 299 Model seemed rather modestly armed, even if it had been admiringly christened a "flying fortress." The 299 possessed no power gun turrets and provided only five .30-caliber machine gun emplacements. Already, before the G models, all machine guns had been standardized at a more deadly .50-caliber. Also, the B-17G brandished a total of twelve guns, including two .50-caliber pieces in the new Bendix chin turret, and could mount a thirteenth if so desired. The aircraft continued to feature a Sperry upper turret behind the cockpit, manifesting two .50-caliber guns, plus a Sperry ball turret, or belly turret, located behind the bomb bay, where the trailing edge of the wing engages the fuselage. The ball turret likewise featured two guns; and a gun was mounted on each side of the waist, as well as each side of the cheek. Two more, of course, provided stingers in the tail. A thirteenth could be placed atop the radio compartment.[8]

The B-17G flew faster than the 299, but not as fast, due to the increased weight and drag of its chin turret, as the earlier E and F models of the fortress. Those planes, with each Curtis-Wright Cyclone power plant developing 1200 horsepower, boasted a top speed approaching 320 miles per hour, quite fast for a four-engine bomber of that era. Most G pilots, however, welcomed the frontal firepower of the chin turret, even though it chopped the top speed of the craft to less than 300 miles per hour. Prior to the chin turret's advent, many German fighter pilots thought a head-on attack offered the best chance of bringing down a B-17. Flying a parallel course but carefully staying out of range of the bomber's guns, the enemy pilot would speed three miles or so ahead of his intended prey, then turn sharply into the B-17's flight path and make a fast-closing, head-on assault. Usually the German fighters flew in waves of two to four, wing tip to wing tip, holding fire until almost certain to strike the bomber somewhere, and diving away only at the last possible instant before colliding with the American plane—sometimes closing to a hundred yards, or even seventy-five yards, before they broke away.

"The psychological impact of such attacks on B-17 crews was understandably chilling," wrote air war historians Stephen McFarland and Wesley Newton. Not only did the bomber crew have to endure "the drawn-out tension from enemy fighters flying parallel for several minutes," continued McFarland and Newton, "but then [they] had the trauma of these planes suddenly turning directly into their faces with guns blazing at a closing rate of over 500 mph." Some forward-facing crewmen became virtually paralyzed with fear that, even if not struck by fire from the German guns, the fighter well might ram them, particularly if an American shot happened to kill its pilot or that pilot miscalculated the breakaway point by so much as a fraction of a second. "Those frontal assaults by German fighter planes put the fear of God in you," said Robert Morgan, pilot of the "Memphis Belle," the most famous U.S. bomber of the European air war. "It was bad in the cockpit, but it was far worse in the nose," continued Morgan. "The bombardier and the navigator were sitting in a big bay window, open to the sky, with nothing but a pea shooter to defend themselves. And sometimes that pea shooter got so hot in combat that it bent." When the B-17G came on the scene, though, with two .50-caliber machine guns firing straight ahead, enemy pilots began reevaluating that tactic. The head-on attacks did not cease altogether, but they became less frequent.[9]

The B-17G had a range of approximately 2,000 miles when carrying a 6,000-pound bomb load at a cruising speed of 182 miles per hour, and its ceiling was 35,600 feet. Takeoff speed was 110 to 115 miles per hour, following a run of 3,400 feet; landing required a distance of 2,900 feet, after touching down at 90 miles per hour. The plane carried 2,810 gallons of fuel in its wing tanks; and it weighed in at 36,135 pounds when empty, with a normal gross of 55,000 pounds and a maximum takeoff weight of 65,500 pounds, while providing for a crew of nine or ten. King really liked the big bomber and reveled in learning to fly the plane: "You had to be able, blindfolded, to touch and describe all eighty instruments before the instructors were satisfied." And certainly he felt a sense of pride upon qualifying and receiving his silver wings as a four-engine pilot of a prime bomber in the USAAF.[10]

Among his most valuable accomplishments, King had learned to fly the Fortress first with three engines, and then with only two. As time would prove, he definitely needed that exhilarating experience. In fact, King practiced making landings with two motors out and both on the same side of the plane. "You really had to kick that wing [the one with both engines out] up in the air," he said. King also reminisced about the smell of a B-17. The strong, unforgettable scent of grease, oil, and high-octane gasoline was perhaps unpleasing to some people but affectionately recalled by King—and probably by many veterans who flew the Fortress and came to know her as a very special aircraft.

D-Day, June 6, 1944, occurred during King's Columbus training. Afterward, whenever possible while flying the B-17, he tuned in to the latest news about the fighting in Normandy. Memorable also was the Independence Day celebration in Columbus, which featured a big, colorful parade, climaxed by a low-level flyover of B-17s, one of them piloted by King. Soon after his graduation as a B-17 pilot, he received orders detailing him to Avon Park, Florida, located in the central part of the state. There he met the crew with whom he would go to war. Thenceforth known as the King Crew—a crew was always labeled by the pilot's last name—eight young men joined King, each having qualified in his specialized program as a gunner, navigator, radio man, engineer, copilot, or bombardier.[11]

From that point on, the King Crew would be training as a team. There would be cross-country missions, formation flying, bombing exercises, and aerial gunnery practice—whatever might be required of them once in combat. The basic objective was to weld the nine men into a finely tuned air unit, both as specialists and in personal relationships. Generally speaking, that is precisely what occurred. "Perhaps at no time in the history of warfare," wrote an intelligence officer of the U.S. Eighth Air Force, "has there been such a relationship among fighting men as existed with the combat crews of heavy bombardment aircraft, notably in the Eighth Air Force in World War II."[12]

No member of the newly formed King Crew pleased Myron as much—and his presence could not have been more unexpected—as the copilot, William J. Sweeney III. King had met Sweeney months earlier, not long after Myron first began his Air Corps training. Sweeney possessed outstanding qualifications and had compiled an excellent record; King quickly sized up the young man as a top-notch fellow. King assumed that Sweeney had gone on to train as a fighter pilot, which King knew was Sweeney's goal. In fact, a superior officer had held Sweeney back when he normally would have gone to bomber pilot school, hoping soon to place him in fighter-pilot training, as the officer knew that fighters were what Sweeney really wanted.

But then came a new commanding officer, and with the Air Corps needing more copilots at that moment, he not only destroyed Sweeney's dream of becoming a fighter pilot but also ended the possibility that he might be first pilot of a bomber. Sweeney, along with everyone else immediately available, was sent to copilot school, his excellent qualifications for first pilot proving of no consequence. King related his surprise, upon seeing Sweeney again, in the following words: "When I climbed into that B-17 in Avon Park and got in my pilot's seat, I could hardly believe who was already sitting in the copilot's seat! None other than William J.

Sweeney III." King continued, "I really felt fortunate. Right then, I decided that I was going to do everything I possibly could to keep him there as my copilot. Because, you see, I knew how good he was. And if it had not been for the two of us, we probably would not have survived."[13]

❧ Sweeney, who grew up in the Philadelphia area, had already completed a premedical program before enlisting in the service, and when King went through preflight training with him at Maxwell Field in Montgomery, Alabama, Sweeney was at the top of their class. After the war, Sweeney earned his medical degree and became a successful, well-known obstetrician and gynecologist in New York City. King thought, based on their conversations, that what Sweeney would have really liked, more than being either a pilot or a doctor, was a career as an actor on the New York stage.[14]

The King Crew's bombardier, initially, was Richard Smith. However, before going overseas, Smith was reassigned and replaced by, as often was the practice at this stage of the war, a gunner who also would release the bombs. He became known as a togglier. A bombardier was only necessary in the lead plane of a formation. At the instant the lead plane dropped its bombs, all other planes in that formation, with a togglier doing the work, released theirs. The King Crew's togglier was Robert E. Pyne.

Pyne hailed from Oakland, California. An interesting character, he was the only member of the King Crew possessing status as a combat veteran. Having flown eighty missions as a gunner in the Mediterranean Theater, Pyne found himself back in the United States with an assignment as a gunnery instructor. The job did not prove to his liking. King described Pyne as an adventurous type, easily bored, who seemed to thrive on the adrenalin rush generated by danger. Thus he volunteered for a third combat tour. However dangerous the mission might be, Pyne never appeared to be the least bit afraid. In fact, he did not wear a flak suit and never bothered to even put on a flak helmet unless he spotted flak. Nor did he see any need for test firing the machine guns over the English Channel when outbound, which was a customary practice. "If you don't fire it, you don't have to clean it," he reasoned. And some missions, indeed, never saw a gun fired.[15]

Richard I. Lowe became the navigator of the King Crew, obviously a key man every time that the plane took to the air. Lowe grew up in Roswell, New Mexico, and particularly remembered being subjected to "lots of shots [inoculations]" upon entering the service. Unfortunately, he said, after he completed his initial phase of training, "the good old army had misplaced my medical records," and thus "I had to take all the shots again." Lowe also recalled that upon being asked what he wanted to do in the Air Corps, "I chose navigation, as I liked mathematics; little did I know that navigators and bombardiers were usually washed-out pilots." The tallest member of the crew, he was a handsome guy, whom King considered an excellent navigator. He said Lowe would have been "an asset to any crew." While a B-17 formation followed a lead navigator, every navigator was expected to plot the course to the target and always be abreast of where he was. The lead ship, a priority target of the enemy, might be shot down. Or, if any plane were forced to leave the formation, for whatever reason, clearly its navigator was the man to guide the ship home. King said he always felt that, with Lowe as navigator, his crew was in competent hands. After the war, Lowe completed a degree in electrical engineering; later he earned an MBA at Harvard and worked in such diverse locales as Pearl Harbor, Peru, and New England.[16]

The engineer for the King Crew, who also doubled as top turret gunner, was Ernest S. Pavlas, from Caldwell, Texas. A B-17 engineer was supposed to know more about the plane—its engines, its equipment, its armament—than any member of the crew, including the pilot. The engineer worked closely with the copilot, monitoring engine operation, fuel consumption, and the like. Positioned immediately behind the pilot and copilot, the engineer often called out the speed on takeoff at ten-mile-per-hour segments: seventy, eighty, ninety, one hundred. Also, he assisted the bombardier/togglier in proper preparation of the bombs and bomb racks. As top turret gunner, the engineer also had a perch that, if enemy fighters attacked, gave him a great vantage point. King had high praise for Pavlas, whose engineering ability proved quite valuable. Returning to Texas after the war, Pavlas spent his career in the insurance business.[17]

Certainly the King Crew represented a cross section of the United States, with New York, Tennessee, Pennsylvania, California, New Mexico, and Texas already noted. The Hoosier State joined the mix as well, represented by the ball-turret gunner, Philip A. Reinoehl of Brazil, Indiana, a small town situated directly east of Terre Haute. The very tight position in the Sperry ball turret was not designed for a large man—

Reinoehl was five feet, nine inches tall—or a claustrophobic person. Statistically, however, according to one source, it proved to be the safest station in the B-17, when numbers and types of battle wounds are considered. On the other hand, in the event of sudden crisis, the ball-turret gunner was the crew member least likely to escape. Reinoehl kept an "Overseas Diary," which he began on October 23, 1944, the Monday that the King Crew left Hunter Field in Savannah, Georgia, flying to Bangor, Maine, and from there ultimately to England and the Eighth Air Force. Reinoehl's diary has proved useful in several instances and in varying ways. All his life, except for the war, Reinoehl has resided in Brazil. A good mechanic, he has worked on cars and farm equipment, maintained a farm, and enjoyed flying his private plane, while he and his wife reared six children, three girls and three boys.[18]

Making up the rest of the King Crew were a radioman and two more gunners. Patsy DeVito, from Long Branch, New Jersey, operated the radio, "the least glamorous job in a B-17," according to authors Dan Patterson and Paul Perkins. Residing in the center of the fuselage, the radioman "sat for hours on end, static crackling in his ears," as he periodically gave position reports. He also helped the navigator in taking fixes on the location of their aircraft and kept in touch with base headquarters. Still other tasks demanded his time, such as sending any distress signal that might prove necessary and responsibility for the first-aid equipment if any of the crew should be wounded. King recalled that DeVito often demonstrated a good sense of humor. For example, King remembered DeVito's voice over the interphone once asking: "Why do the motors have to have those big, three-bladed fans on them? You'd think that rushing through cold air, like 40 degrees below zero, would keep those engines cool without them!"[19]

The waist gunner on the King Crew was K. Hampton Speelman, known simply as "K." Born in Michigan but growing up in Ohio, he hoped to be a pilot and did qualify, on the written examination, for aviation cadet school. However, because of a perforated eardrum (the result of a wrestling-match injury), Speelman failed the physical test. When he was later drafted, his ear had healed, and for a while he still tried to make the aviation cadet program. However, becoming worried that if he did not get into pilot training he might end up with a highly unwelcome position in the army, Speelman requested aerial gunnery school and successfully completed the program at Kingman, Arizona.

A waist gunner, speaking statistically, manned the position where the most casualties were suffered. His was the station least protected, considering the combined threat of enemy fighter attacks and frostbite. Also, the cramped quarters in which he maneuvered might result in entanglement with his oxygen equipment, electrical connections, and interphone—not to mention the possibility of slipping on shell casings. A waist gunner really needed to be agile. Earlier in the war, B-17s usually had two waist gunners, but due to the tight quarters, as well as increasingly effective long-range fighter protection, generally only one person manned the position in the latter part of the conflict.[20]

The crew's ninth member was the tail gunner, George E. Atkinson of South Pasadena, California. When it came to confinement in close quarters, perhaps the tail gunner's position rated second only to that of the ball-turret occupant. A tail gunner had to stretch out and maneuver around the tail wheel well, and then, once in place, kneel on a seat similar to that of a bicycle to fire his guns. The man had to possess good knees. Definitely his station was critical: more than anyone else, he was in a position to spot enemy fighters approaching from behind, one of their favorite tactics. Atkinson celebrated his nineteenth birthday only a few weeks before going into combat. After the war, he worked in construction, eventually establishing his own company in Alaska.[21]

★ ★ ★

Through the summer months and into the fall of 1944, in the hot Florida sunshine, the King Crew honed their skills, and learned to work together well. As the aircraft commander, King was pleased and said, without qualification, that he had an excellent crew. Naturally he felt closer to some than to others, but he considered every man competent in his particular assignment. No doubt the individual crew members, if so inclined, could have recalled varied and interesting events, both in Florida and throughout their service. But most are now deceased.[22]

Once while training at Avon Park, as King recalled, he was flying a practice bombing mission during which the bombs did not release over the target. (Of course, real bombs were not used for training. Instead, smoke bombs were dropped on the practice runs; thereby one could tell if the target had been hit.) At the end of this particular bomb run, which encompassed several miles, a bomb did fall out as the bomb bay doors were being closed. Apparently it dropped over a little community named Frostproof. The next day a newspaper heralded: "Frostproof Bombed!" Luckily, by the narrowest of margins, no one was killed. A woman who was sitting in her chair, according to the newspaper, got up for some reason only an instant before the bomb hit the chair. Myron did not know with absolute certainty that the bomb that destroyed her chair was the one dropped by his plane, but he was not aware of any other plane that had accidentally dropped a bomb some distance beyond the target.[23]

When navigator Richard Lowe arrived in Florida—the last member of the crew to join up—the King Crew began their navigation training flights. Lowe said one of the first was to Cuba, an interesting over-water destination. He also recalled that "King was surprised to see me remain in the nose of the plane on takeoff." Most of the crew gathered in the radio room for takeoff, but Lowe enjoyed the panoramic view from the front as the legendary bomber lifted into the sky.[24]

The objective of another training flight, which also carried the crew over the Gulf of Mexico, entailed finding the Dry Tortugas, that little stretch of small islands seventy miles directly west of Key West, where the pre–Civil War Fort Jefferson stands as a national monument. The Dry Tortugas mission proved easy enough, but the crew's first night mission presented more difficulty. The target was Atlanta—simply to find the city in the dark and then return to home base. After flying north for some distance, King looked down upon a large, lighted community and, being familiar with Atlanta, recognized at once the well known "Five Points" of the city.

Confidently, he announced, "That's it. Let's go home." Navigator Lowe apparently made no objection. King and crew returned to Avon Park and landed, only then to discover, to their surprise, that they had gotten back to Florida an hour or more before the other planes flying the same mission. King soon figured out, after consulting with Lowe and Sweeney, that they had not gone far enough north, and Myron had mistaken Macon for Atlanta. The rather embarrassing episode did convey a positive lesson. Identifying an objective at night could be more difficult than one might have supposed.

Avon Park's location seemed ideal for those who appreciated hot weather. The site lay about 150 miles northwest of Miami in the very middle of the state (thinking east–west), about 65 to 70 miles from the Atlantic Ocean at Vero Beach and an equal distance from the Gulf of Mexico at Bradenton. Phil Reinoehl recalled going into Avon Park on weekends, as there seldom was opportunity to journey as far as the beach. Richard Lowe, however, said he did get to West Palm Beach but never as far as Miami. Copilot Sweeney arranged for his wife, whom he met when both were attending Maryville College in Tennessee, to be with him while the crew was stationed at Avon Park. And when Eleanor Goodpasture, by that time engaged to Myron King, came to visit King for a few days, she stayed with the Sweeneys.

As copilot, William Sweeney often shared flying time with King. Reinoehl remembered that once, while they were landing, with Sweeney at the controls, "a tire went flat, but Sweeney had the plane under control." Reinoehl explained that "a lock ring, that held the tire on, had broken, and the tire came part of the way off." Determined to prove there was nothing wrong with his flying, "Lieutenant Sweeney carried the broken ring to headquarters," said Reinoehl, "to show that he had not lost control [of the aircraft]" but had confronted a problem caused by a failure of equipment—a piece of metal.

Myron King's version of the Sweeney landing differs a bit from Reinoehl's. King remembered that they were shooting landings, and the copilot brought the bomber around rather sharply in his approach to the runway (perhaps, suggested King, indulging his fighter-pilot mentality just a bit) and failed to fully straighten up the big plane before touching down. The result, as all soon learned, was a busted wheel. King said some of the crew proceeded—mostly in good nature, he thought—to give Sweeney the devil once they learned what happened.

While at Avon Park, recalled Reinoehl, "we flew once a day and nearly every day." The goal was to familiarize each man with his position and especially with the use of the guns at that station. Also, they flew a lot, said Reinoehl, "so Lieutenant Lowe could navigate." On days when they did not fly, the crew attended meetings, learning more about "what was expected of them," as Reinoehl expressed it. Lowe re-called a bit of excitement—and King confirmed his account—of the first time they saw a coral snake that "paid a visit to the latrine." King said there was a boardwalk, like one would find at a beach, leading into the latrine, and they became daily accustomed to spotting the brightly colored reptile "hanging around." Nobody bothered the creature—perhaps surprisingly, considering the common fear of poisonous snakes.

One of the last training missions at Avon Park involved high altitude flying. King said he took the bomber up to forty thousand feet, which is about four thousand feet or so above the plane's specified ceiling. The mission went off without any problems, but King remembered it well, for upon landing he learned of the death of another boyhood friend, Michael Hornet, with whom he had grown up on Long Island. Hornet was flying a U.S. Navy fighter, learning to land on aircraft carriers at the time. He had seen flames spew up from the engine and, thinking it on fire, had bailed out, apparently striking some part of the plane in the process. Seriously injured, unconscious, maybe already dead, he never pulled the rip cord on his parachute. Strangely, the plane flew on to land, basically undamaged, in a field. Remnants of a mechanic's oil rag on the engine told the tale. It was the rag that had caught fire, producing the flames that led the unfortunate young pilot to conclude his plane was on fire.

After successfully completing their training at Avon Park, the King Crew's next stop was Hunter Army Air Field in Savannah, Georgia. There they would be assigned a new B-17G in which to fly to England by the North Atlantic route. Before final departure for England, the crew was given a short R&R (rest and recreation). They could fly either to New York or Chicago. "Myron having roots on Long Island," recounted Richard Lowe, "naturally chose New York." Lowe wrote that he had never been to New York "and certainly preferred New York to Chicago." Thus the navigator was quite pleased with the decision and added that "King and his brother who lived in the city treated us all royally." And then it was back to duty for the King Crew.[25]

After the crew's months of preparation in many parts of the United States, war at last was at hand. But no amount of training could possibly have imparted the overwhelming, all-consuming reality of the thing they were about to experience.

3 ★ From Savannah to Northamptonshire

"WHEN WE GOT TO SAVANNAH, WE WERE GIVEN A FEW DAYS TO CHECK out the plane assigned us for the overseas flight," King said. "Then suddenly, in the middle of the night," he continued, "they woke us up, gave us a mimeographed flight sheet, and told us to take that B-17 immediately to Shreveport, Louisiana." Hurricane season on the Atlantic coast is June through December. It was then mid-October, a hurricane was nearing Savannah, and those valuable bombers needed to be flown to safety at once.

"So we took off, sometime after midnight, and flew that plane to Shreveport. We were arriving unannounced, and as we approached the airfield, I called for landing instructions," recounted King, his tone of voice and facial expression showing a touch of amusement. "Tower, this is B-17," he said, mimicking the manner in which he remembered talking. "Give us directions for landing." The tower came back with a simple response: "Follow the plane in front of you."

Accordingly, said King, "I got behind the plane in front of me, going down base leg, preparing to land." Then the aircraft in front, which was a smaller ship than the B-17, turned left, lining up to land on the shorter of the two runways. Myron, of course, was not familiar with either runway. "So I pick up my microphone, excited like," he said, "and call: 'Tower, do you know this is a B-17? Do you really want us to land on the short runway?'" King then heard laughter over the mike coming from the tower, followed by the instruction: "No, B-17. You are cleared to land on the long runway."

Generally speaking, explained King, you were expected to land on the first third of a runway. "As we made the turn to land," he said, "the tower came in again: 'B-17, number one on landing; for your information, that runway is sixteen thousand feet long.'" King would learn, shortly afterward, that the runway he had declined to land on was seventy-five hundred feet long. "The longest runway that I had ever landed on was five thousand feet," he confessed, and "I had never even seen a runway three miles long. Thus I just flew down to the tower, which was about centered on the side of that long runway, and landed. Those guys in the tower obviously got a kick out of that incident."[1]

Meanwhile, the hurricane that threatened Savannah had moved on, its destructive winds staying out to sea and causing minimal damage to the Georgia coastline. The time soon came for the King Crew to head back to Savannah. King decided that en route he should make a slight detour—maybe more than slight—northward to Tennessee. "Now this B-17 we were flying was straight from the factory, and we were headed to England, and there were no numbers on it," he said. "That's very special: a B-17 with no numbers, and every pilot's favorite thing was to buzz, and my fiancé is back in Nashville. Even if they did catch up with you, you are on your way to England and the war. They are not going to say anything except 'Good Luck!'"

Thus King proceeded to Nashville, flying "the Great Circle Course," as he jokingly characterized his return from Shreveport to Savannah. He planned to buzz David Lipscomb College, the school he had attended and to which his fiancé had by then transferred, and for good measure, while so close, to buzz her nearby home as well. Approaching from the south, King swung the big bomber left and made a circle around the college. "We just flew low enough to make some noise, and get everyone's attention so they would come out and look at us." Then, expanding the circle, the B-17 first disappeared to the south, only to come roaring back momentarily and flying much lower. "When I got back to Lipscomb, I came in real low, lower than the smoke stacks," he said. "They would have washed you out, if you had done that in cadets," he added. Next, he banked the bomber sharply around and flew right over Eleanor Goodpasture's house, slightly above the tree tops.[2]

Then King headed for Chattanooga, thinking he might as well buzz his own home in St. Elmo, before turning south and flying back to Savannah. Circling around to the east of the city, he came in over Missionary Ridge. Dropping much lower after clearing the ridge, he headed toward the foot of the famous incline railway on Lookout Mountain, which is still in operation today. "Until then," King said, "I had not fully realized how much space it takes to turn a B-17 around. I'm making this circle, looking at all the sights, and suddenly I glance up and I'm headed straight into the side of Lookout Mountain. I was forced to make a much steeper turn than I ordinarily would have made, and that's really when I learned rule number one of why the Air Corps did not want you to buzz!"[3]

Afterward, it was on to Savannah, where King and Sweeney became confused about the location of the airports—rather an easy mistake when one considers the proximity of the city airport to the Army Air Field. Having already dropped the B-17's landing gear, they radioed for landing instructions. Back came the rebuke: "B-17, pull it up and go away. You are not at our airfield." Retracting the wheels, they flew a short distance farther south, at last touching down safely at Hunter Army Air Field. The hurricane (nobody named them back then) had delayed the King Crew a bit, but after having their picture taken—a good photograph which today is displayed on a wall at the Mighty Eighth Air Force Museum near Savannah—they took off at 7:30 a.m., October 23, 1944, winging first toward Bangor, Maine, and then on to the war in Europe.[4]

But why not do a little more buzzing en route? Their plane still displayed no numbers, and Sweeney's home, just south of Philadelphia, lay almost directly in their flight path. King turned the bomber's controls over to Sweeney, who thought buzzing his home a grand idea, and sat back to enjoy the view. After flying for a short time, suddenly Sweeney exclaimed: "What's all this black stuff just ahead of us?" An array of apparent explosions had appeared in their front. Robert Pyne, the toggler veteran of scores of missions, happened to be in the cockpit at the time, right behind King and Sweeney. "That's flak," he said. "Probably dummy shells, but they are telling us to get the hell out of here." Their plane was approaching Washington, D.C., heading in the general direction of the capitol, and obviously they had alarmed somebody. At once

Sweeney swung the plane away from Washington, of necessity making a little detour on their journey to the Philadelphia area. King mused: "We might have been the only B-17 to ever draw flak in Washington, D.C." Neither King nor Sweeney, however, allowed that episode to deter them from another buzz job.

On to Philadelphia they flew, where Sweeney soon identified his home, and dropping lower, began making a big circle around the place in preparation for streaking directly over it. "I was going to let him buzz his house as many times as he wanted," recalled King, who undoubtedly enjoyed the fun. But alas, unexpectedly, their joyride experienced an abrupt interruption. Over the radio crackled a no-nonsense voice: "B-17, you are cutting off commercial traffic landing at such and such an airport. Get out of here!" Of course, King and Sweeney knew they could not continue interfering with the airfield's landing pattern. Immediately they headed for New York.[5]

Specifically, they charted a course for Long Island, where King, having buzzed his home in Chattanooga two or three days earlier, thought he should not neglect his home in Hampton Bays. After making a couple of low level passes over the house without incident—although King admitted he did have to pull up rather sharply once to avoid some power lines—he resumed the flight to Bangor, which was reached without further delay or interruption. The bomber touched down at Dow Field about 3:30 p.m. Since the plan was to stay at Bangor only one night, Philip Reinoehl and George Atkinson chose to sleep in the plane. Before leaving the next morning, though, the B-17's tires had to be pumped up. In Savannah, the temperature had been quite hot—King remembered ninety degrees as the high—but in Bangor it was below freezing, the sudden change apparently affecting the pressure in the tires.[6]

Takeoff from Bangor was at 9:00 a.m., October 24, the crew heading for Goose Bay, Labrador, approximately seven hundred miles from the northern coast of Maine; from there, the day afterward, they were to wing on to Greenland. They were flying "the great circle route" to the British Isles, and the journey from Labrador to Greenland, where the United States had built bases under an agreement with Denmark, entailed an over-water run of about eight hundred miles. Approaching the gigantic (fifteen-hundred-mile-long) island's spectacular coastal mountains, King could see a seemingly endless icecap stretching before him. Landing at Greenland was a tricky endeavor unless a pilot fully understood the situation, and a number of American airmen had lost their lives attempting it.

First a plane flew up a wide fiord until it approached a small island. Swinging right of the island and continuing up the fiord led to the landing field. If a pilot flew left of the island, however, he would soon be heading into an ever-narrowing gorge in which he could not turn around. His only "out" would be to pull up in time to get above the gorge and then go back and start again. Precarious is the operative word—obviously. "At Goose Bay," said King, "they showed us a movie to familiarize us with the danger, and instruct us about the proper approach." Having been fully apprised of the problem he would face, King experienced no difficulty in identifying the island, then swinging right and flying about twenty miles up a beautiful but alarmingly narrow fiord accented by high, steep cliffs, until he landed the B-17 in an unforgettable setting, where a great barrier of stone and ice loomed ahead, only a short distance beyond the runway. King observed that the site was unique, "the only time that I ever faced such a situation." Also, he added, "you landed uphill; and the runway was pretty steep." That too was a bit dicey. Soon after the war, King painted an impressive picture inspired by the northern lights of the Greenland scene. At Greenland the crew knew they were "into cold weather, sure enough," necessitating putting covers over the plane's engines and the wings. Philip Reinoehl wrote in his diary: "I almost froze while we were putting those covers on."[7]

King and crew never meant to tarry in Greenland. Bad weather set in soon after they landed, however, and for twelve days and thirteen nights they had no choice but to stay there. Reinoehl noted how he and some of the others passed the time. Once they watched a war-training film about how to survive in the Arctic regions. A couple of times or more they saw a Hollywood film. Often some of the guys bowled. Reinoehl obviously enjoyed bowling, heading for the lanes nearly every day— even by himself if no one else seemed interested. Periodically they ran up the B-17's engines, the number-three motor causing a little excitement once when it caught on fire. At least twice they cleared snow off the plane. And once Reinoehl went fishing, snagging one fish. "At least it was supposed to be a fish," he added, thinking that the creature had a very strange appearance. On November 3, he wrote about the northern lights, which certainly impressed him: "It is clear out tonight and the Northern Lights are very bright. You can see them almost every night if it is clear. They are right overhead here." He also recorded that one day forty or more Germans were captured on the Greenland ice cap, from which they had been providing early-warning weather reports for the German military.[8]

There were a couple of mornings in Greenland when the crew was aroused early in anticipation of leaving for Iceland, which would be the next stop. Both times the weather quickly closed in, scrubbing the flight. King became worried that they might get weathered in for the winter. Finally, on November 7, they were cleared to take off for Iceland. The weatherman predicted eight-tenths' cloud cover but was convinced that they could get through. If, in view of what did happen, they could somehow have been guaranteed that the cloud cover would be the sole problem, that would have been welcome indeed.[9]

What they confronted a significant distance from Greenland was a raging storm that was steadily growing worse. "We tried to fly over it," related King, "but when we climbed over five miles up, we still couldn't see the top of it, and were being thrown all over the sky." Crew members, who never anticipated going up that high, had to dig their oxygen masks out of duffel bags in the bomb bay, while being tossed to and fro. King decided to turn back to Greenland. He called the navigator: "Lowe, this is getting too rough. We've got to go back. Give me a heading for home." Lowe's chilling response still rings in King's ears: "We have passed the point of no return"—a phrase meaning that fuel was insufficient for a return to Greenland. Myron said, "I can hear Lowe's words as if it were only yesterday: 'WE HAVE PASSED THE POINT OF NO RETURN.'"[10]

King then called Iceland: "We are into all this bad weather. We can't go back. Give us some instructions." He was told to go down to three hundred feet above the water, which he did, finding the strength of the storm worse then ever. King believed he had flown into a full-blown hurricane; in fact, he thought it was the same storm that earlier threatened Savannah, and now it played havoc with their B-17 as if it were a toy. "We were flying through the spot where the wind is coming down at maybe a hundred miles an hour," he said. "And it's going up at a hundred miles an hour, and it just flipped that plane up vertical—stood it on its wing—and then flipped it back, only to turn it vertical on the other wing. And it kept that up. Kept it up a long time."[11]

At one point Sweeney picked up the microphone and called Iceland. "Tell us *something* to do! We're having an awful time," he said. The reply came in a soft, female voice: "B-17, go down a little lower." The exasperated copilot vented his frustration: "We're already on top of the water! What do you think this is, a submarine?" King said Sweeney possessed a forceful, commanding presence, recalling that once in Florida the crew all piled into a truck for the ride out to their plane, when the driver adamantly and profanely declined to chauffeur them. Instantly Sweeney stood and addressed the man in a booming, no-nonsense voice: "You *will* drive us to the plane. And you will do it right *now*. And that's an order!" King declared, "That man got right up and drove us to the plane."

Of course, King and Sweeney both knew the harsh reality they faced over the North Atlantic. They could not fly below the storm, nor did it seem they could climb above it. And if they could neither turn back nor fly around it, then obviously they had to fly through the raging thing. They could only hope the plane's structural strength proved sufficient to withstand the storm's stress until they made it to Iceland—and hope also that they did not run out of fuel, which was getting low. King said when they finally landed safely at Meeks Field, Iceland, and rolled to a stop, crew members were scrambling out of the plane, and kissing the ground, some of them even before all the props had stopped turning. He added that Richard Lowe, visiting with him in the fall of 2006 and reminiscing about their war experiences, spoke of that flight to Iceland as more frightening than the worst combat mission they ever flew. It was little wonder that Lowe characterized their trip to England as "an adventure in itself."[12]

The crew had one day to recover in Iceland before flying on to the British Isles. Reinoehl's diary records that he did not get out of bed until about noon—making no mention of how late others may have slept—at which time he learned Franklin Delano Roosevelt had been elected to the presidency for a fourth term. That night he took in a show. "The army band was there, and they were good," he noted appreciatively. Early on Thursday morning, November 9, the King Crew took off from Meeks Field for a flight to Valley, Wales, where they touched down shortly after noon. "Sure is pretty country," observed Reinoehl, specifically commenting on the many stone fences and attractive brick houses. The next day, having turned over their new B-17 to the American authorities, who took it to a refitting station for upgrading, King and crew boarded a train for England, heading toward their designated base in Northamptonshire.[13]

4 ★ Concerning Those Who Went Before

WHEN THE KING CREW ARRIVED IN NORTHAMPTONSHIRE, SPECIFICALLY Station 128, Deenethorpe, in November 1944, the war in Europe had been raging a long time—more than five years, in fact. "Never in the history of air warfare," wrote Starr Smith, "has there been a campaign like the heavy bombardment battles waged against Nazi Germany from 1940 through the spring of 1945." And almost certainly, there will never be such a campaign again.

The technology required to fight that unprecedented air war—the maximum development of propeller fighters and bombers—was not achieved until the early 1940s and then, amazingly, by the last days of that incredible clash, it was being preempted by jets, missiles, and the atomic bomb. While the air war raged, however, it proved to be a colossal phenomenon—a battle front in the skies ranging from a height of several hundred feet to an altitude of five or six miles, with a new kind of warrior and entailing combat ordeals totally unknown to history. World War I in the air, especially the bomber war, not only pales in comparison but hardly exists—recognizable, at best, in outlines vaguely distinguishable. Casualties in the 1940s air war were enormous by any standard. The Eighth Air Force had more than 26,000 men killed, and another 29,500 shot down, while the victims of their bombing raids numbered many, many times more. RAF Bomber Command, because they were at war longer, suffered more than 50,000 men killed, while they probably also killed far more civilians than did the American bombers.

For nearly three years the British had fought the air war alone, as Americans did not begin arriving in England until the spring of 1942, and did not launch their first heavy-bomber mission until August of that year. A "get-your-feet-wet" kind of endeavor, the American target was Rouen in German-occupied France, entailing a relatively short flight and conducted with a small force of twelve B-17s, with six others flying a diversionary mission. All the bombers returned safely.[1]

Modestly initiated, the U.S. bomber offensive against Germany, first under the leadership of Brigadier General Asa N. Duncan and then under that of Brigadier General Ira C. Eaker, would in time become a major force in the achievement of Allied victory. Before that occurred, however, significant growing pains plagued the U.S. Eighth Air Force, as the new American bombing command became known. "The Americans," remarked one historian, with a seeming touch of flippancy, "insisted on repeating most of the mistakes the British had already made."[2]

The British, early on, had thought they could do what the Americans later set about: flying in the daytime, in close formation, with their machine guns providing mutual protection, while they bombed specific targets with considerable accuracy. But months prior to the arrival of the first Americans in the British Isles—actually, before the United States entered the war—the British realized, based on costly lessons of experience, that their concept had been wrong. The aircraft losses inflicted by German fighters proved prohibitive. The bombers clearly were not able to protect themselves. And British fighters, chiefly Spitfires and Hurricanes, while excellent aircraft, did not possess the range to escort bombers to even moderately distant targets. Also, British bombs, even when skies were clear and German fighters inconsequential, were not striking the targets with any degree of precision; the majority exploded so far away that the target was not damaged at all.[3]

Consequently, the British resorted to bombing at night, when enemy fighters could not operate as effectively. Also, they relinquished any idea of formation and precision bombing of strategic targets. Instead, they contented themselves with "area bombing," in which they attempted to saturate a general target environment, often a city. A prime objective was to "dehouse" German workers and destroy morale. Of course, this "city busting," as RAF crews called it, inevitably meant the infliction of more civilian casualties. However, their "precision bombing" effort had killed civilians, too. The issue became one of degree, for either way civilians died. The British could also rationalize, if they felt the necessity, that the Germans had been the first to bomb civilians and that they themselves had no choice except to destroy enemy targets any way they could. Besides, killing Germans, for many a Brit, proved to be a great morale booster.[4]

Thus, when the U.S. Eighth Air Force advocated precision bombing by day, in spite of the British experience (and the German, too, for that matter), some critics prophesied that American losses would be prohibitive. *Arrogance, overconfidence,* and *ignorance* were among the terms employed by those who were convinced that disaster awaited the American strategy. In fairness, though, the inexperienced Americans believed they possessed a couple of aces that the Brits lacked, aces that would give them a decisive edge. One was the Norden bomb sight developed by engineer Carl L. Norden. Indeed, it was an excellent piece of equipment, and with it Americans thought they would be able to hit a target consistently and from high altitude. It offered the proverbial placement of "a bomb in a pickle barrel from six miles up"—or so the thing was hyped. The Americans' other ace was a combination of more and heavier fire power than the British bombers carried.

The best British heavy bomber, the Avro Lancaster, which in various ways deserved the many accolades it garnered, carried eight 7.7 mm machine guns in three turrets: two guns in the nose, two on top of the fuselage, and four in the tail. The B-17 Es and Fs, in contrast, mounted either ten or eleven guns, while the B-17Gs bristled with twelve or thirteen guns, all of which were of heavier caliber than the British armament. American strategic bombing theorists believed that by flying in tight formations, with great firepower giving each other protection against German attackers, the bombers, without escort, could successfully fight their way through to a target and back, while bombing it with precision.

"The conflict boiled down to this," wrote Jimmy Doolittle, who would take over command of the Eighth at the beginning of 1944. "We believed that we could destroy the enemy's ability and will to wage war by hitting specified targets with precision, rather than by bombing large areas of cities in which thousands of civilians lived and worked. To us, it was the most ethical way to go."[5]

Since the earliest American raids over German-occupied territory went reasonably well—in coping with enemy fighters, that is—USAAF officers were encouraged to believe their tactics and strategy were sound. Soon British and Americans reached an understanding: the British would continue with the area bombing by night, while the Americans operated by day, concentrating on specific military and military-oriented targets. American results were better than what the British had done, except in overcast conditions. When the Americans got it right, they sometimes achieved impressive accuracy. Their "precision" bombing, however, sometimes proved a difficult quest. Walter Boyne, mincing no words, summarized the difficult situation when he wrote that "the abominable weather over the Continent meant that precision daylight bombing was impossible. The Eighth Air Force was forced to rely on the technical equipment that had been developed for blind bombing. The result was that, contrary to popular belief, the American effort was also largely an area-bombing campaign."

Donald Miller, in his book *Masters of the Air*, wrote, "The Eighth Air Force would never find a way to bomb with maximum precision and maximum protection. This threw it into a conundrum that led irrevocably to carpet bombing, with some bombs hitting the target and the rest spilling all over the place. It was combat realities . . . that led the Eighth inexorably in the direction of Bomber Harris's [head of RAF Bomber Command Sir Arthur Harris] indiscriminate area attacks."[6]

If most favorable factors—clear skies, no wind, an absence of flak, no enemy fighters, and no prop wash from other aircraft—presented themselves (which they hardly ever did, of course), then a single American bombardier employing the Norden equipment just might put his bombs in that pickle barrel from thirty thousand feet. The reality over Europe was quite different. Bombs were dropped from a formation of large aircraft. "If it were possible to fly wingtip to wingtip (which no one would do with an overladen bomber in turbulent air), the combat-box formation would be more than 1,800 feet wide," explained Walter Boyne. "All the airplanes dropped their bombs when the leader dropped, creating a swath of bombs 1,800 feet wide, each one subject to the vagaries of wind at various altitudes," continued Boyne. The exact instant when the leader's bombs were released depended not only upon the Norden sight, but also upon the skill of the bombardier. "With the formation covering approximately 300 feet per second," wrote Boyne, "a decision to drop that was even four seconds off would mean that the bombs would be dropped 1,200 feet short of the intended aiming point or 1,200 feet over." All this meant that a load of bombs delivered from formation would not be less than 1,800 feet wide, and might be anywhere from "1,200 to 5,600 feet or more off target. Precision in the sense of hitting *only* the *exact* targets aimed at was impossible."

Another factor came into play as well. Many strategic targets—aircraft plants, munitions factories, railroad marshaling yards—required large numbers of workers. If those people could be killed, clearly the damage to the strategic target became far greater. On Sunday, October 10, 1943, the Eighth Air Force struck Munster. The target was the railroad marshaling yards, and the nearby neighborhood of workers' homes. "The Munster raid," wrote Donald Miller, "was a city-busting operation. Declassified mission reports and flight records clearly list 'the center of town' as the Aiming Point." Railroad tracks can be repaired rapidly—but only if sufficient labor is available. Bombing the homes of the railroad workers eliminated men the Germans needed for the repair work. Actually, then, the Berlin raid of February 3, 1945, was not the only instance in which civilians were targeted by the Americans. Intentionally or unintentionally, large numbers of civilians inevitably suffered and died as a result of the raids. But the Americans, in Europe, never accepted a general "dehousing" approach to civilian bombing as the RAF Bomber Command did. The Berlin and Munster raids stand as exceptions to general American policy, rather than a "business-as-usual" approach.[7]

Significant also was the fact that the build-up of U.S. planes and crews did not proceed with the speed originally anticipated. The invasion of North Africa in November 1942 and the subsequent fighting there necessitated that several units, otherwise destined for England, be diverted to the Mediterranean theater. And when, in 1943, the Eighth Air Force began striking north and west German targets such as the Rhineland, the Ruhr Valley, and the Saar Basin—areas of prime industrial and military production—the enemy's resistance strengthened remarkably. Flak became heavier because the Germans were correctly convinced that flak could be very costly to intruding aircraft, possibly even more so than their fighter shield. The Luftwaffe responded fiercely, too, rising en masse to exact a heavy toll of the big bombers.

Short on bombers and minus long-range fighter escort, the Eighth Air Force suffered heavy losses as 1943 progressed. Rarely was General Eaker able to send out more than 200 to 300 bombers at one time. In late summer, the Eighth turned its effort to southern Germany. Launching 315 heavy bombers, the targets were the crucial Schweinfurt ball-bearing plants and the vital Messerschmitt fighter-plane works at Regensburg. The mission was the largest raid yet mounted, as well as the deepest penetration into Germany to that date and perhaps the most important effort up to that time.

The fateful date was August 17, and the atrocious English weather played havoc with the Eighth Air Force plan. As originally projected, the Third Air Division would take off first, strike Regensburg, and continue on to U.S. bases in North Africa, making this the Eighth's first shuttle mission. The First Air Division was to take off ten minutes after the Third crossed the enemy coastline, with Schweinfurt as its target, and afterward return to England as usual. American fighters would fly escort for the B-17s to the limit of their fuel, while medium bombers would pursue a diversionary mission. But the fog enshrouding English bases destroyed the timetable of the bombers.

The Third Division's B-17s got airborne on schedule, thanks "to the fact that [Commander Curtis] LeMay's groups had been practicing instrument takeoffs for some time," as Edward Jablonski observed. Unfortunately, the First Division did not get off until three and a half hours later, when the weather finally improved. The diversionary missions were cancelled due to the fog, while fighter escort was limited both by the weather and their short range. The upshot was that German fighters struck the Third Division ferociously, employing every conceivable tactic, including dropping bombs upon the Fortress formations.

The enemy fighters then had time to land, refuel, and rearm before attacking the First Division. Also, the Germans brought in fighters from all across the continent—from Holland to Italy, from France to Austria. The Third Division faced a constant air battle—"one of the most intense of the war," according to writer Edward Jablonski—while the First Division fought going and coming. The Germans succeeded in destroying sixty American bombers—slightly more than 19 percent of the total and clearly a prohibitive loss—at a cost to themselves of only twenty-seven fighters. That August 17 raid, which had the effect of speeding up the German dispersal of their military industry, left the Eighth Air Force unable to attempt another deep penetration of the Reich for several weeks. Then, an attack on Stuttgart saw forty-five bombers shot down or running out of fuel, approximately 17 percent of the total participating.[8]

The worst was yet to come. While bad weather ensued for a time, causing some missions to be scrubbed and keeping losses low for approximately a month, October brought a renewal of the carnage. Three consecutive costly raids—to Bremen, Anklam/Marienburg, and Munster—were followed by a return mission to Schweinfurt on October 14, which can only be described as a disaster. Twenty-six percent of the bombers were lost. "In seven days," as McFarland and Newton summarized, "Eighth Air Force had lost 148 four-engine bombers, each with ten crewmen. The American daylight bombing campaign against Germany had reached a crisis point." In October 1943, fewer than one out of four crew members could expect to complete the twenty-five combat missions then constituting their assigned tour of duty with the Eighth Air Force. Worse, as 1944 came in, the number of missions required was increased to thirty.[9]

Obviously, deep penetrations against strategic German targets demanded fighter escorts for the entire journey; otherwise, losses would be unacceptably high. Fortunately for the bomber crews and the heavy-bomber campaigning, those long-range fighter aircraft were finally becoming available in late 1943 and early 1944. More P-47 Thunderbolts and P-38 Lightnings were being equipped with fuel drop tanks to increase their range. Most significantly, the P-51 Mustang was being delivered in large numbers. In addition to its strengths of speed, maneuverability, and firepower, the sleek Mustang was also a veritable flying gas tank. And like the Thunderbolts and Lightnings, it too could be fitted with drop tanks.

Major General Jimmy Doolittle arrived in England from North Africa to take command of the Eighth Air Force in early January 1944. He succinctly stated the dramatic change occurring in the American fighter forces: "By the time that I arrived in England, 150-gallon tanks were available and we were able to hang two of them on a P-47, so they had a tactical radius of 425 miles. The Lockheed P-38 Lightning and the North American P-51 Mustang had greater range than the P-47s; they began to arrive in the theater in November, 1943. These were given even more range with the addition of drop tanks, so that eventually the escorts could fly a very welcome 850 miles from their bases." In the honest, no-nonsense style characteristic of Doolittle, who soon was promoted to lieutenant general and who believed in giving others the credit they deserved, the general continued: "This steadily increased range of escort fighters was an inheritance from which I benefited as commander of the Eighth; their genesis began long before I took over. It was my job to use this increased capability to best advantage."[10]

And so he did. There were those, including some British as well as Americans, who thought General Eaker should not have been removed from command of the Eighth. For example, Walter Boyne, whose book on the air war is top-notch, clearly sympathized with Eaker. Boyne wrote that Eaker had "built the American Eighth Air Force into a formidable force despite every obstacle; just when it was reaching maturity, it was jerked from him like a toy from a child."[11]

Perhaps Eaker deserved to continue in command. Perhaps he would have performed as well as Doolittle in 1944. Actually Eaker was given a higher level of leadership, as commander of the Mediterranean Allied Air Forces, which included the Fifteenth Air Force. The Eighth Air Force, however, was perceived as the premier command. And Doolittle was the man chosen to lead it—the man upon whose shoulders would rest the prime responsibility for its success in 1944. He would bear that burden well.

★ ★ ★

Nineteen forty-four became the decisive year of the European war. During the first part of the year, the USAAF, with continuing, able assistance from the RAF, achieved air superiority over Germany. In early

June, the Allies launched the long-awaited cross-channel invasion of northwestern France, forcing the Germans thereafter to fight on two major fronts, east and west, while the Italian front continued to drain German resources as well. Already the steadily mounting pressure by the Red Army, driving savagely on the eastern front, had compelled the vaunted Wehrmacht to reluctantly give ground. As if for good measure, Rome finally fell to the western Allies in June, with an invasion of southern France following shortly thereafter.

Some American and British advocates of air power, tracing their philosophical lineage back to the Italian prophet of air supremacy, Giulio Douhet, and his widely influential 1921 book, *The Command of the Air*, had earlier believed that strategic bombing could defeat an enemy by smashing its industrial base and destroying civilian morale, with no need for a land invasion. "That had been the hope of both Churchill and Roosevelt in 1941," observed historian Michael S. Sherry. Churchill, in fact, had "pioneered" strategic bombing during the Great War, according to Jorg Friedrich. As minister of munitions, he planned a thousand-bomber raid on Berlin. World War I, however, ended prior to any possible realization of such a fantasy. And by early 1944, bitter experience convinced most political and military leaders on both sides of the Atlantic that final victory in Europe could not be achieved by air power alone. The continent must be invaded.

For the USAAF this meant an all-out effort to achieve air supremacy before the invasion would be launched. "The difficulty, from the point of view of the Army Air Force," as stated by Wesley Frank Craven and James Lea Cate in their excellent history of the Army Air Forces in World War II, "lay in the fact that the German Air Force and its supporting industry had been able to absorb increasing punishment without declining in combat strength. Indeed, as the loss of 60 . . . bombers attacking Schweinfurt on 14 October emphasized, the German Air Force gave every sign of increasing rather than declining strength."[12]

General Doolittle wasted no time addressing the problem, making a critical decision that was formalized on January 21, 1944, less than three weeks after he assumed command of the Eighth Air Force. In fact, "as far as I'm concerned," he wrote, "this was the most important and far-reaching military decision I made during the war. It was also the most controversial." Doolittle's decision was to unleash the

American fighters to go after the German fighters, rather than strictly to protect the bombers. Previously, the duty of the escorting fighters was merely to defend the bombers and not desert them to pursue a German attacker whatever the circumstances. The fighters must bring the bombers safely back to base. Now, as Doolittle phrased it, "The first duty of the Eighth Air Force fighters is to destroy German fighters."[13]

Several factors prompted Doolittle's action. For one, he had the necessary strength available. "The organization I had inherited was formidable," he acknowledged. "There were 25 heavy bomber groups assigned to me on arrival, plus 15 fighter groups. Also, the 9th Air Force, organized largely for tactical operations in support of ground forces, but independent of the 8th, gave us an additional 18 fighter groups if we needed them. . . . That meant more than 5,000 combat aircraft were in the theater."[14]

Also, German rocket-firing ME 109s and FW 190s, as well as twin-engine planes firing rockets, had become quite lethal. Jimmy Doolittle acknowledged this new menace in his memoir. The Germans could stay out of range of the American bombers' .50-caliber machine guns and launch their deadly missiles with terrible effect. The rockets would cause "clusters of explosions from time or contact fuses," explained McFarland and Newton, the barrage dispersing a combat box. "This was quickly followed by an assault, like a cavalry charge, by fighters flying cover for the rocket-launching planes." By the autumn of 1943, the Eighth Air Force, according to McFarland and Newton, "characterized the technique as the greatest threat to massed bombers over Germany."

And, too, German fighter pilots, in order to conserve their strength, were concentrating on the big bombers and avoiding combat with Allied fighters. This strategy promised time for the German aircraft industry, still building more planes in spite of the destruction visited upon it by the Allied bombing campaign, to replenish the Luftwaffe's losses while simultaneously inflicting huge losses on the American heavy bombers.

If air superiority were ever to be achieved, Doolittle concluded that American fighters must aggressively seek out the enemy fighters. Clearly, time was of the essence if command of the sky were to be achieved before D-Day in France. Furthermore, he would be carrying out General Hap Arnold's directive to him only days before he took command of the Eighth: "Destroy the enemy air forces wherever you find them, in the air, on the ground, and in the factories." For Doolittle, who believed that fighter pilots tend by nature to be pugnacious and aggressive and that "fighter aircraft are designed to go after enemy fighters," Arnold's message to him fully justified his new policy, which he characterized as "escort the bombers but pursue and destroy the enemy."[15]

In implementing the new approach, some fighters were assigned to escort duty, but the majority of them went hunting for the enemy air force, wherever they could find it. "Flush them out in the air and beat them up on the ground on the way home," instructed Doolittle. "Your first priority is to take the offensive," he declared. Fighter pilots, predictably, were enthusiastic when they heard the news, but many bomber crews were apprehensive. Some of them were angry. If fighters were being unleashed to fight for air superiority, the crews manning the bombers realized that they had become the bait to lure the German fighters into combat.[16]

Whatever the airmen thought, pro or con, the new strategy worked. No less a figure than Adolf Galland, a top German fighter ace and for a time commander of their fighter force, later said the Luftwaffe lost the air war when Doolittle freed the U.S. fighters to go after the German fighters. Most historians of air power have agreed. The turning point came in February, even though that month, to quote Doolittle in an obvious understatement, "is not noted for fine weather over Europe."[17]

On February 19, 1944, the atrocious weather over Germany began to moderate, permitting the Allies to launch a major series of attacks on German warplane plants, ball-bearing factories, and related facilities. The Eighth Air Force and the Fifteenth Air Force joined with RAF Bomber Command, mounting intense assaults day and night which, continuing through February 25, came to be collectively known as "Big Week." While the Eighth and Fifteenth Air Forces suffered a loss rate of 6 percent—a total of 226 heavy bombers—American fighters, flying 3,673 sorties, lost only 28 aircraft for the whole of "Big Week," during which they wreaked havoc on the Luftwaffe. For the Germans, the entire month of February proved devastating. They lost 2,121 aircraft.

Worst of all, the Germans lost, during "Big Week" alone, an estimated 425 to 450 pilots—losses that damaged the Luftwaffe a great deal more than the destruction of their aircraft. In fact, according to Galland, the German Air Force lost approximately 1,000 pilots between January and April 1944.[18]

Luftwaffe pilots faced possible attack at all times, from takeoff to landing. (Actually, a few of their marvelous new ME 262 twin jets were taken out by U.S. fighters when the German planes were in highly vulnerable takeoff and landing attitudes, especially the latter.) While Germany replaced lost aircraft remarkably well in 1944—producing, despite all the devastation dealt out by Allied aircraft, about 25,000 planes, the most they manufactured during any single year of the war—experienced pilots could not be replaced. "After March," wrote Walter Boyne, "there was an obvious decline in the quality of Luftwaffe pilots." For that matter, March was almost as destructive for the Germans as February had been. Some 2,115 aircraft were lost, in addition to the continuing depletion of pilots. At the same time, American strength, both in numbers and quality, continued to mount. When June at last brought the great, long-awaited invasion of the continent, the Allies firmly commanded the skies over Normandy. The German Air Force had pulled back, both to escape utter destruction and to defend the heart of Germany, above all Berlin. In sum: "Air Superiority had been won not by bombing the enemy factories into oblivion," said Boyne. Rather, it was "by the long-range fighter, using the bombing formations as bait to entice the Luftwaffe to fight."[19]

By the fall of 1944, the German Air Force—regardless of having achieved the first development and deployment of a formidable jet fighter (and bomber, too, with Hitler's insistence that the majority of ME 262s be used as bombers)—had been reduced to a drastically weakened position. Above all, the Luftwaffe was irreversibly damaged by the loss of experienced pilots, while the pool of seasoned Allied flyers became larger and larger. Additionally, the Germans were overwhelmed by the sheer weight of numbers. The marshaling of an ever-increasing American armada of fighters and bombers guaranteed the inevitable reduction of the German Air Force to dire circumstances from which it never recovered.

5 ★ Into the Thick of It

MID-NOVEMBER IN THE BRITISH ISLES IS TYPICALLY COLD AND DAMP, and 1944 proved no exception. When the King Crew detrained at Stone in Staffordshire, Philip Reinoehl noted in his diary, "I almost froze." Cold, gloomy weather would be a frequent companion in the days and weeks to come. If a chilling rain were not falling, then fog or snow likely might be the alternatives. Bright, sunny days would be relatively few as the late fall progressed into winter.

Spending the night at Stone, the King Crew heard a lecture the next day about poison gas. Each man was afterward provided with a gas mask as a standard part of his equipment. According to reports of some scientists and technicians, the Germans were likely to strike Britain with the so-called "Red Death": a poison gas they would shoot across the channel in huge dispensers, with the objective of "destroying every living creature in the British Isles." If not the "Red Death," there was fear that the Germans, as their situation became ever more desperate, might opt for another kind of poison gas. (After all, argued some, the "Boche" tried mustard gas and chlorine gas in World War I; surely the same, or worse, could be expected again.)[1]

Following a second night in Stone, the crew journeyed on to Kettering, a rail station near Deenethorpe, from which they were unceremoniously trucked to their airbase. Deenethorpe, officially designated

Station 128 by the USAAF, lay in the English Midlands. The beautiful, normally peaceful region—a green, gently rolling, pastoral setting dotted with sheep and cows and stretching northward from Bedford to Peterborough—was filled with bases for war planes. Like adjoining East Anglia, located to the east, the Midlands hosted an American heavy-bomber base, or a fighter base, about every six to eight miles in any direction. These areas constituted the heartland of American air power in the British Isles.

"When we came to our squadron area, and I approached the assigned barracks," recalled King, "the first thing I noticed was a strange word over the door: 'Peenemunde.'" King wondered, "What's Peenemunde?" That was the first time King, or anyone else in the crew, had heard of the secluded spot on the Isle of Usedom in the Baltic Sea, where the Germans had been developing the four-thousand-mile-per-hour V-2 rocket. "Peenemunde" was over the door, they soon learned, because the squadron they were joining, the 614th (known as the "Lucky Devils," according to the squadron logo), regarded a recent mission in which they struck that rocket station as one of their more significant targets and the bombing results as one of the group's best efforts. Eighty percent of the bombs were judged to have fallen within a thousand-foot circle. The flight had been long and the flak heavy, with two of the group's B-17s suffering major damage and twenty-three others sustaining minor damage. It was a memorable foray.[2]

Thus the King Crew arrived at one of the premier bombardment groups of the Eighth Air Force, the 401st, stationed at Deenethorpe and commanded by Colonel Harold W. Bowman, who had shepherded the group through training and 175 missions. Called to become deputy chief of staff to General Carl Spaatz at U.S. Strategic Air Forces Headquarters in Paris, Bowman was replaced in early December 1944 by Colonel William T. Seawell, an original squadron commander in the group. The 401st would finish the war with the second-best overall bombing record of the forty heavy bombardment groups stationed in England, clearly establishing it as an elite force. It was customary, in general conversation, to refer to a bombardment group by its place name: Deenethorpe, in this case, rather than Station 128. Ordinarily, four squadrons composed a group, and the 401st had the usual four: the 612th, 613th, 614th, and 615th.[3]

On combat missions, normally three of the four squadrons participated; the group put up all four only if a "maximum effort" were mandated. While a full squadron consisted of twelve aircraft, maintenance problems and battle damage sometimes limited the number available for a particular mission to nine or ten—possibly even less. It was also customary that a crew not fly more than three successive days, afterward standing down for at least one day of rest.

For organizational purposes, three bombardment groups composed a wing. The 401st belonged to the 94th Combat Wing, which included the 351st Bomb Group at Polebrook, a few miles east of Deenethorpe, and the 457th at Glatton, a short distance east of Polebrook. The 94th Wing was commanded by Brigadier General Julius K. Lacey. Three or more wings, in turn, made up an air division, and the Eighth Air Force had three divisions. The First and Third Divisions flew B-17s, and the Second Division was equipped with B-24s. The 401st, as a member of the 94th Wing, became a part of the First Air Division under the command of Major General Howard M. Turner. Also, the 401st was the initial group to arrive in England solely equipped with B-17s which had been fitted with chin turrets. All the planes were B-17Gs, except for one. That single exception, a late production B-17F, received a chin turret because the Boeing company recognized the desperate need for protection from German head-on attacks. Hence, Boeing had rushed to secure a chin turret for the last few F models of the Fortress. Of course, all G models brandished the chin turret.[4]

When the King Crew joined the 401st Bomb Group, the base at Deenethorpe had been operational for nearly a year. Originally planned in 1942 as an airfield for RAF Bomber Command, it became instead, in October 1943, Station 128 of the United States Army Air Force. Three hundred thirty feet above sea level, the excellent site boasted clear approaches to all three runways, and Deenethorpe officially opened for operations on Wednesday, November 24, 1943. Less than two weeks later, on Sunday morning, December 5, the group's B-17s were taking off for a mission to the environs of Paris when an unfortunate accident, as the group history expresses it, "virtually wiped the quaint old village of Deenethorpe off the face of the English countryside."[5]

A Fortress with the striking name of "Zenobia El Elephanta," piloted by Lieutenant Walter B. Keith of Hodgenville, Kentucky, was taking

EUROPE DURING THE WAR, WESTERN FRONT

off west to east, and had just cleared runway number 23 when something went terribly amiss. Failing to gain altitude, the bomber "half-skimmed, half-flew over the ground," and out of control, "crashed into an old stone barn . . . and burst into flames." Eight members of the crew managed to escape unscathed, while men who rushed to the scene extricated the injured navigator and bombardier. Knowing a terrific explosion was imminent, since the plane was loaded with fuel and bombs, several airmen ran from house to house, warning residents to flee for safety. When the six thousand pounds of bombs went up, the explosion shook the earth for miles around, and several of the homes and barns vanished. Deenethorpe lay in ruins. Because of the warnings, however, no one was killed.[6]

Let it be noted—perhaps surprisingly in view of that early crash—that the first *fatal* crash of a B-17 on takeoff at Deenethorpe did not occur until the 144th mission. That is an impressive record, and a tribute to the reliability of the B-17, when one considers the frequent bad weather and the heavy loads of fuel and bombs that always burdened the Fortresses on takeoff. The record also speaks well of the leadership, dedication, and competence of the maintenance crews, who sometimes worked through the night to insure the aircraft would be in the best possible condition each time they went to war. In fact, the 401st Bomb Group required the teamwork of approximately thirty-five hundred airmen and support personnel to accomplish their job; and, of course, the support personnel outnumbered the airmen by a huge margin—five to one or more.

The 401st maintained a fleet of sixty B-17 aircraft, parked at concrete hardstands surrounding the field, except on the northeast side of runway 23. Most of the planes shone in a natural silver finish, indicative of their construction since January 1, 1944. Prior to that date, Boeing had painted the Fortresses in the well-known olive drab camouflage scheme. Only a few of those yet survived at Deenethorpe. Like every bomb group, the 401st planes were readily identified by colorful, distinctive markings on the big tail fin and waist area of the fuselage.

The fin sported a broad, yellow diagonal stripe, accented with black bordering. At the top of the fin, superimposed over the yellow stripe, was a black triangle with a large, white letter S painted inside. The black triangle signified the First Air Division, the yellow diagonal stripe indicated the 94th Combat Wing, and the white S inside the triangle represented the 401st Bomb Group. Below the triangle, about midway down the yellow stripe, was the serial number of the plane in black. Just below that number, also painted in black, was a capital letter—the code letter of that specific B-17. That code letter appeared also on the fuselage, immediately behind the U.S. national insignia, as did, in front of the waist gunner's window, two black capital letters. Those signified the squadron to which the plane belonged, the 614th Squadron's letters being IW.[7]

Like all new airmen joining the 401st, King and crew went through a brief orientation period. The number of missions they were expected to fly had recently been increased again—from thirty to thirty-five. (Initially it had been twenty-five.) "It sort of bugged me at the time," Myron said, "realizing that if I had been a few weeks earlier, I would have had five less missions to fly for a full tour." Also, the week they got to the base, posters were being put up that pictured the first jets the Germans had flown, a topic of concern for all. The crew met with Group Commander Bowman, listened to several lectures, and watched a number of training films. (Phil Reinoehl particularly noted a film about prisoner-of-war camps, should such a fate befall the crew.) "From the films and lectures," King said, "we learned more about the real war in a few days than all we heard during training in the U.S. put together." They flew some training jaunts, too, before their first bombing mission. King remembered that twice they took off with the group, forming up and proceeding to the coast the first time before turning back; the second time they flew across the channel before returning to base. He found the view of Dover's famous white cliffs memorable, calling to mind one of the popular songs of the day and the line, "There'll be blue birds over the white cliffs of Dover . . . when the world is free." Then, on the last day of November, the wait for the real thing at last came to an end.[8]

★ ★ ★

The target for November 30, 1944, was the Leipzig region, about eighty miles southwest of Berlin. There were located some of the Third Reich's most valuable aircraft component and assembly plants; also, and even more important, were the synthetic oil plants in the area, producing 25 to 30 percent of Germany's total oil supply. Only five days earlier, the Eighth Air Force had bombed the same general target with results that were deemed unsatisfactory. Thus, on the last day of November, the heavy bombers would be making the long flight again—550 miles one way. Specifically, many of the planes, including the 401st Bomb Group, were going to Bohlen, on the outskirts of Leipzig, where oil, the lifeblood of Germany's vaunted war machine, constituted the main target. Other bombers would strike other targets, but all would be in the same 40- to 50-mile-square flak area.[9]

Group briefing took place well before daylight, at 0445 hours. Engines would be started at 0750 and taxiing at 0805, with the first plane taking off at 0820 and using the longest runway, number 23. The bomb load consisted of twenty 250-pound general-purpose bombs, and each plane's fuel tanks were filled to capacity. Formation assembly altitude was at eight thousand feet over the Cottesmore Buncher. The King Crew, having arrived at Deenethorpe without a plane, would be flying a bomber assigned to another crew, who were enjoying a well-deserved day of rest. Navigator Richard Lowe said he either paid no attention to the nickname of the B-17 they flew on that memorable day, or if he did know the name at the time, he later forgot it. It was dark when he climbed aboard, explained Lowe, and therefore he could not see the plane's name anyway. Phil Reinoehl did record the number of the aircraft they were flying (44-6464) in his diary, as he would for every mission. This means, obviously, that the King Crew did not fly "Maiden U.S.A." (44-6508) on the mission to Bohlen.[10]

As the time to start engines drew near—less than thirty minutes away, in fact—new orders came down, notifying the waiting airmen that all times had been set back one hour. Engines were to be started at the new time of 0850, with the customary fifteen-minute intervals following for taxiing and takeoff. Such delays, whenever they happened, were always a bit disconcerting. Seldom did crews know the reason for the delay. Possibly the mission might be scrubbed, which usually would not be welcome to pilots and crew mentally prepared to fly that day, psyched to face whatever dangers the sky might bring. Waiting with a touch of apprehension, King finally saw—and right at 0850—the green flare go up from flying control, the signal to start engines. It was also the signal, as some airmen thought of it, that they might die that day.[11]

Takeoff, thankfully, proved uneventful, with the last of the 401st's thirty-nine heavily laden bombers airborne at 1030 hours. King's 614th squadron put up ten B-17s that morning, smoothly assembling in formation and heading for Germany at the fully loaded cruising speed of about 160 miles per hour. A host of fighter escorts soon rendezvoused with them, "the little friends" weaving back and forth so as to not outdistance the slower bombers and providing nearly flawless protection from enemy aircraft all the way to the Bohlen area. But there the bombers faced a hellish concentration of antiaircraft fire; according to one source, it was twice the density usually encountered at heavily defended Berlin. George Menzel, a bombardier who flew with the 614th squadron, wrote that "the flak was intense and accurate, with all but one of the 401st thirty-nine B-17s getting damage from the shrapnel; seven of them major damage."[12]

The weather was clear over the target as the first American aircraft began their bomb runs, and those airmen had a good view of the oil plants. Crewmen could see huge explosions and fires in the refinery areas. But soon the smoke screen the Germans put up, together with the rising smoke from the bomb explosions, obscured much of the target for the men in succeeding planes. Ball-turret gunner Reinoehl wrote in his diary: "We were the third group over the target. I saw planes go down out of the group ahead of us. The sky was black [with flak] and . . . I was never so scared in all of my life as I was when we started over the target." Reinoehl was struck by a sliver of shrapnel. Fortunately the injury proved inconsequential.[13]

Myron King simply said, "They shot the hell out of us." The plane had 150 holes in it when they got back, he added. A B-17's skeleton is strongly built, but its aluminum skin is relatively thin. One can punch a hole in it with a knife or a screw driver. Pieces of flak readily tore through, naturally; some of the metal left only tiny holes and others gaping openings. Clearly the large pieces were dangerous, but a missile ripping even a very small hole sometimes could be deadly. And if no flak fragment wounded an airman, a piece of the plane itself sometimes caused injury. During the bomb run, togglier Pyne was knocked backward by the concussion of a blast that blew a hole in the Plexiglas nose, leaving particles in one of his eyes. Luckily he did not sustain any permanent injury, although he missed the next two missions.[14]

"We never saw anything like what we saw at Bohlen," remembered King. There being no wind that day, King said, the black smoke from flak could be seen hanging over Bohlen from one hundred miles away. As each group made its bomb run, still more smoke appeared—never dissipating, he added—and turned the sky ever darker. A lot of B-17s were going down, some exploding in a big ball of fire and smoke, others spiraling out of control, their engines on fire and trailing smoke or with part of a wing or tail shot away. First reports were that fifty-six bombers had been lost on the mission, a figure later officially fixed at twenty-nine, when others were located at continental bases. Some of those, of course, had been badly shot up and forced to crash land. Several of them never flew again.[15]

King said he actually saw most of the bombers that were shot down that day. "Our position made it so we could see the planes ahead of us and the ones behind us. They were just all over the target, you see, going down all around us." The scene was forever etched on the mind of the young pilot. When King returned home after the war, he painted a panoramic picture of that awful day over Bohlen, as he remembered it from the B-17's cockpit. King's plane was one of the 401st's many stragglers returning from Bohlen. Fortunately, though, the American fighter escorts kept the Luftwaffe from getting close enough to attack any of the group's late-returning bombers.[16]

When King landed, he said, a fire engine and ambulance followed the plane down the runway. Unknown to anyone on board, the exhaust pipe on one of the outboard motors had been shot away, thus giving an appearance to those on the ground that the engine was on fire. As soon as the B-17's motors were shut down, King said, every member of the crew kissed the ground as he left the bomber. King somehow learned that the ball-turret gunner had crawled out of his confined space earlier than he should have. He said he felt compelled to warn Reinoehl not to do that again. "I told him that if a German fighter were following us, and approaching from below our plane, the entire crew's

safety could depend on whether or not he spotted that enemy fighter."
Reinoehl would never again get out of the turret early. King continued
to elaborate on the incident: "I knew he was cramped and scared, but
I also knew that I couldn't just ignore the matter." Then, he added, "I
was in shock myself. And I was wondering if all the missions were going
to be like this one." If so, then clearly there would be little to no chance
of surviving thirty-five of them.[17]

The November 30 mission to Bohlen truly was one of the rough-
est of the war. It was the thirteenth time that the Eighth Air Force had
bombed that region, and Roger Freeman wrote in his history of the
Eighth that "the flak [on the thirtieth] was the most formidable yet."
The group history of the 401st states that on the mission to Bohlen,
"more of our aircraft were damaged and crews had more difficulty
than on any other mission to date." Vic Maslen, in his 614th Squadron
history, wrote that "our formations were met with deadly accurate flak
and many members of the Group were wounded." As costly as the mission was and considering how many planes the Eighth lost that day, it
is perhaps surprising that the 401st, while suffering major damage to
several planes, did not actually lose a single bomber over Bohlen.[18]

6 ★ Berlin, Bad Weather, and "the Bulge"

WHEN THEY LEARNED THE TARGET OF THEIR SECOND MISSION, KING AND crew likely felt that the fates were aligned against them. In the briefing room, as the curtain covering the large map of Western Europe was drawn back, King saw that the mission ribbon led even deeper into Germany than on their first assignment. This time they were going to Berlin. Crews always found the flak over the German capital to be very accurate and deadly. Little time was required for a new crew to hear about the dangers of a mission to "Big B." Besides, common sense said that the Germans surely would have their capital heavily defended. Thus, Berlin had soon won, and ever held, the understandable reputation as the toughest target in the Third Reich. Specifically, the target of the mission was the Rhein-metal Bersig A.C. plant at Berlin/Tegal, a munitions and tank works northwest of the city center.[1]

The date was Tuesday, December 5—one year to the day, incidentally, since B-17 number 42-39825, Zenobia-El Elephanta, crashed on takeoff, its exploding bombs leveling the little village of Deenethorpe. This day, thankfully, there would be no accident on takeoff—and no delay. Right on schedule at 0635 hours, the green flare went up, arcing and drifting across the field, signifying time to start engines. Almost as one, the bombers began coming to life, one big propeller after another spinning and then the motor roaring. Takeoff that morning, as so often in winter, was in darkness; each bomber taxied single file into position at the head of the runway, the pilots holding hard on the brakes, pushing throttles wide open, and then, at thirty-second intervals, releasing brakes for the takeoff roll. Formation assembly was in the darkness, too. Nevertheless, and in spite of bad weather as well, assembly was accomplished on schedule, and the bombers headed for "Big B" on time. Fighter escorts soon joined up, and Phil Reinoehl declared, "We had three fighters to every bomber."[2]

The First Division put up 222 aircraft that day, and the Third Division 229, both divisions en route to Berlin. At the same time, the Second Division's B-24s were bombing the Munster rail yards. The flight to Berlin was largely uneventful—"We did not experience much flak on the route," observed Reinoehl, and no enemy fighters got through the escorts to attack the bombers—but the 401st found heavy cloud cover over the target. In the 614th Squadron history, Vic Maslen wrote, "The weather over the target was 9/10ths to 10/10ths cloud cover." Not surprisingly, the bombing that day proved rather inaccurate. As a matter of fact, most of the bombs fell way off target. "The strike was found later," wrote Maslen, "to be about four and one half miles east of the MPI." Then he added, perhaps with a touch of sarcastic humor, "but within the city limits of Berlin."[3]

Sometimes an airman might wonder, in the words of a bombardier from another group, "God, how many people would die today because of us!" And then, perhaps he would think, and "How many of US would THEY kill?" Undoubtedly, on December 5, as bombs struck far from the targets, a lot of people died in Berlin. Phil Reinoehl's diary comment only underscores that reality: "We did not get our bombs away [as something impeded the drop mechanism] for about two minutes after the rest of the group." He did believe that "we got them out over town though." If an airman obsessed about the civilians—especially the women and children who were suffering and dying—he might well become mentally unhinged. Probably most preferred not to think in the terms of Colonel Darr H. Alkire, who bluntly told a group of men who had recently received their wings, that they might as well face the fact that they were "going to be baby-killers and women-killers." To the contrary, bomber crews saw themselves, if the war were to be won, as carrying out the highly dangerous and indispensable work of crushing Nazi war production.[4]

While perhaps few airmen would have classed the December 5 mission as a "milk run," the Berlin target, which had been expected to entail a very dangerous journey, turned out to be a fairly easy one, "all things considered," as they experienced "moderate to intense flak" with relatively few planes lost. Reinoehl recorded that the King Crew "bucked a pretty strong head wind coming back," having fallen behind at the target and actually flying back with another group. The flight had been long, nine hours and fifteen minutes, said Reinoehl, with the crew on oxygen about six hours, at an altitude of 26,500 feet, and the temperature at forty-nine below zero. Then he added, "We did not get any holes today. Thank goodness." Finally, he noted that his ball turret "did not work very good today." But King and crew had made it to Berlin and back. Mission Number Two was in the books.[5]

If any airman expected that the Berlin mission would earn him a day of rest, he was quickly disappointed. In fact, the King Crew was awakened even earlier on the morning of December 6 than it had been on the previous day. Briefing for the mission in the darkness of 0330 hours revealed the target to be the Merseburg-Leipzig area, with the primary objective once again oil refineries. This time it concentrated on Merseburg and a strike against the Leuna oil refinery of I. G. Farben.[6]

It was a big day for the 401st Bomb Group. The group was hitting a major target for the third consecutive day, having bombed the large, important marshaling yards at Kassel on December 4. Also, for only the second time in 178 missions, the group was putting up "a massive force," to borrow Vic Maslen's phrase, of fifty-one aircraft. Such an impressive achievement speaks powerfully of the competence, dedication, and hard work of the ground crews. After putting up thirty-nine B-17s on each of the two previous days, to then ensure that 204 engines were all running smoothly for December 6 qualifies as a magnificent feat. And this is not to mention everything else the ground crews had to check out in preparing fifty-one aircraft for a combat mission.[7]

December 6 was a special day for yet another reason. The 401st, flying as the 94th Combat Wing's "A" Group, was actually leading the First Air Division, with Lieutenant Colonel Burton K. Vorhees as the air commander. And the 614th Squadron, having launched twelve bombers, with King and crew aboard B-17 number 42-97931 (an aircraft known as "Madam Queen Delivered"), was serving as a screening force. This meant the squadron was flying ahead of the main group formation in order to drop "chaff" in the target area. "Chaff" consisted of thin strips of metallic aluminum foil, "appearing like Christmas tinsel," said King, adding, "It looked like icicles, and we even decorated Christmas trees with it." On German radar, however, the fine strips looked like airplanes, and the purpose was to confuse the German flak gunners.[8]

Every one of the 614th's twelve aircraft carried a load of fifty ninety-pound boxes of chaff. "We flew across Merseburg on the windward side of the city," King explained, "and you would rip the box open with a cutter and drop it down the chute. When it hit the air, it would blow apart and all that chaff would spread out, making what appeared to be a mass of airplanes on the enemy's radar. So the Germans would be shooting their flak guns at all of the aluminum, while the planes loaded with bombs were coming over the target at a higher altitude, above the level where the flak was exploding." Phil Reinoehl said that Patsy DeVito, the radio operator, cut open the boxes and shoved them out. He added that they were "bouncing off the ball turret," which was perhaps a bit disconcerting, although Reinoehl did not say that. Whether the chaff affected the German gunners to the extent desired seems questionable, for eighty-one of the First Air Division's B-17s suffered some damage from flak. None were lost, however. Four bombers from the Third Division did go down.[9]

Overall, the day was a good one for King and crew, as well as for the 401st. Reinoehl noted that no flak was encountered on the flight to the target and thought that "we had a good P-51 escort all the way in and out." He further observed, "We did not keep very good formation." Nevertheless, according to Reinoehl's count, their plane "only got two holes today," and he concluded that "we were very lucky." As for the group, Maslen's *Deenethorpe Diary* records that every one of the planes was safely down at base by 1634 hours, "making good landings amidst stinking weather conditions."[10]

★ ★ ★

Another mission, which would have made four missions in four days for the Eighth, was in the works for December 7. The 401st was briefed at

0500 hours, with takeoff, thirty-nine planes strong, scheduled for 0800. The mission was scrubbed, however. The "stinking weather conditions" had become stifling. "December, 1944, brought the worst winter weather in England for 54 years," wrote Martin Bowman in his history of the Eighth Air Force's B-17 crews. "Water froze in the pipes and a thin film of ice coated the runways at bases throughout eastern England. The temperature dropped to as low as minus 18 degrees Centigrade." Navigator Richard Lowe remembered the weather as "always cold and damp," saying, "Through November, December, January, we always felt cold." But the worst feature of the weather for an airman, according to Martin Bowman, "was lack of visibility during missions." Addressing the visibility issue, Roger Freeman wrote, "In the first three weeks of December the B-17 and B-24 bombardiers had little opportunity to make visual sightings on any target."[11]

For the next three days, which took in the weekend of December 8–10, the 401st stood down. Probably this was one of the occasions when Richard Lowe headed for London, which he liked to do whenever sufficient time between missions permitted. "Sweeney, the copilot, and I usually went to London where we saw at least three movies in a row," Lowe said, "and then we would have a meal at the Grosvener House, an officers' club." He wrote that "Myron, on the other hand, stayed closer to the base and searched out local bookshops and antique shops." King himself commented that he made good use of a bicycle, not only for transportation around the base but also occasionally for an excursion to a nearby town, such as Kettering or some other community. Lowe also said of King: "He was quite artistic and did some painting and making handcrafted objects."[12]

The comments of Lowe and King well underscore the unique nature of the American bomber war against Germany: hours of flirting with danger, terror, and death in the skies, occasionally broken by periods of essentially normal life—good food, entertainment, sports, books, art, friendships, and other welcome aspects of a civilized existence. "There was always something exciting on the ground," wrote Lowe, "such as a mid-night raid on the mess hall to 'liberate' a can of peaches, or whatever. . . . Occasionally a prankster would drop a flare down the chimney of a next-door Nissen hut, which would vacate that building in a hurry." Lowe also recalled that "we often got a kick out of listening to Axis Sally or Lord Haw Haw for information, or mis-information, about our war effort."

A memorable saying developed about the American airmen, which well characterizes the peculiarity of the war they fought: "Bombing Germany in the morning, and dancing at the Savoy in the evening." Realistically, of course, even with tens of thousands of airmen based in England, such dancing pleasure didn't happen often or involve very many of the guys. But literally it was possible. And, albeit infrequently— very infrequently—it did actually happen and symbolizes the vast difference in the war fought by the Eighth Air Force and the war of the U.S. Army on the ground in Europe. The war, nevertheless, could never be far removed from the thoughts of an airman, whose chances of being killed or seriously wounded were obviously great; and early Monday morning, December 11, King and crew once more steeled themselves for a combat mission.

The target was the railroad yards at Frankfurt; and on this day the Eighth Air Force launched its largest air strike to that time: 1,467 heavy bombers dropping tons and tons of high explosives on rail targets and bridges. Interestingly, Phil Reinoehl wrote in his diary that "we did not see any flak on the bomb run" and that everyone "wondered if we were close to the target. Lt. Lowe said he thought we dropped a little short of the target. I hope we didn't." They flew the next day too, again striking Merseburg, which, commented Reinoehl, was "the old favorite oil target"—and with good reason, for it was the eighteenth time the Eighth Air Force had bombed Merseburg in 1944. Then, for the next three days, bad weather closed down all the Eighth's bomber and fighter operations.[13]

"The weather conditions were not much better on [December] 15th," declared Vic Maslen, "when 39 aircraft of the 401st took off in semi-darkness." The weather was so bad that the King Crew fully expected that the mission would be scrubbed, but at 0820 hours, right on schedule, the lead B-17 headed down runway 23 on takeoff roll; the target was Kassel. Enemy fighters presented no serious problem on the mission, with the bombers well protected by P-51s, Thunderbolts, and Lightnings. Flak over the target proved minimal, and cloud cover was so thick that Reinoehl said he did not see any flak bursts, only heard them, and occasionally felt the jolts, while the plane suffered no damage. When they returned, however, the awful weather over England had Deenethorpe closed in, forcing all of the planes to land elsewhere, farther to the east. King and thirty other bombers from the 401st landed at Old Buckenham, a B-24 base near the city of Norwich in East Anglia.[14]

"I remember waiting to take off the next morning to return to Deenethorpe," recalled King, "when a B-24 in front of us called the tower requesting permission to take off on three engines." King said he and Sweeney both laughed. "In a B-17," explained King, "we would never have asked permission to take off on three motors. We would have just done it. That B-24 however, was a lumbering aircraft. Probably it barely got off on three engines."[15]

There is no question that a Fortress, all factors being equal, could take off with greater ease than a Liberator. In bad weather, though, even a B-17 at full power might experience difficulty; and King and Sweeney barely managed a harrowing takeoff one morning about this time. No living member of the King Crew who contributed information for this book recalls exactly which mission it was. Probably, considering the evidence available and the collective judgment of King, Lowe, and Reinoehl, the range must have been about the eighth to the fourteenth. No doubt the hazardous takeoff, rather than the mission target, became the event forever imprinted on their memory.

The morning was very cold. Richard Lowe described the experience in the following words: "That B-17's wings were frosted with ice and our crew took brooms to try to get the frost off; the crew chief for that plane refusing to use de-icing fluid to clear the wings. On take off, with a maximum load of fuel and bombs, the plane barely was able to lift off. I think the copilot actually pulled up the wheels at the end of the runway, and somehow we flew. We were all frightened, and when we returned to base, we lit into that crew chief something fierce." Phil Reinoehl recalled that the crew thought the mission would be scrubbed, "but no such luck. There was quite a bit of ice and snow on the plane when we took off, and I sure did sweat it out until we got in the air."[16]

The very next day King learned, of all unwelcome surprises, that he and his crew had been assigned, as their permanent aircraft, that very B-17—the plane with a crew chief whom all of the King Crew considered unacceptable. When asked about the incident, King remembered it vividly and spoke passionately: "No sir, we were not going to fly any plane serviced by that crew chief again. I protested strongly. Why, the man had told me, when I talked to him about de-icing that bomber: 'It doesn't weigh much.' That's what he said. 'It doesn't weigh much.' That man sure got in trouble with his superiors. And that's when, a few days later, they gave us the 'Maiden' as our permanent aircraft."[17]

The bad weather during the winter of 1944–45 took the lives of many men in the Eighth Air Force. That they flew under such dangerous conditions testifies, in the strongest terms, to the significance of the air war in the minds of the high command. As King succinctly put it, speaking of several missions that winter, "We flew in unflyable weather." He remembered flying one mission during the period of the worst weather when, "if I remember correctly, not a single bomber was lost to either enemy fighters or flak, but ten or twelve went down because of the weather; most of them victims of mid-air collisions." And when a crew successfully returned to England from a mission during that awful winter, the weather often rendered the landing a dicey affair. Usually the pilots found coats of ice covering the runways, which made braking, before exhausting the length of the runway on rollout, a tricky proposition. Always, however, visibility proved the greatest trial of flying in the terrible weather.[18]

On one of the missions, King remembered, "We formed up under the clouds, and then went up into the clouds and flew the entire mission in the clouds. Most of the time I could see only one other plane— the B-17 on my wing. If we got out of formation, I knew there would be no way to get back in." All one could do then would be to "drop below the formation"—hoping, of course, that in doing so a collision could be avoided—"and then head for home. If you stayed up there with everybody else, and out of formation, a collision was a virtual certainty."

Occasionally, continued King, "We would break out of the clouds momentarily, and I could see all of the planes in our squadron. Sometimes I could see another squadron as well; maybe even a third squadron. And then we were back into the soup again." King declared, "I guess that was the most scared I ever was on a mission. As long as I saw just one or two other planes I was OK. But when I suddenly saw the whole squadron—and maybe another squadron too—and all of us flying close—planes ahead, planes above and below, planes to the side, and then all disappeared once more into the clouds—that really scared you." And then he added, "Scared the shit out of you."[19]

★ ★ ★

By mid-December 1944, American airmen knew the war had swung decidedly against Germany. After Allied ground forces broke out of the Normandy beachhead in midsummer, German resistance in France quickly collapsed, while massive Russian troops continued their irresistible advance into the Nazi Reich from the east. Overly optimistic observers, some no doubt succumbing to wishful thinking rather than making a careful analysis, predicted the war might be over by Christmas. In September, the British and the Americans launched a daring plan for a combined airborne and ground offensive to circumvent the formidable German Siegfried line, gain a bridgehead on the Lower Rhine, and drive to the Zuyder Zee. From this region the Allied armies could fan out across the Westphalia Plain, an area suitable for armored maneuver, and pour into the heart of Germany.

Conceived by Field Marshal Sir Bernard Montgomery and approved, somewhat reluctantly, by General Dwight D. Eisenhower, the operation, if successful, promised to be the decisive campaign of the war in Western Europe, a master stroke enabling the western Allies to administer a death blow to the Third Reich. Unfortunately, "Market Garden," the code name of the endeavor, proved a bit too ambitious. Afterward, Montgomery curiously pronounced the operation 90 percent successful, though clearly it was an overall failure.

The Germans prevailed in the intense struggle for the key bridge at Arnhem and thus effectively checkmated the Allied strategy. While this "bridge-too-far" campaign, as it later became popularly known from Cornelius Ryan's book, certainly demonstrated that the war would not be over by Christmas, the Wehrmacht was perceived as having been reduced to a strictly defensive posture. Supposedly the Germans, still dangerous when fighting defensively to be sure, were incapable of mounting a major offensive campaign.

And then suddenly, in mid-December, it happened. Initial ominous warnings of a German offensive in the Ardennes sector of Belgium were hard to believe. Perhaps, thought some Americans, a few limited attacks on U.S. units were being magnified and misinterpreted. Mystifying though the reports may have seemed at first, the rapidly mounting evidence of a major enemy assault became undeniable. In the fog-enshrouded early morning hours of December 16, Adolph Hitler had launched the greatest offensive in the west since the spring of 1940.

A quarter of a million German soldiers—thirty divisions equipped with thousands of artillery pieces, armor, and military vehicles of various types—swept through the Ardennes Forest. Their objective was to capture the port of Antwerp and split the Allied Armies. It was a desperate strategy conceived in the demented mind of the Fuhrer. Gambling that the Russian summer offensive had run its course, Hitler struck where he thought the western Allies were weakest.

Contemptuously regarding both England and the United States as "decadent democracies," Hitler believed a hard blow might divide them politically. The Americans, he thought, were in the most vulnerable situation. Thus, the German Fuhrer would power his way over them, drive to the coast, and trap the British in the north—in essence, a second Dunkirk. The campaign would be the greatest military reversal in history, the all-surpassing genius of Adolph Hitler transforming imminent defeat into glorious victory.

Hitler's assault indeed took the American troops by surprise, strategically and tactically. The Germans massed their men effectively, too, far outnumbering the American forces at the point of attack. And Allied air power, that great strength against which the Germans no longer possessed any meaningful defense and which their commanders feared might well prove decisive in turning back their assault, was grounded by bad weather. While the "Hitler weather" of damp, heavily overcast skies shielded the German armor, infantry, and communications network from retaliatory air strikes, the concentrated enemy assault broke the three, thinly stretched American divisions holding the line in the region of Luxembourg and eastern Belgium.

The German attack tore a huge hole in the Western Front, achieving a deep penetration of about sixty-five miles into Allied territory and creating a distinct bulge in the line, from which the struggle became known as "the Battle of the Bulge." As a hell of desperate, confused fighting raged in a befogged, spooky atmosphere, with English-speaking Germans outfitted in G.I. dress infiltrating American lines to sabotage and terrorize, Supreme Allied Headquarters at Versailles determined what must be done. Stunned by the strength of the German counterattack, Eisenhower decided to commit his strategic reserve, the First Allied Airborne Army, to plug the gap. As soon as possible, Allied armor and infantry reinforcements in large numbers would be brought to the support of the Airborne troops. So also the American air force—as quickly as the weather moderated.[20]

But for several days after the German assault began, a period of particularly bad weather, characterized by low clouds and heavy fog, was so persistent that flying, as Roger Freeman wrote, "was out of the question." On December 19, the weather did improve, although not very much. Nevertheless, because of the crisis in Belgium, the Eighth Air Force took to the sky in limited strength, attempting to strike communications centers supporting the German offensive. Myron King and Richard Lowe both testified as to the dire circumstances in the Ardennes, recalling that they and all the flying officers at Deenethorpe were asked to turn in their side arms (.45 caliber Colt automatics), so the weapons could be sent to the hard-pressed American ground troops. "They needed them more than we 'fly boys,'" as Lowe wrote. King and crew, perhaps with few regrets considering the forbidding weather, were not among those scheduled to fly as the 401st bombers took off on the nineteenth, their target Koblenz.[21]

Getting the squadrons airborne proved nerve-racking and time-consuming. Thirty minutes before scheduled takeoff at 0815, the time of departure was delayed an hour. Then, only five minutes before the new takeoff time, Wing Command postponed departure "until further notice." At least that notice came soon but entailed another delay of a half hour. When at last the bombers started roaring down the runway and disappearing into the fog on takeoff roll, still more time was lost because one B-17 ran off the runway. The flying control log reads, "SC-C [the bomber's identification code] reports he is off the runway about half way down. Visibility very poor—we cannot see him. All aircraft stand by." Finally, according to the log book, fully two hours behind the original schedule, thirty-five aircraft were airborne "in very poor visibility." Four planes scheduled for the mission, including the B-17 that ran off the runway, were never able to get into the air.[22]

Poor visibility seemed ubiquitous as the bombers winged eastward toward the continent. Over the target, the bad weather caused the 401st's squadrons to become separated and bomb three different places: one hitting Koblenz, another Schleiden, and the third striking Stadtkyll. Upon returning to England, the airmen found that weather had Deenethorpe completely socked in. The result was, to quote one of them, "the mother of all diversions," as the group's bombers landed at several bases. A dozen let down at RAF Tangmere, a base not far from London. Many pilots were desperate for a place to land, their gas tanks nearly depleted, only forty or fifty gallons left when the wheels of their planes touched earth once more. The most extreme diversion involved a few bombers that flew west and south all the way to Cornwall, finally landing not far from Land's End. Some aircraft did not get back to Deenethorpe for three or four days, as they were called home one squadron at a time. This was done to avoid confusion in the event the weather worsened again before they got back—which it did in some cases, forcing several planes to divert once more.[23]

Meanwhile, though the war raged, Christmas season was at hand, and the American military, whatever the circumstances, was not inclined to ignore the occasion. Myron King recalled a nine- or ten-year-old boy named Jimmy Wright, whose mother washed clothes for the squadron's officers. Jimmy, along with his dog, became a frequent visitor to the base, as he delivered the washing for his mother. "We decided to surprise him with a Christmas tree and presents," said Myron. "We cut the top out of a fir tree and decorated it with chaff to look like icicles." When Jimmy saw the tree, his response amused King and the others. "Oh, you have cut down the King's tree," the boy said, reminding the airmen that one was supposed to get royal permission before cutting an evergreen.[24]

On December 23, continuing the base policy of befriending the local people, the 401st Bomb Group hosted a Christmas party. USAAF trucks brought to the base more than five hundred children from nearby villages and towns, where they were treated to various "goodies," of which many had been deprived for years. One of the favorite treats was ice cream. Also, on December 23, the bad weather finally began to lift, and by Christmas Eve, which fell on a Sunday in 1944, the Eighth Air Force at last was able to launch a major effort against communication targets in the Koblenz area, which were supporting the German offensive in the Ardennes.[25]

Maiden U.S.A. sitting on the tarmac, together with a B-24 and a C-47. Courtesy of the Mighty Eighth Air Force Museum, Pooler, Georgia.

The King Crew at Savannah, Georgia, prior to crossing the Atlantic. Kneeling, left to right, are Sweeney, King, and Lowe. Standing, left to right, are DeVito, Pyne, Pavlas, Speelman, Atkinson, and Reinoehl. Courtesy of Myron King.

Covering the engines at Greenland. Courtesy of Myron King.

Myron King, with B-17
in the background, at
Greenland. Courtesy of
Myron King.

Five of the crew in Greenland. Left to right are DeVito, King, Pyne, Lowe, and Pavlas. Courtesy of Myron King.

Eleanor Goodpasture, Myron's fiancée, in a studio portrait taken during the war. Courtesy of Eleanor King.

401st Bomb Group B-17s flying through the clouds. Courtesy of Mighty Eighth Air Force Museum, Pooler, Georgia.

Three 401st Bomb Group B-17s in formation above the clouds. Courtesy of the Mighty Eighth Air Force Museum, Pooler, Georgia.

A B-17 from the 401st Bomb Group over Ludwigshafen, Germany. Courtesy of Mighty Eighth Air Force Museum, Pooler, Georgia.

Close-up view of flak damage to the nose of a 401st Bomb Group B-17. Courtesy of the Mighty Eighth Air Force Museum, Pooler, Georgia.

Flight jacket of the "Maiden U.S.A." Courtesy of Mighty Eighth Air Force Museum, Pooler, Georgia.

U.S. military personnel and others in Egypt. King is in front, third from the left, with Lowe standing beside him. Sweeney is third from the right, in front, and Leon Dolin is on the extreme right. Courtesy of the Mighty Eighth Air Force Museum, Pooler, Georgia.

Eleanor and Myron King on their wedding day. Photo courtesy of Eleanor King.

7 ★ From Christmas Eve to Berlin Again

THE CHRISTMAS EVE MISSION WAS, IN FACT, THE LARGEST AMERICAN AIR strike mounted during the war up to that time. The Eighth Air Force put up every heavy bomber that was in condition to fly, including several that had been retired from combat. The total force numbered 2,046 four-engine aircraft, escorted by more than 850 fighters. Crews were told that the route to the target would take them over the positions of the ground troops fighting in "the Bulge" and at lower altitude than normal. This was done for morale purposes. In the clear sky over the Belgium/Luxembourg sector—as Phil Reinoehl observed from his belly-turret position, "Today it was clear as a crystal ball"—the long stream of American planes, steadily winging eastward as if there were no end to their numbers, was plainly visible to both the American troops and the Germans.[1]

Anyone who saw that air show, whether as observer or participant, watched a spectacle unmatched. Never before had such an armada, almost three thousand strong, taken to the air. "I was way back in the crowd that day; several hundred back," said Myron King. "The sky was perfectly clear. All I saw were planes, stretching as far ahead as my eyes could see. And when I looked back, planes as far to the rear as I could see."[2]

Mounting such a huge raid, even under the best of circumstances, presented a challenge for all involved. The Christmas Eve mission, because a significant number of planes never got back to their base after the last raid, entailed a particularly difficult operational problem. King's 614th Squadron, for example, actually contributed thirteen aircraft to that maximum effort on December 24, but only six of them, including King and crew, took off from Deenethorpe. Seven crews of the 614th flew from other bases. To some degree, what was true of the 614th was true of many squadrons throughout the Eighth Air Force. And at Deenethorpe, in addition to launching its own bombers, flight control also put up eight planes from Polebrook and one from Grafton Underwood, aircraft which earlier had been diverted from their own bases due to bad weather. Obviously, operational difficulties were widespread, but most seem to have been well handled.[3]

The Christmas Eve mission, besides massing the largest force of bombers ever dispatched on a combat operation, also witnessed the death of Brigadier General Frederick W. Castle, the air leader of the Eighth Air Force on that historic day. Castle was flying his thirtieth mission. Tired and in need of rest, he had no intention of making the flight initially. However, learning that his Third Division was scheduled to lead the entire Eighth Air Force, he changed his mind, reportedly saying that in such a maximum effort—"and because we have to stop that [German] breakthrough"—he would be expected to fly and lead: "This is the kind of thing they pay me for."[4]

Flying in the copilot's seat of the lead B-17, the customary position for the Eighth's air leader, and while still over friendly territory, a flight of ME 109s suddenly and unexpectedly assaulted the general's aircraft, as well as other planes in Castle's leading formation. Myron King was too far back in the stream of bombers to see anything of what happened at the front. Nor did he hear anything about the attack until after the mission. He did readily recall the speculation of many airmen who thought the Luftwaffe's surprise foray probably was facilitated by the rather similar appearance, in general lines and at a distance, of the P-51 Mustang and the ME 109. Their look-alike profile might have enabled the Germans to sweep in close before the Americans, who were not expecting an attack so early in the mission anyway, realized the danger. According to Roger Freeman, the Luftwaffe achieved surprise by attacking out of the sun. Whatever the precise explanation, and perhaps both of the above contributed, the B-17 with General Castle aboard, known simply as "Treble Four" from its last four identification numbers, suffered mortal damage from the attack.[5]

It was then that General Castle took control of the doomed bomber and ordered the crew, three of whom were wounded, including the copilot riding in the tail, to bail out. "Castle deliberately took control of the stricken aircraft in order to give the pilot a chance to parachute," wrote Freeman. "It was also apparent," he continued, "that Castle did not order the jettisoning of the bomb load . . . for fear of killing Allied troops or Belgian civilians, probably hoping to drop them behind enemy lines." All of the crew, except the pilot and the general, managed to get out of the burning plane, and most of them survived. Before the pilot could make his escape, however, the right wing tank exploded and sent the bomber into a spin from which it never recovered. General Castle's heroic actions in trying to save the crew through the willing sacrifice of his own life, brought a posthumous award of the Medal of Honor. King recounted the story with admiration for Castle's bravery, remarking that he believed Castle was the only general in the nation's history to die in a direct attempt to save the lives of his subordinates, both officers and enlisted men. That is why the story of Brigadier General Frederick W. Castle occupies an exalted position—one all its own—in the hallowed lore of the Eighth Air Force.[6]

The excellent weather over the continent was still holding when the Fortresses and Liberators reached their target over Koblenz, and all the bombing was visual. "We got quite a bit of flak," remarked Reinoehl. "I guess we saw almost every kind of flak they have. We were in it about thirty minutes." Despite the flak, described as "accurate," though not intense, in the squadron history of the 614th, the bombing results were good. King said the appearance of the exploding bombs, from altitude, reminded him of trees—"as if they were suddenly springing up, full grown, one right after another, row after row of them." Reinoehl was watching the explosions, too. "I saw all our bombs hit," he wrote in his diary. He then briefly commented, "It was not pretty." Nevertheless, the Eighth Air Force could take satisfaction, as the planes turned back toward England, in knowing they had delivered a major blow against German communications supporting the Ardennes offensive.[7]

Winging westward to home base, even with clear sky over the continent and after running the gauntlet of enemy flak and fighters, experienced airmen well knew that danger could still lie ahead. Bad weather often confronted them after recrossing the channel. No crewman could really relax until he heard that familiar screech indicating that a bomber's wheels were once more safely contacting an English runway. So it was with the Christmas Eve mission, as the English Midlands became socked in by late afternoon.

In the entry for 1630 hours on December 24, Deenethorpe's flying control log book reads, "Weather at base is poor and getting worse. Polebrook [home of the 351st Bomb Group, which, like the 401st, belonged to the 94th Combat Wing] almost forcibly restrained from sending us their aircraft!" The 401st had already been diverted to Lavenham, an American base in East Anglia, not far from the coast. There the majority of its bombers, including the B-17 flown by King, were able to make safe landings. A handful of 401st planes put down at other fields in East Anglia. Deenethorpe's flying control entry for 2130 hours reads: "After many agonizing hours and hundreds of fruitless phone calls on our part, and thousands of foolish ones on other people's part, all our aircraft are accounted for!"[8]

King talked at some length about his stay at Lavenham. Initially he had an impression that the base was a bit disorganized. That was before he learned of the death of General Castle, who had flown from Lavenham that morning. Also, as more and more planes landed, the base facilities were hard-pressed to accommodate the unusually large number of airmen. King soon decided that Lavenham was handling the problems as well as could be expected.

"There were no sleeping quarters available for the whole crew," he said, "and some of us stayed in the Officer's Club Christmas Eve night, and waited up for Santa Claus." He remembered a big Christmas tree in the club and "one of those large, set-back, English fireplaces with benches along the set-back, so that, with a small fire, several people can sit close on a bench and keep warm." He said the room also contained some big, overstuffed chairs in which one could sleep. King alternated between spending time in a big chair and warming himself beside the fire, as the night became quite cold. "So we had Christmas spirits on

Christmas Eve night," he continued. "There was a picket fence around the Officer's Club, and when fuel for the fire ran low, we went out, tore down that fence, and burned it to keep warm. When we ran out of fence, there were some wooden chairs around which suffered after that. And thus we stayed warm that night."[9]

If any of the King Crew reflected on his situation that Christmas of 1944, particularly the possible alternatives a man might face when engaged in a war, he perhaps felt fortunate—even if, like Myron King that Christmas Eve night, he had to sleep in a chair, rather than on clean sheets in his bunk at Deenethorpe. The chances are that not a single airman would have wished to swap places with the men they had just assisted and, indeed, would continue to support. Some of those beleaguered American ground troops in Belgium were totally surrounded by superior numbers of German infantry and armor. Yet it is a curious fact that several hundred of those soldiers involved in the Battle of the Bulge would enjoy a New Year's Eve treat that many servicemen, whatever their circumstances, would have considered quite special.

Among the first of George Patton's army to reinforce the Airborne troops in the Belgium/Luxembourg fighting was the 317th Regiment of the 80th Infantry Division. "There was little to ease our suffering from the extreme cold, the incessant artillery fire, and the ferocity of the fighting," recalled James H. Hayes, a member of the 317th, who said that they "were suffering about 200 casualties a day." However, among the prized supplies fortunately obtained by his regiment was a movie starring the gorgeous and brilliant dancer Rita Hayworth. During World War II, no female star surpassed, if indeed any equaled, the stature of the glamorous, red-haired Hayworth as a pinup favorite among American military personnel.

Thus the troops set up a movie house to view *Cover Girl,* in which she starred with Gene Kelly. There was an old barn, about five hundred yards back of the front, which was converted into "a blacked-out theater, complete with some scrounged stoves that were able to heat the building," continued Hayes. "We ran the movie continually and were able to accommodate about 200 men at a time, so in one evening we were able to get almost all the remaining members of our regiment through to see the movie and have some relief from the severe weather." Years later, when Hayworth died, Hayes said he had ever after remembered the actress fondly, for she enabled him that night to block from his mind, at least for a little while, the awful reality of his situation.[10]

★ ★ ★

Bad weather over the English Midlands continued through Christmas day. Most of the 401st bombers could not return to Deenethorpe until December 26, and fifteen of them did not get back then. Even so, a mission was scheduled for the next day.

For the first time, on Wednesday, December 27, King and crew were assigned to fly the Maiden. It was anything but a good day for flying in the Midlands, as freezing rain and fog were everywhere. A predawn inspection revealed that runways and perimeters were coated with ice, and flying control requested that sand and salt be distributed over them. The weather was so cold that a number of B-17 engines refused to start, and several aircraft had to be scrubbed from the mission.[11]

"It was not very good weather to take off this morning," commented Reinoehl in a bit of understatement. Despite the difficulties—takeoff was delayed an hour later than scheduled—the 401st put thirty-eight bombers in the air, a few flying from fields other than Deenethorpe. The entire Eighth Air Force launched 575 four-engine aircraft. The specific target for the 401st was the railroad marshaling yards at Gerolstein, about thirty miles east of the Belgium border with Germany. The purpose, explained at briefing, was again to disrupt German lines of communication that supported their forces in the Belgium/Luxembourg sector.[12]

Once the bombers crossed the channel, the weather from the coast on in to the target cleared. A good visual bomb run was permitted for both the 401st's lead squadron and its low squadron. The latter was the 614th, which included King and the Maiden. Their bomb run was deemed excellent, as 50 percent of the bombs fell within one thousand feet of the MPI, and all within two thousand feet. The high-flying squadron, however, actually bombed the wrong target. Compelled first to make a 360-degree turn before starting their bomb run, they bombed the marshaling yards at St. Vith. They had somehow become confused about the location of the Gerolstein target while making their wide, sweeping turn, which obviously encompassed a large area of the sky. The miscue was an example of the difficulties sometimes experienced in attempting to identify a target, even in clear weather.[13]

Back in England, little had changed as the bombers returned home to Deenethorpe. The awful weather still held the area under siege, making landing a hazardous undertaking. Finding the runway proved a dangerous challenge. "We had a hard time getting in here when we got back," wrote Reinoehl that night. "There was quite a bit of fog. We could not see to line up with the runway." In fact, two and a half hours were required to land all the 401st bombers "under extremely poor weather conditions," as the flying control log book expressed the problem. One officer took up a position at the end of the runway and from there assisted Major Charles Baldwin, in the control tower, to guide and "talk" the pilots onto the runway. Obviously, the situation was tense for everybody—"We sweated them all in," commented Reinoehl—but all of the B-17s finally touched down without an accident.[14]

King and crew flew two more missions before the end of 1944. On December 30, their target was a railroad overpass at Kaiserslautern, Germany, and the plane they flew was becoming one of the most famous in the Eighth Air Force. Only a handful of B-17s ever survived 100 missions. "Chute the Works," aircraft number 42-97395, which carried the King Crew to Kaiserslautern (and in which they would fly two more times), long seemed to lead a charmed life. She would not survive the war, however, going down on her 111th mission in late March 1945, shortly before the conflict ended in Europe.[15]

Interestingly, the B-17 with which the King Crew ultimately became primarily and prominently associated, "Maiden U.S.A.," came within inches of destruction on her New Year's Day mission. The target that day was oil storage facilities at Derben, Germany, and the Maiden, flown by the crew of Lieutenant Wylie White, suffered the most serious damage of her lifetime, as she was repeatedly struck by flak. The worst single hit came when a shell entered the fuselage from the bottom, ripped through the roof, leaving a two-foot-square hole, and exploded a short distance above the plane. If the shell had exploded inside the fuselage, or if its path had varied slightly and severed the major control cables to the tail, almost certainly the Maiden would have been doomed. As it was, she had to be grounded for several days before all the damage could be repaired.[16]

In the meantime, as January progressed, England's worst weather in half a century continued to plague air operations, with the fields of the Eighth Air Force covered with snow, ice, and fog. "In this terrible weather the Fortresses of the 401st were serviced in the open air in temperatures well below zero," stated Vic Maslen in the 614th's squadron history. "Servicing aircraft under these conditions can only be described as heroic work," continued Maslen, especially as "most of it was carried out in the pitch dark of the night before take-off."[17]

During January the King Crew chalked up nine more missions, five of them in the Maiden. Nearly all missions, though characterized by certain similarities, had peculiarly memorable moments. Sunday, January 21, so qualified. Phil Reinoehl's diary entry notes that he was awakened early, at 0200 hours, and told that the target would necessitate a long haul. After several days of bad weather had held up operations, the 401st was flying once more, assigned the primary target of a tank factory at Aschaffenburg.[18]

Takeoff, starting at 0735 hours, saw the group put up thirty-six aircraft, ten from the 614th Squadron, with the King Crew flying the Maiden. The mission was their sixteenth, the route taking them southeast across France and, after winging into Germany, turning back north in the direction of the target. "We were skirting flak areas all the way to the target," remarked Reinoehl, who confessed that "I am still scared to death when we get in flak." And the crew did witness a close-flying B-17 destroyed by flak. That bomber, from another group, had come up on the left side of the Maiden shortly before the deadly shell struck. As the crippled plane started going down, "We saw at least one chute open," recorded Reinoehl, and then the bomber "exploded in flames. We watched it until it went through the clouds."[19]

Once over the target, the group found the all-too-familiar ten-tenths' cloud cover and, as a result, bombed the secondary target, the railroad marshaling yards. King knew, of course, that with heavy cloud cover, the bombing could hardly be precise, whatever the target. King said he thought—and clearly it troubled him—that the time was about right for some people, on that Sunday morning, to be going and coming from church. However disturbing that realization, at least the Maiden did not fly through flak on the way out, and there were no signs of the Luftwaffe. Phil Reinoehl did note another problem with the ball turret. "I lost the access plate off the left side of the ball," he wrote. "That cold air sure did cool me off. I thought I was frozen." As for flak, he thankfully pronounced it "meager and inaccurate" for the mission as a whole. Then, exactly one week later, came the mission many considered the most memorable endeavor of the month at Deenethorpe.[20]

★ ★ ★

Sunday, January 28, 1945, certainly was a big day for the 401st. The group flew its two hundredth mission—which had been delayed for five days by terrible weather over northern Europe. Finally, with the German weather improving, the big mission was on. The Eighth Air Force would strike bridges, marshaling yards, and oil installations, with the 401st attacking the marshaling yards at Cologne. Takeoff, scheduled for 0825 hours, would be to the northwest, using runway 33. Although 33 was one of the two shorter runways, the customary early-morning airfield inspection found 33 to be in the best shape, because high winds had blown the snow off. The King Crew had flown the Maiden on their last four missions, but she was not ready to go on that Sunday. Thus, they flew "Shark Tooth," another of the group's better-known Fortresses.[21]

Since Cologne is near the western German border, the mission did not require a long trip, with the IP actually in Belgium. Consequently, the planes crossed into Germany with bomb bay doors open. About a minute before "bombs away," there was a break in the clouds, enabling the lead bombardier to make a slight course correction. As a result, the bombs were said to have created "a concise and neat pattern right in the assigned marshaling yards." The Luftwaffe made no effort to thwart the attack, and there was very little flak at the target, prompting Reinoehl to comment that the latter "eased my mind a lot." Doubtless, many another airman would have seconded that thought. While fourteen of the group's planes did suffer some battle damage, most of it was light—one hole in "Shark Tooth" was Reinoehl's assessment—and not a single B-17 was lost. By 1521 hours all of the 401st's Fortresses had touched down safely at Deenethorpe, smoothly completing the two hundredth mission.[22]

The grand achievement was celebrated on February 1 with a huge party, described as "a carnival-circus" by one writer, for all enlisted men and officers. Inside Hangar One, a large tent measuring two hundred feet by forty feet was set up to shelter the formal portion of the festivities. Elsewhere a popular bar provided a thousand gallons of beer, and the cooking facilities were said to have served at least five thousand hot dogs. Musical entertainment came from both the Eighth Air Force's "Flying Yank Orchestra" and the 401st's own thirteen-piece dance band, "The Bomb Beats."

Perhaps some airmen, upon such an auspicious occasion, might have hoped for a return engagement by the sultry Marlene Dietrich, who had entertained the base back in September, but there was no such luck. The party did not lack for celebrities, however—that is, celebrities in the form of high-ranking brass. Among them were Brigadier General Howard M. Turner, commanding officer of the First Air Division, and Colonel Eugene Roemig, commander of the 457th Bomb Group and former executive officer of the 401st. Above all, without a doubt, was Jimmy Doolittle, commanding general of the Eighth Air Force, who delivered the principal remarks of the evening.

Particularly, Doolittle spoke of the group's work supporting the ground troops in the Battle of the Bulge. "History will record the job done by the heavy bombers as being largely responsible for stopping the recent German breakthrough," he declared. "The Hun is on the ropes," he continued, drawing upon boxing terminology, a subject the general knew something about from personal experience. "Now is the time to knock him out. You've done a splendid job so far. Now give him everything you've got and get it over with."[23]

Myron King was pleased to learn of Doolittle's presence and soon sought out the illustrious airman, with whom a myriad of topics might have been possible conversation pieces. Perhaps many people, if presented with such an opportunity, might have turned to the daring, unforgettable Tokyo raid, a mission that had brought Doolittle yet more fame, a promotion to brigadier general and the Medal of Honor. However, King said that what he and Doolittle talked about, primarily, was the Gee Bee, that hot-to-handle racing gem flown to victory by Doolittle in the 1932 Thompson Trophy Race—a model of which King built, as noted in an earlier chapter, and which somehow still survives, albeit rather worn. King thought that Doolittle possibly welcomed the chance to focus, for a few moments, on a fascinating airplane that involved a great triumph and was not war-related. He found Doolittle very personable, an impression entirely consistent with the memorable, popular image of the great flyer.[24]

★ ★ ★

And then came, for the King Crew and the "Maiden U.S.A.," the fateful mission to Berlin on February 3, 1945. On that Saturday, the Eighth Air Force mounted a massive armada of over one thousand B-17s. Benefiting from near-perfect weather over the target and excellent bombing skills, the Eighth administered a blow to Berlin from which, according to the 401st Bomb Group history, "the Nazis never recovered." However, the American bombers themselves suffered heavy blows from the German ground defenses.[25]

The intensity and accuracy of the flak constituted "the most fearful concentration the Eighth ever experienced over the [Reich] capital," declared Roger Freeman. One or two bombers "were taken out of nearly every formation," he said, with "twenty-one actually going down over the city" and another six managing to crash land behind Russian lines. Ninety-three of the aircraft returning to England had suffered major battle damage. Among those severely hit and heading for the Russian lines, as earlier recounted in the prologue, was the Flying Fortress "Maiden U.S.A.," with King and his crew aboard.[26]

8 ★ Behind Russian Lines

FLYING EAST FROM BERLIN WITH TWO MOTORS GONE AND THEIR FIGHTER
escorts having turned back because of dwindling fuel, King and crew
faced the unknown. Yet, bad as their situation may have seemed, it
could have been worse. Their crippled bomber might have gone down
over the capital of the Reich. The crew might have been compelled to
bail out over the city they were attacking, a fate that very possibly could
have meant death. In the earlier days of the war, an airman who successfully parachuted from a doomed plane usually received reasonable
treatment as a prisoner of war. By this late stage of the conflict, however, he was as likely to be murdered, perhaps beaten to death, by those
he had been bombing.

The Berlin mission of February 3 is thought by some Americans to
have killed twenty-five thousand Germans, making it one of the most destructive raids of the war. With the bomber stream stretching for well
over three hundred miles, the devastating pounding of Big B continued
incessantly for hours. To have parachuted into the capital of Germany
upon that traumatic occasion well might have resulted in an American
airman experiencing the bloodthirsty fury of an enraged mob. Such a
perspective, however, likely may occur to a man only in retrospect, when
the pressure of a crisis is not upon him and he reflects at leisure about
what might have been.

King remembered that the demands of the moment weighed upon him as they continued winging eastward. "For the first time in my life, I was totally in charge," he said. "Always before there had been some-one—mother, father, teachers, military officers—directing me, telling me what to do. Now the responsibility was mine. I might advise with Sweeney, or Lowe, or the others, but as first pilot, I knew that ultimately I had to make the decisions."[1]

The foremost question, obviously, was where to land. During the early morning briefing, the 614th crews had been given coordinates for an emergency landing field behind Russian lines. At once King headed for that location, which seemed, both to him and Sweeney, the natural choice—a no-brainer, in current slang. All they found, however, was a plowed field, totally unsuitable for landing. "So we continued flying eastward, hoping to spot a field smooth enough and long enough to accommodate a B-17," said King. "I thought we needed to get near a city and a hospital, if somebody should be injured in the landing. That was my number-one thought, as we picked up the Vistula River and flew up the Vistula toward Warsaw."[2]

As Warsaw came in view the sight proved shocking. "We crisscrossed the city and were horrified at what we encountered," King said. "I had seen heavily damaged cities, but nothing like Warsaw." King's impression was that nearly every building appeared to have been destroyed: "Some-times there was a wall or two and a chimney still standing. Many times there was nothing left but rubble. When we found the airport, the run-ways had been totally bombed out, and the adjacent fields plowed up into trenches." People could be seen filling in bomb craters, he said, work-ing to create a runway for future use. But the job was not even close to being finished: "There was no way an airplane, any airplane, could have landed there without crashing."

The Maiden, at that point, had been flying on only two engines for a long time. The distance from Berlin to Warsaw, in a straight line, is close to 350 miles, and of course, the flight had not been altogether in a straight line. Twice King's hopes for a satisfactory landing field had been dashed. He realized they needed to get the bomber down soon; yet there seemed to be no chance of landing at Warsaw. "So I thought the only thing to do was continue flying east," he recalled, "and find a farm field big enough to land on, even if we had to make it a wheels up affair."[3]

That is when, flying away from the Warsaw airport, King and crew found their Fortress suddenly in the gun sight of a Russian fighter plane. It was a low-wing, single-seat Lavochkin La–5FN. Powered by a 1700-horsepower radial engine, the Lavochkin was armed with two 20mm cannon mounted in the upper fuselage deck and synchronized to fire through the propeller. The aircraft was one of the best Russian fighters, and its two cannon were certainly capable of bringing down a bomber. As King expressed it, "That Russian could have blown our plane to pieces."[4]

The Russian pilot was Major Jaskulsky Vikenty Ivanov, and the issue for him was whether the B-17 in his gun sight was manned by Americans or Germans. The Germans had been known sometimes to attack the Russians using a captured American plane. Ivanov could speak English, and he later told King that as he was coming around in a pursuit curve, with the American Fortress in his sight, he twice took up the slack in the triggers to his 20mm cannon, preparing to fire, only to let the slack out each time. He alternated between thinking, "Nazi," and then, a split second later, "No, American."

For the third time, said the Russian pilot, he took up the slack in the triggers. Then he saw that the B-17 pilot had fired a flare and lowered the landing gear. Myron said that one of the crew, spotting the Russian plane, had called out, "Fighter," giving the location—"ten o'clock," as best King could recall. Seeing the Russian insignia on the plane, Myron fired the flare, and "we put our feet down." Apparently it was in the nick of time before Ivanov began firing. Once convinced that an American crew manned the bomber, Ivanov directed and escorted the Maiden to his own base, called Kuflevo, a short distance east and south of Warsaw, near Minsk Mazowiecki.

King and Sweeney, however, still faced a big problem: landing their aircraft. The runway was very short, barely adequate for a fighter plane and not nearly long enough for a heavy bomber. Nor was the quality of the runway state of the art—far from it. Actually, the landing "field" was just that, a farmer's field with irrigation terraces across the landing area, about every eighteen to twenty feet.

The Russians had prepared a runway by flooding the field, knowing the water would quickly freeze in the very cold weather, thus providing a flat, smooth, but short runway for smaller aircraft. King said the whole field was no longer than the first third of a typical runway on which he and Sweeney were accustomed to landing a Fortress. Considering all factors, though, there seemed to be no other choice. They would have to land where the Russian directed.

"I don't remember ever concentrating in my life like I did approaching that landing," King said. "When I think of it today, it's just like I am right there again. I ordered the crew to assume their positions in the radio room, according to authorized procedure for crash landing. I was thinking that I've got to set the plane down immediately after crossing the fence or, for sure, we'll crash at the other end of the field." He gestured to indicate the extreme angle of descent he used, declaring "I bet our tail didn't miss that fence three feet, and the plane came down so hard, with such a crashing sound, that I first thought I had broken the landing gear."

Thankfully, the gear was intact. The noise came from ice breaking up under the weight of the bomber and crashing into the underside of the plane. According to King, Richard Lowe told him during a recent visit that he did not believe that one could crash a plane and make as much noise as that ice did. Lowe also said that he thought the sound was "very much like flak," something with which "we had plenty of experience." When King realized the noise came from pieces of ice pummeling the plane, he feared for the flaps.

Extending more than half the length of the wings and three feet wide, the fully extended flaps certainly were taking a beating as the wind from the props hurled big chunks of ice into them. Nothing could be done, however, except ride it out. "And so," concluded King, "we made a big skidding, sweeping turn . . . and going sideways too . . . and finally came to a stop at the end of that field." Breathing a sigh of relief, King shut down the engines. The Maiden had landed.[5]

The crew scrambled instantly from the plane, each man kissing the ground as soon as he touched it, according to King's recollection. Their landing attracted considerable attention, with a rather large number of people quickly gathering around, some in Russian military uniform and others apparently civilians. Customarily upon returning to Deenethorpe from a mission, the 401st crewmen were offered a two-ounce shot of whiskey—"right when you got out of the plane," explained King. Nobody expected that at Kuflevo. Nor were they anticipating hot coffee, usually provided by the Red Cross upon landing in England. What some crewmen did want was water.

Richard Lowe said he was very thirsty. However, neither he nor any other member of the crew spoke Russian, and none of the people closely packed about the plane could converse in English. "But through gestures we expressed a desire for water to drink," Lowe said. Promptly the Russians provided each man with a large tumbler filled with a clear liquid that Lowe assumed to be water. Unsuspectingly, he took a big swallow, and experienced his first-ever taste of vodka. "What a shock!" he said. And, one might add, what a welcome to Russian-controlled territory.[6]

★ ★ ★

Myron King and his crew assumed they soon would be returning to England. As it turned out, for them the war was over, and a Russian adventure was now underway—one that would eventually include a court-martial and considerable intrigue. But the King Crew, of course, had no inkling of any of that. For the moment, they were just glad to be on the ground.

King said they were escorted to an underground headquarters base, which reminded him of a command post in World War I trench warfare—at least as such operations appeared in the movies. The Russians brought in a high-school-age girl who spoke a little English, and she served as an interpreter. King then proceeded to explain, through the girl's interpretation, who they were and that they had just bombed Berlin. He said the Russians really warmed up when they heard about the Berlin raid. "They then were very cooperative. It was as if they couldn't do enough for us," he added. According to his understanding, the Russians would begin trying to get clearance for him, once the B-17 could be repaired, to fly to Lublin, Poland, where high-octane petrol could be obtained for the plane. At that point, King assumed he would then fly to an American base in Italy.

Also, to the blushing embarrassment of his young interpreter, the Russians wanted to know if the Americans desired "front-line wives." If so, the Russians would be pleased to provide female companionship for the crew for the night. Myron said that he carefully and politely declined on behalf of the entire crew—a decision, according to King, that was quite disappointing to togglier Sergeant Robert Pyne.[7]

The Russians then proceeded, recorded Reinoehl in his diary, to "throw a party for us." Waist gunner "K" Speelman was more specific. He said the Russians fed them well and then treated them to a dance. He didn't think the two-piece band (banjo and accordion) was very good, but he gave them credit for enthusiasm. After the dance, several of the crew were billeted separately in three or four small Polish homes. Speelman and Patsy DeVito were paired together and spent quite a while talking that night to the Polish family who hosted them. The family had brought in an English-speaking neighbor to act as an interpreter. Reinoehl said he slept in a house with some Russian pilots and the next morning discovered that his watch had disappeared.

King was billeted with the pilot who intercepted them. Myron said he had the impression that Major Ivanov commanded the base. Since he spoke English, they talked at length. In fact, the Russian pilot gave King his photograph with his name and a Kiev address, written on the back of the picture. King remembered the Russian as a handsome man who "looked like a Hollywood movie star."[8]

The next morning, Sunday, February 4, King and some of the crew set about examining the engines in hope of making repairs. In fact, Ernie Pavlas, whom King considered "an expert engineer," was already working on the number-two motor when King arrived. Soon appearing as well was copilot Sweeney, who King thought possessed a good knowledge of engines. King added that he himself had done a lot of mechanical work and that "in the late thirties, I was planning to build a 'do-it-yourself airplane.'"

The three men worked well together. There were also some Russians assigned to help them, but the language barrier presented problems. Pavlas had removed the cowling by the time King got there to help and thought the main problem lay with the oil cooler. Once they got the cooler out and discovered holes in it, King said, "we went up to a farm house and found a box of old tractor tools, a blow torch and some scrap lead." They fired up the blow torch, soldered the holes in front and back of the cooler, reinstalled the piece, and started up the engine. "It ran hot," King declared, "but it ran. Ran just fine."

The number-four engine, as luck would have it, appeared to have taken care of itself. King said they figured that the extreme cold, freezing up a water line, had caused the motor to run away. Apparently, the problem was not the result of any flak damage. Once thawed out, the motor seemed OK. The plane had a number of holes in it administered by the flak; there were also some noticeable dents from the ice that had been slung into the underside. But that kind of damage would not keep the aircraft from flying. Flaps, ailerons, elevators—all the control surfaces—appeared to be responding properly. "I wonder," mused Myron, "how many crews, forced down in Russian lines, managed to repair their plane themselves. I bet there would not have been many."[9]

The following day, February 5, Pavlas worked on the ship all day, attempting to ensure that everything was functioning well. Myron spent most of the morning with Major Ivanov, who was trying to help King get clearance to fly to Lublin, where they thought he could get sufficient fuel for a flight to Italy. King's understanding from talking with the Russian was that he could be cleared to fly to Italy. However, the only information they could get from Lublin was that gas was not available there. King hoped some favorable news would develop later in the day, or at least by the next day.[10]

Then would come the crucial test. Could a B-17 actually take off from that incredibly short field? Landing there had proved a tough challenge. Taking off promised to be an even greater one.

9 ★ A Bizarre Affair

KING AND SWEENEY EXAMINED THE AIRFIELD CAREFULLY. FOR THAT matter, the entire crew scrutinized that runway. Two of the men had learned to fly small planes before entering the service, and every member of the crew obviously had spent a lot of time in a B-17. All knew how much distance and speed it normally took to get one of those bombers airborne. Understandably, every man had a keen interest in that airfield, and the chances are they all harbored serious doubts that the Maiden could take off from such a short runway.

King said one end of the runway rested on a slight hill, from which there was a gradual descent to the other end of the field—"maybe ten to fifteen degrees," he speculated. If he took off into the wind, as a pilot is supposed to do, then the plane would be going uphill, because the wind customarily came from that direction. After walking the field and mulling over the matter, Myron "figured the downhill run would give us the best chance. Usually, there was only a little breeze anyway, and building sufficient speed seemed the critical issue—more important than a slight wind. Even going downhill, I knew it would be very difficult to reach flying speed before we ran out of runway."

He also observed that a road crossed the lower end of the runway. Roughly speaking, the intersection of the road and the runway composed a "T" configuration. The top of the T was the road and the stem the runway. King said the road surface was built up above the runway well over a foot, maybe two feet or more. That road, as events turned out, would be a factor in the takeoff. King believed they might be able to lift off going downhill if they first removed everything from the plane that was not absolutely essential for it to fly. Clearly, he did not think much of their chances in the other direction.[1]

The plan, once the Maiden was airborne, was to head south to Lublin, a city no more than seventy miles distant, where Major Ivanov said they would find an adequate runway and suitable fuel. From there, King thought, they would fly to an American base in Italy. By Monday afternoon, February 5, the bomber seemed to be in flying condition, and the crew was preparing, if they got clearance, for what all anticipated would be a hazardous takeoff. King and Sweeney were in the Maiden's cockpit, warming up and further testing the engines, when, Sweeney said, "a Russian C-47 buzzed the field, buzzed it again, and came in and landed."[2]

The American-designed, twin-engine transport taxied up at once, parked right beside the B-17, and a Russian general emerged from the ship. Sweeney related that he immediately exited the Maiden via the nose hatch and walked over to the general, while King finished shutting down the engines. Sweeney began conversing with the general through a young man who acted as an interpreter. Soon King came up and joined the conversation. King described the young man, who became a key figure in subsequent events, as a boy, maybe eighteen or nineteen years old. Both King and Sweeney naturally assumed he belonged to the general's party in the C-47—which he probably did. All the King Crew, in fact, thought the young interpreter arrived with the general, although apparently none of them actually saw him get out of the plane. The situation, with the boy interpreting for the general, just made it seem reasonable that he had flown in with the Russian officer.[3]

When the general learned that the Americans intended to fly to Lublin—which he well may have known before he landed—he told King and Sweeney that they could not go there. He gave them no explanation, but clearly his decision was not subject to discussion. He did inform them that they could fly with him to Lida, which was in the opposite direction from Lublin, and nearly two hundred miles northeast of Kuflevo. Indeed, the general would be escorting them to Lida, a city where, he said, they could obtain aviation fuel and then fly to an American base at Poltava, which lay some distance east of Kiev. His invitation to fly with him to Lida perhaps constituted the proverbial offer that one does not refuse. Thus, as Sweeney expressed it, "We decided that we would fly to Lida." That the Russian general arrived at Kuflevo by mere coincidence seems rather unlikely. Again, Sweeney's apt words on the matter: "The Russian general said, 'You are going to fly on my wing.' So we flew."[4]

Until this time, King and his crew knew nothing about the existence of an American air base at Poltava, and only later would they learn what had been occurring in Lublin—the latter likely explaining the Russian general's determination to prevent the Americans from flying there. Operating in Lublin was a self-proclaimed provisional government of Poland. The regime was a Communist puppet, developed and recognized by Moscow, and functioning in a closed city. For their part, the United States and Great Britain favored the Polish government-in-exile, headquartered in London. At the very time the King Crew arrived at Kuflevo, the Soviets were in the process of transferring the Lublin government to Warsaw, and Joseph Stalin, at the Yalta Conference, was speaking of that regime as the Warsaw government.

The legitimacy of Poland's government had become a major international issue between the Americans and the British on the one hand and their Russian ally on the other. King, Sweeney, and the rest of the crew had been too busy fighting the war to know much, if anything, about such high-stakes political maneuvering over the future of Eastern Europe. Also, no member of the King Crew held a rank higher than that of first lieutenant, and all they desired from the Lublin airport was fuel, after which they wanted to fly to Italy as soon as possible. Nevertheless, it appears that at Kuflevo they inadvertently came too close to the political action. Even if they were not high-ranking brass and knew nothing of the Lublin government, it was too close for the comfort of the secretive Russian leaders, who disliked Americans—any Americans—being in Russian-controlled territory in the first place and who were irrevocably committed, as the world would learn in months to come, to the domination of all of Eastern Europe.

EUROPE DURING THE WAR, EASTERN FRONT

Although a trifle puzzled by the general's brusque negation of their intended flight to Lublin, King and Sweeney quickly focused once more on their monumental challenge: getting the B-17 into the air. The general was in a hurry. He said that he would not fly at night, and the time was then late afternoon, about five o'clock, as King remembered it. The general did agree to take with him part of Myron's crew, plus equipment removed from the bomber in order to lessen the weight. The smaller, lighter C-47 could take off from the short runway without difficulty.

Thus, anything heavy that could be removed—particularly machine guns, ammunition, and flak suits—were transferred to the general's plane. "There was a lot of confusion," recalled Sweeney, "everyone running around transferring stuff from one ship to the other." Sweeney painted a hectic scene, and the tone rings true, given the peculiar circumstances. As he remembered, "They would talk to us in Russian," which of course the Americans did not understand. "There were Russians running around inside both planes," he said, "and Americans running back and forth between the planes. . . . It was awfully hard to convey anything."

The Maiden's skeleton crew for the takeoff, in addition to King and Sweeney, included Lowe and Pavlas; the other five members of the crew were to ride with the general. As King and Sweeney began running up the Maiden's engines, a piece of the cowling blew off one of the motors, and King feared that it might have struck the tail. He instructed Pavlas to go back, take a good look around, and see if any damage had resulted. Returning to the flight deck with a welcome report of no harm done to the tail structure, the engineer also brought unexpected word that the general's interpreter had gotten on board their plane.

King immediately turned to navigator Lowe, who had just come up from the nose of the ship, and said, according to Sweeney's later testimony, "Tell that boy to get the hell out of here, and into the C-47." But when Lowe looked out the waist door of the B-17, he saw that the general's plane had already taxied into takeoff position, and thus the boy could not be transferred to the Russian's aircraft. Unlike American flyers, who warmed up their engines, the Russians started their motors, immediately taxied out to the head of the runway, and, never running up the engines, simply took off. Consequently, as Lowe informed King, it was too late to make the transfer. "We will have to take him with us then," said King, according to Lowe's testimony. Ordinary courtesy dictated, given the situation, that they carry the general's interpreter with them, knowing their next stop would be where the general landed. "So," concluded Sweeney, "we told him to get back in the radio room and we would take him to join the General."[5]

Clearly, pilot and copilot had little time to concern themselves with their uninvited passenger. A quick glance at the B-17's performance specifications leaves no doubt that they faced a very dangerous takeoff. A speed of 110 to 115 miles per hour and a takeoff distance of 3,400 feet, according to the Boeing company, were necessary for a Fortress to lift off. The runway at Kuflevo was markedly shorter than 3,400 feet—"approximately 2,000 feet long," testified King—and King knew he could not reach a speed of 110 mph before the end of the runway would be upon them.[6]

Nevertheless, King thought he had a reasonably good chance of getting the B-17 into the air. Three factors would work in his favor. For one, the plane would not be as heavy as it usually was on takeoff. Second, he would give the engines a boost in power by pushing the throttles into the "war-emergency" range. While an engine could not be run long in war-emergency power because cylinder heads would begin developing cracks and ruinous damage would soon result, it was possible to increase the horsepower from the normal 1200 to 1380 for a short time—a total of 5520 horsepower for the combined four motors rather than the customary 4800. Still another important factor would be increasing lift, the instant the plane became airborne, by dropping the flaps. The flaps could not be extended during the takeoff run, of course, since the drag would hinder the buildup to maximum speed. But the second the ship was in the air, the flaps were to be deployed.[7]

Yet another factor came into play, and it was an intangible but highly significant consideration: King's ability to fly the bomber. Those were the days before computers assisted pilots. It was the era of "stick-and-rudder" flying, when a pilot's "feel" for handling his ship could mean the difference between life and death. King said that when he first began flying a B-17, the plane "felt like I was driving a Greyhound bus." By this stage of the war, though, he had flown it so much that he felt very comfortable with it—"almost as if I were flying a fighter plane." He added, "And all that buzzing I did back in the states, even if they did not want you doing it, improved my ability to fly that ship. So I told Sweeney to take care of everything in the cockpit [meaning particularly the gear and the flaps]." As King also told Sweeney, "If this big-assed bird will fly, I'll get it out of here. I'll fly this thing by the seat of my pants." King explained that "the old timers" used to say that.[8]

Another intangible should be noted: the plane itself. Just as some cars perform better than others of the same make and model, there are some aircraft that are superior to others of the same make. Possibly, the Maiden was one of those special airplanes. The pilot who flew the ship on more missions than any other man, Lieutenant Norman L. Sisson, clearly considered her a superior plane. "Aircraft 6508 was a flying dream, a Cadillac of the Fortresses," Sisson wrote. "This bomber would fly without trim and respond instantly to any control. It was a breeze to fly in formation. . . . It could maintain the Group's airspeed on three engines and would land with the touch of a feather." Wisdom dictates a bit of caution when contemplating such a subjective issue, but it is just possible that King was at the controls of a Fortress with extraordinary flying characteristics.[9]

When he taxied the bomber up on that slight rise of ground, facing that short runway, locking the brakes and pushing up on the power, King had to know—and Sweeney, Lowe and Pavlas knew as well—that their takeoff run required a total commitment. The runway was too short for any second guessing once they had started down it. They must either take off or crash. King said that when he removed the restraining rod and pushed the throttles into war-emergency power, while holding hard on the brakes, "that plane was shaking like I never felt shaking." And then, releasing the brakes, down the field they went, rapidly building speed—but not fast enough. "We were going about eighty miles per hour, maybe a little more, when we reached the end of the field, and when our wheels hit the edge of that road, we literally bounced into the air," said King. "Sweeney had one hand on the gear control and one hand on the flap controls, and the very instant we were in the air, he had the wheels coming up and the flaps going down. I'll bet he didn't waste a split second getting that job done."[10]

Even so, King described how the plane dropped down close to the ground; so close that he thought the propeller blades, for a second, might have bitten into the snow, which was more than a foot deep. Undoubtedly the whirling props were so close to the snow that they were blowing the white stuff everywhere. But the Fortress was in the air—barely. The aircraft needed to build more speed before King could hope to climb. And dead ahead lay a clump of trees.

The only hope of avoiding the trees was to go around them. However, using the ailerons, normally second nature for a pilot in making a turn, was out of the question because the plane was so close to the ground. The ailerons would drop the wing on the side to which the plane is turning. Thus, King had to guide the turn with nothing but the rudder. "We had to make a flat, skidding turn, breaking all the rules of turning," as he expressed it. With little room to spare, he managed to skirt the trees successfully.

"I still didn't try to climb," remembered King. "Didn't think we had enough speed and lift. We went across another field after the one containing the clump of trees. That airplane was in a sort of cocked-up position, like all that wind was blowing on the ground. And then finally, it just took off itself. The lift had become so strong that the plane went up. It went up steeply," continued King. "I didn't pull it up steep; she had at last gotten enough speed and enough lift to go up by herself." King added, "That was the most heavenly feeling—going up like that—I can ever remember in flying." A great sense of relief flooded over King: "We had been down on a field that we couldn't take off from, which was the case with many downed American bombers. But we did. We had taken off from a field that should have been impossible to take off from."[11]

As soon as the Maiden was safely in the air and fully under control, King took the engines out of war-emergency power. A later examination would reveal the motors had gotten so hot and stressed that every one of the engines had some cracked cylinders. Despite that, the motors were providing the necessary power, as the Maiden flew on the wing of the Russian C-47, heading toward Lida, the place where the general said he was taking them. Then, when they were perhaps halfway to Lida and King was relaxing just a bit after the harrowing takeoff from Kuflevo, he learned from Pavlas that the general's "interpreter" was no such thing.

Pavlas said he had gone back in the plane to check further on the tail structure, when the young man told him that he had an uncle in London and that he was not the general's interpreter. Once the engineer got back to the flight deck, he informed King of what the young fellow had said. King was taken completely by surprise. In fact, he testified, "I was dumbfounded . . . and did not know exactly what to do." Years later, King said that when he heard Pavlas's words, "I sensed that we had a problem."[12]

Indeed they did. At that time, however, King had no idea of the incident's eventual magnitude. When he had first learned the young man was on board the B-17 and had ordered him out, King said the fellow responded, apparently to Lowe or Pavlas, "I want to fly in your airplane." That statement led King to believe that the man, after seeing some of the American crew get into the general's plane, and much like a boy back in the states might try to finagle a ride in a Fortress if he got a chance, thus decided that "he would ride in our ship for the thrill of it"—to use King's words. Since he was thought to be the general's interpreter and could not then be transferred to the Russian plane, King was not particularly concerned about the matter—beyond realizing that the boy probably had no concept of how dangerous their takeoff would be. It was too late to do anything about that, however.[13]

After learning that the boy, whom they came to call Jack Smith, was not the general's interpreter, King understandably viewed the incident in a very different perspective. He and Sweeney exchanged thoughts about the matter—"the usual procedure," according to Sweeney, "just talking back and forth and deciding to send him to the American authorities." Of course, the responsibility for the decision to take him to the American authorities at Poltava, and not turn him over to the Russians, was King's—for better or worse. "I figured," King said, "not knowing the situation, . . . and what [the Russians] would do with him . . . , that it would be best to turn him in at Poltava, where the [American] authorities there would know better how to handle the situation than I did."[14]

As the testimony of both King and Sweeney certainly conveys, pilot and copilot expected to fly to Poltava as soon as they gassed up the plane at Lida, possibly that night but the next day for sure. King's decision, as Sweeney's testimony confirms, was consistent with the typical American practice, when flying in foreign countries, of reporting infractions and violations of regulations—such as an attempt by an unauthorized foreigner to stow away on a military aircraft—to U.S. authorities. And so the matter was determined as they winged toward Lida in the late afternoon's gathering darkness. For some unexplained reason, however, possibly because darkness came on so rapidly, the two planes did not go all the way to Lida. Instead, the general's plane led King's B-17 to an airfield some thirty to fifty miles southwest of Lida, at a town called Szczuczyn.[15]

The general's plane first buzzed the Szczuczyn field, intending for the B-17 to land before the C-47. The airfield was a fighter-bomber base with a steel-mat runway considerably longer than the Kuflevo field, a welcome sight to King and Sweeney. Myron estimated the runway's length as approximately a mile and said that he made a straight-in approach, all the while enamored of the breathtaking, panoramic scene unfolding around him. A foot or more of snow covered the ground, and a long row of tall, snow-blanketed fir trees stretched beside the base, "silhouetted against a deep purple sky," in the last few moments before darkness settled over the field.[16]

King said the Russians turned a high-powered search light upon the Fortress as she touched down and followed the plane to the end of the runway with that light. King painted an impressive picture in words of the landing: "So, there was a giant circle of white light, about the height of those tall, snow-enshrouded trees, moving along those trees, with the B-17's shadow right in the middle of that circle." Recalling the great scenes from the movie *Dr. Zhivago*, King asserted that none of them "could touch the scene I saw just before dark when we landed at Szczuczyn."[17]

The general's C-47 then landed behind King, using only about half of the runway, after which it turned around and taxied back down the runway, where the pilot parked the ship on the opposite side of the field. When the B-17 came to a stop, all four Americans exited the plane through the nose hatch. Soon a Russian drove up in what Sweeney and

Pavlas both said was a jeep—still more evidence, along with the C-47 and the steel mat runway—of major American assistance to the Russians through the lend-lease program. By means of gestures, plus a bare minimum of words, the Russian driver instructed Sweeney, Lowe, and Pavlas to get into the jeep, while making motions for Myron to reboard the plane. King was to take the bomber to the other side of the field, parking it beside the general's transport, while the Russian drove the rest of the crew to the operations room.[18]

By the time King taxied the Maiden to the opposite end of the field and pulled up along side the C-47, it was obvious that all of the general's party, and the Americans who flew with him, had left the aircraft. King said that he then went through the plane, front to back, checking it prior to exiting at the waist door. Still in the radio room was the young, uninvited passenger. Myron observed that he had put on some American flying clothes, which undoubtedly came from the crew's emergency bag.

"The emergency bag," explained King, "contained an extra pair of shoes and a complete assortment of emergency flying clothes for altitude flying." King readily understood that the boy must have gotten cold, as the B-17 had been even colder than normal because of big holes in the fuselage from flak damage. He still did not know quite what to think of the young stowaway who wanted to spend the night in the plane. Myron said that his English was "excellent," with a marked British accent: "I figured he was telling the truth about wanting to go to London and see his uncle. I thought he probably was from England." King said that neither he nor any of the crew was "looking for intrigue; [we were] just trying to take everything one day at a time." Phil Reinoehl also believed the boy's story about wanting to get to England. Only later, declared King, when he learned more about U.S.–Soviet relations and the problems that had been developing between the countries, did the possibility occur to him that the Russians, seeking ways to get Americans out of the Soviet Union, might have planted a stowaway on the Maiden in order to cause trouble.

King finally had to order the fellow out of the plane, after which the two walked together to the operations room where the rest of the crew had gathered. As for the clothing the young stranger had appropriated, King said the weather "was very cold and I did not see any point in having him change his clothes." At the operations room, King hoped to get clearance to fly to Poltava, possibly that night. "I thought surely we would get out of there the next day, or at worst, the day after that," he said. "Little did I know we would be at Szczuczyn for the next five weeks."[19]

When King reached the operations room, the general and his party were nowhere to be seen; nor would they reappear that night. Soon it became apparent to King and all the crew that they would not be cleared for an immediate flight to Poltava. "We waited at operations approximately thirty minutes," testified King, "while they fixed the dining room for us to eat." The crew was in a large, fine building, which King described as essentially a palace and probably, he speculated, had once been the centerpiece of a great plantation. He likened the mansion, with its magnificent white columns, to the White House in Washington, D.C. "When everything was ready, they directed us into the dining room," King said, "where ten places [with clearly one for Jack Smith] had been prepared, in a very elaborate manner, the best they had." When Sweeney later testified about the occasion, he said, "They treated us like kings. . . . Gave us the best food they had and Vodka."[20]

Following the meal most of the crew, and Jack Smith along with them, were directed to sleeping quarters elsewhere, while the officers— King, Sweeney, and Lowe—were billeted in the mansion. King said they were given a large bedroom upstairs, over the entrance. "And after we got in our room," related King, "some musicians below us started playing 'Chattanooga Choo Choo.'" Then, with emphasis, he said, "That blew my mind. There we were in Russian-controlled Poland, and the Russians were playing 'Chattanooga Choo Choo.' Half of my life had been spent in Chattanooga and the Russians were playing that song, obviously it seemed, for us. They played it several times." Later, Myron learned that only a few days before he arrived, the base at Szczuczyn had obtained an American movie in which "Chattanooga Choo Choo" had been featured. The musicians had listened closely and learned to play the tune.[21]

The first order of business the following morning was to transfer the B-17's equipment, which had been transported in the C-47, back to the American aircraft. King and crew were also advised that weather conditions would not allow them to be given a clearance to fly to Poltava that day. That line would become all too familiar in the days and weeks to come, leaving no doubt in the minds of the Americans that inclement weather provided a convenient excuse for the Russians to detain them. Why they were being detained remains an enigma to this day. Eventually, the King Crew would learn that the Russians never informed the American base at Poltava that they were safely down behind Russian lines. King said—and Lowe verified his account—that he requested more than once that the Russians notify the American authorities about their safety and was assured that they had done so. Speculating about the matter six decades later, King said, "They just got rid of anybody who gave them a problem. That's why they never reported my crew's location and safety to Poltava. If they had decided to get rid of us, they would not have had to answer to anybody."[22]

During the morning of February 6, according to King, the Russian general who led them to Szczuczyn called him into his office, along with a Russian interpreter, and asked for a list of everyone on the plane. Myron included the name of Jack Smith. Actually, he did not know the name of the young man and explained that he wrote "Jack Smith" because that was the name of a navigator who had trained with the crew for a while before being transferred elsewhere. Who among the King Crew first called the fellow Jack Smith probably is impossible now to determine. Every member of the crew must have known that Jack Smith was not his real name. Myron said some also called him "Jocko."

The general next wanted to know, as he pointed to each name on the list, if that person was an American. When he pointed to the name Jack Smith, King replied, "No." Then the general asked if he was Polish, and King indicated that he did not know the man's nationality. ("I never thought he was a Pole, however," declared King in an interview many years later.) Turning to a large map on the wall, the general inquired where Jack Smith got on the American bomber. That well may have struck King as a strange query, one to which the general presumably knew the answer. King patiently told the general that he boarded at Kuflevo, from which they flew to Szczuczyn on the general's wing, discovering en route that the boy was not the general's interpreter. King said he also told the general of his decision to take Jack Smith with his crew and turn him over to the American authorities on the charge of violating U.S. regulations that prohibited unauthorized persons from riding in an American military airplane.[23]

Following King's meeting with the general, he and Lowe decided to go into the town and stroll around for a while. Szczuczyn was a small place, only about five blocks in length and three blocks wide. The history of the village dated back to the late seventeenth century, when it served as the administrative center for the estate of Stanislaw Antony Szczuka, vice chancellor of the Grand Duchy of Lithuania. Through the years, Szczuczyn had come under the rule of Prussia, Czarist Russia, Imperial Germany, the Polish Republic, the Soviet Union, and Nazi Germany. On the eve of World War II, the population numbered approximately fifty-seven hundred, with Jews constituting more than half of the town's inhabitants. For them, the war had been devastating.

First, in September 1939, came the German army's invasion, which led to the immediate deportation of some three hundred Jewish men to Germany and the burning of the village synagogue. By the end of the month, the Germans turned over Szczuczyn to their ally at the time, the Russian army, which soon exiled a number of prominent Jewish families to Siberia. Gangs of Polish anti-Semites joined in the persecution, organizing a pogrom and killing scores of Jews. Then, in June 1941, the Germans came again to Szczuczyn, having attacked their former Soviet ally. The Nazis at once killed some six hundred Jews, and established the rest, perhaps two thousand people, in a ghetto. By late 1942 and early 1943, these Jews were deported to the Auschwitz and Treblinka death camps and killed. By the time King and his crew arrived in Szczuczyn, the general population probably numbered less than twenty-five hundred, and all the Jews had been killed or removed.

While King and Lowe explored the town, Sweeney and the rest of the crew stayed at the base, hanging out with some Russian pilots. Sweeney said that during this time Jack Smith told him that he had been upstairs in the barber shop when the general had come in and recognized him. Clearly, thought Sweeney, the boy was worried. He remained with Sweeney and the others. "Within five or ten minutes," related Sweeney, "a Russian Captain came in and took him away. I never saw him again." Neither did King nor any other member of the crew.[24]

There was never any satisfactory explanation from the Russian general concerning the matter—which came as no surprise to King. In the weeks that followed, as various members of the crew visited the town, they encountered more than one English-speaking Pole who inquired about the welfare of their crew. In particular, they asked about the one who had been wounded. Richard Lowe, who had suffered a superficial neck wound over Berlin, did not seem to be the crew member the Polish questioners had in mind. When told that the crew were all fine, King said, the Poles replied that they had heard one of the crew had been shot. Phil Reinoehl recalled specifically that some of the crew were out walking when they met some Polish men, one of whom could speak English and who said, apparently expressing the testimony of all, that the Russians had shot the young man. Reports also circulated that gunshots had been heard on the base, coming from behind a building, on the day Jack Smith disappeared.[25]

Probably the closest anyone in the Russian military ever came to an explanation of the Jack Smith mystery involved the navigator on the general's C-47. One night, according to tail gunner George Atkinson, the navigator went to the room of the B-17's enlisted men, with whom Jack Smith had spent one night. Having obviously consumed a large quantity of vodka, the Russian pointed to the spot where Jack Smith had spent the night. He then pointed his thumb and forefinger as if it were a pistol and indicated that the young man had been shot.[26]

King had hoped that when the stowaway realized the Americans had simply landed at another field in Poland and were next intending to fly several hundred miles into Russia that he would give up trying to reach England with them—or whatever it was he had in mind—and disappear. King, of course, never envisioned such a mysterious disappearance, which left a host of questions and no satisfactory answer.

★ ★ ★

Later in February, back in the United States, the King family and Eleanor Goodpasture received word that Myron was missing in action. Eleanor also received a letter from Ward J. Fellows, chaplain of the 401st Bomb Group, a major portion of which follows:

Dear Miss Goodpasture:

Sometime ago, when he was first here, 1st Lieutenant Myron L. King . . . asked me to write you if he were ever missing. . . . From what Myron said to me I know how hard this must be for you, and I speak for the Commanding General, Eighth Air Force, and the Commanding Officer and others of the 401st Bombardment Group in assuring you of our regret and sympathy. It is our hope and prayer that he will return and that the two of you will be able to fulfill your plans together. But in any event I want you to be assured of Myron's love and loyalty toward you, and to know that he showed himself a courageous, fine, and truly Christian man while serving in the uniform of the air force here. May you find help and strength from God in this trial, and may your faith be equal to anything, as is the love and power of God in Jesus Christ.

In an interview decades later, Eleanor shared her thoughts at the time she received the letter. Specifically, did she feel that Myron likely had been killed? "No," she said, explaining that only a few days before he was reported missing, she had received a letter from him in which he told her, "Don't worry if you should hear that I am missing, for a lot of things can go right, even when you are reported missing." Eleanor, who was also concerned about her older brother, then serving with the Marines and soon to be landing on Okinawa, said that Myron's letter "helped a lot. Of course I knew that he might be gone, but that letter helped keep up my spirit."[27]

10 ★ The Russian Adventure Darkens

ON THE DAY AFTER A RUSSIAN OFFICER TOOK JACK SMITH AWAY, KING was again summoned by the general who led them to Szczuczyn. He wanted a detailed written account of everything King knew about Jack Smith. King said that he "wrote the complete story of how [Jack Smith] had interpreted for the General, and how we thought he was the General's interpreter, and how our engineer later found out that he wasn't." King went on to explain that "I intended to turn him in [to American authorities] at Poltava, and that I did not want to cause any trouble with our Russian friends." King also said, "I wrote FRIENDS in big letters."[1]

The general's interpreter could not speak English very well, but he possessed an English-Russian dictionary, using it to translate King's statement into Russian. "At first the General was very stern," according to King. But as he read the statement, "he nodded approval at each sentence." When he finished the statement, "The General seemed well pleased with the explanation," thought King. Then occurred, quite suddenly, an intense and frightening moment. The general emphatically uttered something in Russian, became very excited—or so it seemed to King—pulled out his pistol, walked quickly around King, and pointed the muzzle into King's back. Just as quickly, he pulled the weapon away, returned the sidearm to its holster, and appeared to resume his normal mood. The general's dramatic action, as best King could eventually understand, was nothing more than the Russian's way of conveying that supposedly Jack Smith would have shot King in the back.[2]

After that unnerving episode, the general attempted to explain to King that he should forget about the Jack Smith incident. "He finally got it over to me," testified King, "by mentioning Jack Smith, then making me say the name, and making out as though he didn't know what I was talking about." King gathered that the general was telling him that the incident was a local affair, would be dealt with at that base, and would never go any further. "That," related King, "was the interpretation that I got."[3]

Following his meeting with the general that day, February 7, King said, he and the crew found armed guards stationed outside their rooms that night. Also, two Russian airmen came to their quarters—"one of whom could speak English fluently," recalled King. They began associating with all of the crew. He said they would spend "three or four hours [with us] every night and a couple of hours in the day." King soon drew a reasonable conclusion that "the General was deciding whether we had told him the truth about Jack Smith or whether we were trying to put something over on him."[4]

Obviously the Russians were not going to allow their American "guests" to leave Szczuczyn anytime soon. In fact, "They pulled a big [piece of equipment] in front of our plane so we could not leave," wrote Phil Reinoehl in his February 7 diary entry. King explained that the large, heavy machine was a snow scraper, with which the Russians cleared the runway. He estimated its width as thirty feet. "They would hook it to a tractor and pull it down the runway to scrape off the snow," he recalled. "Well, they parked that thing right in front of the B-17. Placed guards there too." For several days "our movements were very restricted," said King.[5]

One day while the crew members were closely confined, the Russian guards came in with instructions for them to strip off their clothes and take a shower. When some of the men indicated that they did not want to take a shower, they were ordered to strip anyway. Clearly, the Russians had no concern for the cleanliness of the crew but were merely using the shower, said King, "as an excuse for an opportunity to search our clothing." King recalled that Sweeney became worried because he had "some identity papers, passports, or something of that nature, which he said Jack Smith had left with him." King said he personally never saw those papers and supposed they disappeared at that time.[6]

After several days passed, the Russians relaxed their hold a bit, permitting the crew to visit the Maiden, run up the engines, and clear the snow off the wings. Judging from Reineohl's diary, snow must have fallen, on average, about every third day and in large amounts. Given such snowy weather and very cold temperatures (often twenty degrees below zero), they really needed to get the snow off the plane and warm up the motors. Various mechanics, pilots, gunners, guards, and even civilians showed a lot of interest in the bomber. Consequently, the crew conducted tours through the plane, answering questions and relating interesting facts about the B-17 whenever anyone was present who could serve as an interpreter. King and the others hoped such openness and patience would reassure the Russians about the Americans' proper motivations and good will.[7]

While passing the time, some of the crew examined the big snow scraper stationed in front of the Maiden. Curious about how much it weighed, they pushed and pulled on the thing, discovering that if several of them applied enough muscle, they could move it around, which they proceeded to do, a decision that was not among their wiser moments. "When we got out there the next morning," said King, "the Russians had not put the scraper back. Instead, they had brought up four runway rollers, placing one in front of each motor."

The rollers were big, heavy, steel-cast-construction machines that were used to pack the snow on the runway. Whenever the snow became too much of a problem, the Russians, instead of clearing the runway, "just packed it with those rollers, making it like ice," said King, "and the planes could take off without a problem." Not only had the Russians positioned one roller in front of each engine, but they had also turned each of the rollers on its side with a bulldozer. "And only a bulldozer could move them," King declared.[8]

Apparently unwilling to forget the matter and choosing to kid around about it, one or more of the crew informed the Russian guards that the rollers could never stop a Fortress. The American aircraft was so advanced, they claimed, that it actually could back up. The irony is that, in fact, both King and Sweeney could back up the bomber. "Sweeney was really good at it," King said. He explained that by locking the left brake and running up the number-one engine, the right side of the plane could be swung back. Then, unlocking the left brake and idling the number-one engine, while holding hard on the right brake and running up the number-four engine, the left side of the aircraft could be swung backward. "If you continued to alternate like that," King declared with a touch of a smile, "why you could just back that B-17 up with no difficulty. Sweeney could do it fast." Evidently the Russians were convinced that the Fortress could back up. The next morning, King and crew found the Russians had dug an impassable trench behind the Maiden.[9]

★ ★ ★

The King Crew generally seemed to get on well with the Russian flyers, who loved to party. "The Russian flyers were friendly," noted Richard Lowe. "One or two of them spoke some English, and one taught us to play chess." Lowe said they flew most of their missions at night, and "whenever a mission was scrubbed they would come and wake us for a party, . . . which mostly amounted to drinking huge quantities of Vodka, with raw bacon chaser, music and Russian dancing." Phil Reinoehl particularly remarked about the celebration of "Red Army Day"—which he said actually continued for two days—featuring "a big dance," heavy drinking, and a great deal of noise. "I never heard so much noise," Reinoehl wrote in his diary.[10]

Of particular interest to the Americans were the Russian women pilots. King and the others knew that American and British women were engaged in ferrying various kinds of warplanes. Sometimes they piloted them from the factory to a military base or from one base to another. But American and British women never flew in combat, as the Russian women were doing. A few of them flew the best Russian fighter planes and became aces. Most of the female pilots at Szczuczyn, though, flew old, rickety, canvas-covered biplanes. King said they "looked like somebody might have built them in his back yard." The majority of these aircraft were Polikarpov PO-2s: two-seater, open-cockpit, sixty-miles-per-hour planes, which carried no more than four small bombs. On the positive side, however, the aircraft was cheap, simple, and surprisingly reliable.

Through the hellish Russian winter, exposed to extreme cold in the open cockpits, the women flew both day and night—more often at night. Many of them died, for German antiaircraft fire could be deadly, while a few racked up incredible numbers of missions. Flying four or five, maybe even eight or ten sorties per night, some of those women became veterans of seven hundred, eight hundred, or a thousand missions by the end of the war, and were decorated as heroes of the Soviet Union. Germans who were attacked by them came to call the women "the night witches." Often the night witches would cut their engines, gliding noiselessly over the German lines to drop their bombs, or sometimes the woman who was not piloting the plane would drop hand grenades into the German camps. Such tactics interrupted sleep, spread terror, and killed and wounded Germans at random—occasionally in large numbers.[11]

Myron said he talked with some of the women about the number of missions they had flown. "I didn't want to tell them we had flown twenty missions," he confessed, "for they wouldn't have thought that was anything." Thus, to save face, he said, "We added all our missions together, twenty for each member of the crew, plus Pyne, who was on his third tour, and that came to a total of over two hundred." One of the Russian women, hearing from King that the crew had flown more than two hundred missions, commented to him in her broken English, as she patted his arm, "Oh, . . . you are an old pilot."[12]

King also recalled a discussion with the women concerning procedures for takeoff. As noted earlier, Russian pilots, both men and women, started a plane's motors and, with no warming up or checklist for safety, taxied at once to the head of the runway. Then, without pause, they took off. One of the women, upon learning how the American flyers went through a detailed procedure and warmed the engines thoroughly, bluntly told Myron, "You waste a lot of petrol." He replied, "Well, you fly your way and I'll fly mine."[13]

Perhaps no occasion during their five-week stay at Szczuczyn created more of a stir for King and Lowe than the celebration of Woman's

Day in the Russian army. The date was March 8, according to Reinoehl's diary entry. "They woke us up at 12:00 or 1:00 at night," said King. "'Get up,' they were saying. Then 'Szczuczyn and Frau,' and 'Szczuczyn and Vodka,' they repeatedly told us. They intended for us—the officers, that is—to help them celebrate woman's day in the army, and they were not about to let us refuse." Myron said Sweeney was sick with a bad cold, but the Russians insisted that King and Lowe join them for a party. "So Sweeney stayed in the room and Lowe and I went to the celebration, and what a party it was," he declared.

"Probably there were twelve of us sitting around a table, with Lowe and me together at one end of the table, where several large plants were positioned nearby," King continued. Already some of the Russians were inebriated and singing Russian songs—apparently crooning with considerable gusto. From time to time, the boisterous Russians wanted King and Lowe to sing, while they sang along with them. "I couldn't think of anything that seemed appropriate for the situation," Myron said, "except the Air Corps song. So I would lead them in 'Off we go, into the wild blue yonder . . . ' and so on. While I kept their attention, Lowe dumped his vodka on the nearest plant. Then when he led the Air Corps song, I dumped my vodka on the plant. They kept filling our glasses and we kept dumping the drinks on that plant. We also began keeping a hand around the glass so they couldn't tell how much Vodka remained. And that's how we managed, as the celebration went on and on, to keep from getting drunk. I would have liked to have seen what those plants looked like the next day, after we poured all that vodka on them."[14]

King recalled that their guide, who directed them across snow-covered fields back to their quarters, had gotten drunk. "He hardly knew what he was doing," said King. "Supposedly he picked a shortcut through a wooded area, although it did not seem especially short. At one point Russian guards suddenly appeared, yelled for us to halt, and shoved a rifle into our stomach. Our guide managed to explain what we had been doing, and they let us pass."

King said that when they reached the gate into the big house where he and Lowe stayed, Russian guards again halted them. "Our guide then spoke to the guards in perfect English," related King, "telling them,

'These men are my American friends that I am guiding back to their quarters.' After that, he turned to us and, speaking in Russian, apparently told us what he had told the guards. Well, that gives you an idea of how much vodka he had consumed; our translator talking to the Russians in English, and to the Americans in Russian. I guess the guards understood the situation, maybe recognized Lowe and me. Anyway, they allowed us to pass on into our quarters without any question."

There was also a wild sleigh ride at Szczuczyn that left a lasting impression on King. Sweeney, Lowe, and King were walking back from the town, when a Polish fellow with a sleigh, drawn by a couple of horses, offered them a ride. They accepted, thinking that a ride would be fun, and the Pole obviously set about to give them a thrill. Myron said the driver was standing and whipping the horses to go as fast as possible. "That sleigh was going thirty-five miles an hour, I guess, but it felt like fifty," King said. "He was flying through that snow, and he took us on a long ride." Upon finally returning to the mansion where they were quartered, the Americans tried to tell the Pole to stop the sleigh at the gate. Russian guards were always stationed at the gate, and the accepted procedure was to walk, not ride, from the gate to the house. When the driver turned the sleigh toward the gate, apparently with no intention of halting, so far as the Americans could tell, King said that he, Sweeney, and Lowe simply leaped from the sleigh into a snow bank, for fear the guards would shoot the Pole if he did not stop: "If we had not bailed out of that sleigh, and that driver had gone through the gate, those guards might as soon have shot him as not."[15]

★ ★ ★

As the days at Szczuczyn became weeks, the Russians treated the Americans quite well, according to Sweeney's account, particularly once the Jack Smith episode had seemingly receded to the background. "They could not do enough for us," testified Sweeney. "They treated us like kings, I would say. Gave us the best food they had and vodka, and wanted to make sure we had plenty to do to take up our time. We tried to chop wood ourselves so that we could have some exercise, but that was out. They treated us exactly like we were guests, and honored guests."[16]

Except, of course, that the Russians would not allow their guests to leave. Again and again King requested permission to fly to the American base at Poltava. Time after time he was told that the weather was too bad, and clearance for takeoff was denied—politely but firmly. After many days of frustration, the Russians told him they had good news. Moscow, so they said, had cleared the Americans to leave Szczuczyn whenever the weather permitted. Did this mean, King wondered to himself, that Moscow had been holding them up all along? The Russians seemed totally unconcerned about the obvious implication of such "news" from Moscow—that they had simply been lying for days about the weather problem. But still the bad weather, according to the Russians, never seemed to lift.

Sometimes when the weather at Szczuczyn was clear, King requested permission to fly part of the way to Poltava—perhaps to Kiev, or if not there, as far as the weather allowed. The first time he made such a request, King said the base commander vigorously nodded his head in approval, saying with complementary emphasis or possibly an air of condescension, "Good thinking." Nothing changed, however. Always the Russians had some reason why King could not be cleared for takeoff. One time, when the weather seemed good, he was told that the runway at Poltava was under repair and unserviceable. And it was not until March 9, more than a month after the crew's arrival at Szczuczyn, recorded Phil Reinoehl in his diary, that the Russians even gave Richard Lowe the maps he would need to navigate a flight to Poltava.[17]

Meanwhile, the Russian ground forces had driven the Germans so far westward that the Szczuczyn location became of little use to them. The Russians at Szczuczyn said they were therefore moving to a new base, farther to the west, from which they could more readily strike the enemy. King was told that when they did, the Russian planes would escort the American bomber to the new site. Seemingly, Poltava no longer was an option for King and crew. Clearly the Russians, for reasons unexplained, intended to keep the Americans with them at their new location. The Russians also said there was no runway at the new base, and according to their information, the ground was muddy.

Obviously—at least it was obvious to King and Sweeney (and, one would think, to the Russians also)—they could not land a heavy bomber on such a field. However, for a time, it seemed that King would have no choice in the matter. He then told the Russians that if compelled to go with them, the only thing he could do was "belly in," for landing with the gear down in such circumstances would result in a crash. Fortunately, the Russians altered their plans for King, although, as usual, giving no reason for the change. They simply informed him that he would be flying northeast—with Russian escort, naturally—to Lida, the base where he thought they were headed weeks earlier. Although the weather at Szczuczyn was not good at takeoff, noted King, the Russians seemed to have no hesitation about him flying to Lida that day.[18]

Food and supplies were running low at Szczuczyn, as the resources there were transferred to the new western base. King and crew fared better at Lida—much better, in fact, than in the last days at Szczuczyn. At Lida they found themselves eating with the highest-ranking Russian officers: the majors, colonels, and generals. "Every meal was like a feast," remembered King. He recalled an interesting ritual as well. "At the head of the table was a doctor, along with the commanding officer. Each time that a dish was brought in, they . . . gave it to the doctor, and he would sample it, to test for poison. That way we knew whether or not to eat it. After tasting the dish, the doctor would smile and pass it around the table. It did not make us feel particularly better to think that they were expecting poison."

King said the Russians at Lida provided three men to wait on them; King was convinced they were actually assigned to spy on the Americans. Guards armed with machine guns were stationed outside their quarters, and guards were also assigned to watch the B-17, in part to insure that the plane was protected and in part, thought King, to insure that the Americans did not attempt to leave. King said the Russians permitted his crew to examine Russian aircraft at the base, and in return, the Russians expected to study the American bomber. He said, in fact, that Russian officers and mechanics went over the Maiden meticulously.

Then suddenly, unexpectedly, after only five days in Lida, the Russians cleared King to fly the three hundred miles to Kiev. Figuratively jumping for joy, the crew hurriedly climbed aboard the B-17 to take off as quickly as possible, lest the unpredictable Russians should change their decision. Once in the air and encountering no bad weather on the way to Kiev, King decided, understandably, to continue hauling it all the way to Poltava, although he gradually dropped lower and lower because of the thickening, low-hanging clouds. He landed safely at the American base on Sunday, March 18. According to Richard Lowe's recollection, they "barreled for Poltava at tree top level."[19]

The airfield at Poltava was located about two miles west of the city and served as the headquarters for American personnel stationed in the Soviet Union. Because the longest runway prior to the Americans arriving was only thirty-three hundred feet, the top priority had been laying down a runway of steel-matting, a mile-plus in length, that could handle B-17s. Myron was pleased to see, for the first time since leaving Deenethorpe on February 3, a runway fully adequate for a heavy bomber. As for Poltava itself, the city that once constituted the center of an enviable agricultural area, boasting a population of 130,000, had obviously suffered the ravages of war. The population had been reduced by two-thirds, and the Germans had destroyed every public building.[20]

After the Russians reclaimed the city, they removed considerable rubble and reconstructed a few areas, at least in part. Far more labor would be required before Poltava could hope to be returned to its former status as "the pride of the Ukraine." As for the airfield, King and crew got something of a shock as they landed, immediately spotting numerous B-17s either utterly destroyed or having suffered various levels of serious damage. They soon learned the Fortresses were victims, some months earlier, of a devastating German night attack by HE 111 and JU 88 bombers.

Roger Freeman wrote that the enemy bombers first "illuminated Poltava with flares and proceeded to drop over 100 tons of assorted ordnance before flying off without hurt to themselves. Ammunition dumps were hit and 450,000 gallons of fuel [were] ignited." The next morning, Freeman continued, "brought a fantastic sight—44 of the 72 Fortresses on the field were burnt out or blasted wrecks and another 26 had damage. [Several] other U.S. . . . aircraft were also smashed." King would soon learn that the Germans' surprise attack had fueled the tension already building between the Americans and the Russians. The Russians had insisted—in essence, demanded—that they shoulder the defensive responsibility for the American base, only to fail miserably. In fact, the total failure of the Russian "defense" caused some Americans to speculate that the Russians wanted the Germans to strike the U.S. planes; perhaps they had even leaked information to the *Luftwaffe* about the presence of the aircraft. Or, at the least, they had left the sky open for German reconnaissance planes in the area. The *Luftwaffe* raid resulted in the worst single loss of U.S. aircraft on the ground during the European conflict.[21]

For weeks Myron had assimilated information, firsthand and more than he ever desired, about Soviet duplicity. Poltava deepened this education. He discovered that the Russians, despite their assurances, had never notified Poltava, or any other U.S. forces, of his crew's safety and location. Then came a surprising bit of luck, however, as King encountered a familiar face from Tennessee. Soon after being assigned to a barracks at Poltava, he was taking what gear he had and putting it in his lower bunk when he looked up to see the fellow on the top bunk next to him. "Both of us, at the very same moment," declared King, "said, 'Don't I know you?'" The young man in the top bunk was Howard Youree from Nashville; he had been in college at Lipscomb when King was there. Youree was a B-17 crew member who had bailed out near the German-Russian lines when his plane had been shot down. He told King that both sides were shooting at him as he floated down. Fortunately, he was not hit and, after landing safely, crawled to the Russian lines. Eventually, following further adventures, he arrived at Poltava.[22]

The small-world cliché seems irresistible. Howard Youree's family knew the family of King's fiancée. Youree immediately wrote home, informing his family that King was safe at Poltava, and they at once passed the good news to Eleanor Goodpasture, who then got the word to King's family. Until this time, both the King and Goodpasture families knew only that Myron had been reported missing in action and had thought that he likely was a prisoner of war and/or wounded or that he was possibly dead.[23]

As for Youree, the young Nashvillian, having been at Poltava longer than King, had grown increasingly frustrated with the Russians. They routinely declined American requests for flight clearances and detained U.S. airmen who sought to leave Russia and return to their bases in England or Italy. King remembered one night when Youree came in late, so upset and disgusted with the situation that he pulled out an automatic sidearm and fired it into the ceiling. King and the others could well sympathize with Youree's anger. Eventually, Youree did return safely to his base and ultimately to the United States.

At Poltava the Maiden finally received the maintenance and repair service that had been sorely needed. Engines with cracked cylinders were changed out, flak holes were patched up, and all instruments and controls were thoroughly checked. While King and the others waited for their Fortress to be readied for a flight back to England, they did enjoy some measure of mental comfort and relaxation that had been unknown during their retention by the Russians at Szczuczyn. Phil Reinoehl, for example, said he enjoyed receiving some clean clothes at the base and that "those Luckies [Lucky Strike cigarettes] sure are good; the eats are good; and they also have a nice E.M. [enlisted men's] club." In the days to come, he spent a number of hours watching movies at the base, as did other members of the crew. King observed that "the PX at Poltava was as good as anything in England." All the crew felt that the dangers and frustrations of recent weeks, most of them anyway, were probably behind them at last. Again they were among Americans at a USAAF base—even if the location was in Russia.[24]

Becoming acquainted with some local Russians when he learned they could speak English, King was intrigued by their reaction to the Bible's New Testament. He said they had asked him if he had any English writing that they could read. Taking from his pocket a small red-letter edition (the words of Jesus printed in red) of the New Testament, which he always carried, he opened it to the Sermon on the Mount, found in Matthew, chapters 5, 6, and 7. When they had read those chapters, the Russians commented to King that it was a "good book." Furthermore, he said, they claimed that "Marx and Engels wrote this"— a response that, of course, fascinated King. That was when he began to realize the extent of Communist indoctrination among the Russian intelligentsia.[25]

★ ★ ★

On March 30, without explanation, the Russians grounded all American aircraft in the Soviet Union. Day after day the grounding continued, with the Soviets never stating any reason for their action. News also came of the sudden death of President Franklin D. Roosevelt at Warm Springs, Georgia. King recalled that the Russians with whom he associated generally had a favorable attitude toward Roosevelt. He remembered more than one Russian commenting to him about "the Big Three": Stalin, Roosevelt, and Churchill. "They would say, 'Stalin: Good; FDR: Good; Churchill: Nyet' (not good)," he recalled. When the Russians at Poltava learned of Roosevelt's death, King said, a company of Russian women in the military—perhaps fifty strong, he thought—marched around the base in honor of the American president.

But the real shocker for King came just when he expected a clearance any day to fly out of Russia. Instead he received a summons to Moscow, supposedly to answer questions about the five weeks spent in Szczcuzyn. Actually, charges would be served against him by U.S. military authorities for allegedly violating the 96th U.S. Army Article of War, which forbade transporting an unauthorized civilian in a military aircraft and "thereby bringing discredit on the military service of the United States." Ordered to Moscow by U.S. authorities, along with Sweeney, Lowe, and Pavlas—the skeleton crew that made the hazardous takeoff from Kuflevo—King and the others flew the five-hundred-mile trip in a Russian transport, since American aircraft were still grounded. King's Russian vexations clearly would continue. Some Americans, disappointingly and disconcertingly, would contribute to the ordeal as well.[26]

King had become, as only in time he would realize, both an innocent victim and a pawn in the increasingly complex machinations of Soviet-American relations. Joseph Stalin's policies, with Soviet strength burgeoning and victory over Germany imminent, already were birthing the great divide between East and West that came to be known as the Cold War. Americans fared poorly in the early stages of that eventual half-century-long conflict. At that time, they hardly looked beyond the defeat of Germany and Japan. Americans who attempted to foresee the future of U.S.-Soviet relations too often seemed handicapped by rose-tinted lenses. Worse, Stalin held a clear advantage in Eastern and much of Central Europe—meaning "boots on the ground," in the current cliché—while some American leaders had not fully realized that there was a new game in town.

In the on-going "march of folly," to apply Barbara Tuchman's pertinent and depressing phrase, optimism, ignorance, and occasionally arrogance once again combined to prevail over knowledge, understanding, and realism. True, some Americans vaguely sensed—and a few actually seemed to realize—what was happening; but their warning voices, only faintly and intermittently audible, proved inconsequential. And thus in the perplexing milieu of American-Soviet relations, in which some U.S. leaders had yet to grasp the real nature and evolution of the alliance in which they had been participating, First Lieutenant Myron L. King became deeply entwined.

11 ★ The Eagle and the Bear

IN WILLIAM FAULKNER'S BOOK *REQUIEM FOR A NUN*, THIS FAMOUS STATE-
ment appears: "The past is never dead. It's not even past."[1]

Franklin Roosevelt and Joseph Stalin, while only two years apart
in age, shared little in common otherwise. Roosevelt had a privileged
upbringing, while Stalin, the son of a cobbler, grew up in the lowest
grade of society. Roosevelt graduated from Harvard, although by his
own admission his scholarship was less than impressive, and he generally
earned "Gentleman's C's." Afterward he studied at Columbia Law School
and, though he never graduated, gained admittance to the New York bar.
Stalin's deeply religious mother, hoping to make her son a priest of the
Russian Orthodox Church, sent him to theological seminary. There he
proved an able student, a voracious reader, and an avid debater. Instead
of becoming a priest, however, he became a revolutionist.[2]

Profoundly influenced by Marxism, Stalin came to view Russian capitalism as "the most atrocious and bestial in the world" and the government under the Tsars as "the most corrupt, cruel and inefficient." Shortly
before his scheduled graduation, the young Marxist was expelled from
the seminary—his revolutionary views being totally unacceptable to the
church. Stalin soon thereafter became active in the Social Democratic
Party, siding with the radical Bolsheviks when they separated from the
movement's more moderate wing. He ceaselessly labored to foment revolution and was banished to Siberia four times prior to World War I.

Three times he escaped. Upon his fourth deportation, Stalin remained in Siberia until the revolution of 1917. Fighting in the field during the civil war of 1918–21, Stalin, like many Bolsheviks, never forgot the Allied military intervention, during which the United States sent thousands of troops into the northern Russian ports of Archangel and Murmansk and the Pacific port of Vladivostok.[3]

While this intervention developed into an enormously complicated issue—which neither Stalin nor President Woodrow Wilson fully understood, particularly regarding Vladivostok and the forty-thousand-strong, staunchly anti-Bolshevik Czech Legion—the venture's overall impact "confirmed the Bolsheviks in their hatred and distrust for the capitalist nations," as diplomatic historian Jerald A. Combs put it. Stalin well remembered, too, that in 1924 most of the major powers, including Great Britain, France, and Italy, had officially recognized the Soviet Union. Yet the United States, in the words of Stalin biographer Isaac Deutscher, "stubbornly refused, up to 1933," to extend the hand of recognition. No doubt the "Red Scare," which had been sweeping the United States, played a considerable role in America declining to recognize the Soviets, but that factor, if anything, served only to disturb them more.[4]

By early 1924, the widely revered Vladimir Ilyich Lenin was dead, and Stalin—who Lenin, shortly before his death, had said should be removed from the general secretariat of the party because he was "inclined to abuse power"—soon confirmed both that he was a cunning, unscrupulous, and vicious political in-fighter and that Lenin's assessment of his lust for power was a notable understatement. By the 1930s, Stalin reigned supreme and purged untold thousands who might possibly have opposed his exercise of absolute authority. On the international scene, Stalin found the burgeoning strength of the United States impressive but also troubling. "America's rising star filled him with forebodings," wrote Deutscher, "for he saw the United States propping up the decaying European capitalism, mainly through loans granted to Germany." And by the middle to late 1930s, Stalin became quite concerned that Western appeasement of Germany aimed to promote Nazi militarism against Russia. He claimed to be particularly troubled that Britain and France had accepted Hitler's demand for Czechoslovakia's

Sudetenland, interpreting their action as designed to keep Germany on the path of *Drang nach Osten* (drive to the east), a course likely to end in war between Germany and the Soviets. As Brigadier General John R. Deane, who would head the United States Military Mission (USMM) in Moscow, expressed the matter in his memoir: "The attitude of the Western Allies toward the Soviet Union in the first twenty-five years of its existence could hardly be characterized as friendly."[5]

As for Roosevelt, the New York patrician seemed to rise almost effortlessly, first from the practice of law to the state senate, next to the position of assistant secretary of the Navy under Wilson, and then to the Democratic vice-presidential nomination in 1920. However, in the summer of 1921, Roosevelt's career experienced a major setback when infantile paralysis struck the handsome, thirty-nine-year-old. His long struggle to recover a partial use of his legs perhaps instilled a strength of character in the man that some people thought had not been evident before that ordeal.

A gifted speaker and charismatic individual, the New Yorker staged a marvelous comeback in 1928, when he became governor of the Empire State. His reelection two years later served as a springboard to gain the Democratic nomination for president in 1932. Winning by a wide margin over the unfortunate Herbert Hoover, whom millions blamed for the miseries of the Great Depression, FDR won the presidency three more times, while leading the nation out of the Depression and through the most all-consuming war known to history.

Clearly Roosevelt was a person of substance, deservedly remembered as one of the nation's few great presidents. Demonstrating impressive abilities at home and abroad, he essentially conducted his own foreign relations for some time, in part because of Secretary of State Cordell Hull's illness and in part because FDR liked being in charge and doing the job himself. A man whose smooth, eloquent, powerful speech manifested optimism, determination and a "can-do" spirit, Roosevelt considered himself a good judge of men, and he believed that his charm and presence could win people over to his point of view. Often he was right.

While FDR never went so far as to claim that he had looked into Stalin's soul, the president's confidence in his ability to woo the man he nicknamed "Uncle Joe" seemed almost boundless—evidence that even the most capable men certainly make mistakes. Stalin "doesn't want anything but security for his country," said Roosevelt upon one occasion, "and I think that if I give him everything that I can, and ask for nothing in return, *noblesse oblige,* he won't try to annex anything and will work with me for a world of democracy and peace." In such manner the president sought to blunt Soviet imperialism. During the summer of 1944, Roosevelt instructed the Polish premier, Stanislaw Mikolajczyk: "Don't worry, Stalin doesn't intend to take freedom from Poland." For emphasis, FDR also said, "Of one thing I'm certain; Stalin is not an imperialist."[6]

The president long thought that the United States could get along with the Soviet Union, and he downplayed the pertinent warnings, especially those from W. Averell Harriman, the U.S. ambassador to Moscow, and William C. Bullitt, the former ambassador, of Uncle Joe's relentless and uncompromising territorial ambitions. Harriman warned FDR that Stalin was inclined to be a "world bully," and Bullitt prophesied that the Soviet dictator would never honor his pledges. The president's knowledge of Marxist philosophy, as historian Thomas A. Bailey expressed the matter, "was less than profound," and unquestionably FDR's hope for Stalin's cooperation with capitalism after the war had little foundation. In essence, about the only things Stalin and the Soviet Communists had in common with Roosevelt and U.S. capitalism, as well as with Great Britain, was a resolve to destroy Hitler and the Nazis.[7]

Once Stalin saw the chessboard of war turn decisively against Germany, he quickly realized that the massive Red Army, just as he had hoped, was in a dominant position to control all of Eastern and Central Europe. A man who knew something about history, Stalin was keenly aware of Russia's great national struggle against Napoleon and the French, who had attacked through Poland in 1812. And twice during Stalin's own adulthood, the Germans had poured through Poland to assault Russia. In the interests of Soviet security and a general expansion of territory, Stalin was determined to push his boundaries westward—absorbing Estonia, Latvia, Lithuania, eastern Poland, and part of Rumania—all areas the Soviets believed were unfairly taken from them after the Great War. Above all, he wanted to establish Poland as a buffer state under the firm control of the U.S.S.R. For Stalin, regardless of what he might say in praise of democracy and free elections, Soviet dominance was simply nonnegotiable. To borrow the pertinent words of Cornelius Ryan, "the Russians were becoming more demanding and arrogant with every mile they advanced into central Europe."[8]

Thus, for Roosevelt and Stalin, whose personal histories had evolved in dramatically divergent manners, the past probably negated any realistic chance of long-term alliance as the Hitlerian crisis waned. Also, the pronounced mutual mistrust of one nation toward the other immensely complicated their international alliance. From the beginning, American capitalism had despised Bolshevik Russia, while Soviet Communism not only abhorred capitalism universally but regarded America as a premier example of that which it sought to destroy. "Soviet Russia," declared Glen Infield, "had no intention of collaborating during or after World War II except in those instances in which the Soviet Union would benefit."[9]

The United States and Great Britain admittedly had their problems in trying to understand one another and work together, and they were tied to each other by a common heritage and by innumerable cultural bonds, such as language, laws, representative government, trade and finance, human behavior, and more. Between the United States and the Soviet Union, however, a great gulf existed, not only in politics and economic philosophy, but also in language, values, culture, and way of life. "The wartime unity of two alien ways of life," wrote historian Howard Jones, "could not permanently dispel their fundamental differences." Indeed, even their temporary unity scarcely survived the great conflict. The upshot, for both nations and their leaders, was that history held captive their wartime alliance. Once again, to quote Faulkner, "It's all *now*, you see. Yesterday won't be over until tomorrow and tomorrow began ten thousand years ago."[10]

★ ★ ★

By February 1945, when Myron King and his crew arrived in Russian-controlled territory, the early rush of enthusiastic cooperation between the United States, Great Britain, and the Soviet Union against Nazi Germany had lost much of its dynamic—particularly when viewed from the Soviet perspective. It was difficult to believe that Joseph Stalin had ever said, as he did on July 30, 1941, to Harry Hopkins, President Roosevelt's envoy, that he "would welcome American troops on any part of the Russian front, under the complete command of the American army," to fight the German invader. Stalin spoke those words, of course, before the United States was even at war, when he was disheartened, probably in despair, as the German *blitzkrieg* had thrust 450 miles deep into Soviet territory in less than a month. Some military authorities predicted Soviet defeat within three to six months at the most, and the Russian dictator sought help wherever he might find it. He had to know, unless one assumes that the shock of Hitler's surprise attack rendered him temporarily deranged (which it may have), that American troops were not coming to his aid. Perhaps he hoped, through such friendly, unqualified overtures, to encourage the United States to provide even more lend-lease military equipment than had already been committed.[11]

Whatever the explanation of Stalin's apparent bid for U.S. troops during the early weeks of the Nazi onslaught, Americans soon launched a not-so-subtle agenda of their own. Even before the Japanese attack on Pearl Harbor, the United States was eyeing far-eastern Russian bases in anticipation of a likely war with Japan. Air bases in the Vladivostok region would place most of Japan's homeland within relatively easy striking distance of U.S. heavy bombers. Thus, on the pretext of surveying delivery routes for lend-lease materials for the Soviets, transported from Alaska across the U.S.S.R., the United States sought to obtain information on Soviet air bases. The Russians declined, of course, instantly aware—one writer suggested that two seconds might have been required for them to see through the ruse—that the real American interest lay in bases from which Japan could be bombed.

The Soviets, understandably, proved unwilling to take any step that might encourage Japan, a partner in the Berlin-Rome-Tokyo Axis, to attack the hard-pressed Russians in support of Germany. Once Japan launched its highly successful, far-reaching assault of December 1941, then the possible establishment of American air bases in the Soviet Far East, from which Japan could easily be raided, obviously became immensely desirable. Equally obvious to Stalin was the fact that such policy ran counter to Soviet interests, and Uncle Joe's temper flared readily when Americans broached the subject, even if they did so indirectly.[12]

Meanwhile, the Russian troops, struggling to survive, received major assistance from the early arrival of winter. According to an ancient proverb, Russia has two unbeatable commanders on her side: General January and General February, who could provide a decisive one-two punch. Fortunately for the Soviets, yet a third appeared in the winter of 1941–42: General December. The early winter played havoc with the Germans, whose clothing proved inadequate to protect them from the severe cold, while their equipment broke down as well, the engine blocks of tanks and other vehicles freezing solid. And the soldiers of the vaunted *Wehrmacht* were reduced to half rations. At the very gates of Moscow (the Kremlin towers were visible in the distance to Gunther Von Kluge's army group), their triumphal drive had stalled. The Germans had to fall back, shorten their lines, and take up defensive positions. Enraged, Hitler fired the chief of the general staff and, soon after, all three army group commanders as well.

The worst news for the Germans was that the Soviets not only still had life, but they also showed they had plenty of fight left in them. True, they had sacrificed masses of men as they retreated, but secretly they had been concentrating huge reserves with which to counterattack when the time was right. The arrogant, overconfident Germans, having grossly underestimated Soviet strength, suddenly found themselves under attack by masses of Russians, dressed for the cold, of whose existence they never dreamed. The Soviets launched major attacks in the Crimea and also in the north. Their greatest success came in front of Moscow, where they broke the German army group both north and south of the city and drove them back almost two hundred miles. The war in Russia was far from over, but Stalin and the battle-hardened Soviets were breathing strongly when the spring of 1942 arrived.

All along the line, throughout 1942 and well into 1943, from Finland to the Black Sea and the Caucasus, the Germans and the Soviets grappled in a ruthless, titanic struggle that ground ever so slowly against the Nazis. When the Soviet army finally went over to the offensive at Stalingrad, it had, as John Keegan wrote, "been ravaged by eighteen months of losses on a scale never experienced before in history." In fact, "more people fought and died [on the Eastern Front]," observed Gerhard Weinberg, "than on all the other fronts of the war around the globe put together." Perhaps the Russian triumph at Stalingrad provided the single greatest breakthrough of the awful conflict, for the battle probably smashed any realistic hope of a German offensive victory. If not Stalingrad, then maybe it was Leningrad—when the symbolic city at last survived the long, brutal German siege—that became a decisive turning point in favor of Russia.

Or, yet again, it was possibly Kursk, the greatest tank battle of World War II—with each side employing nearly three thousand tanks in an unprecedented collision of blood, steel, and iron in mid-summer 1943 that rendered the Germans unable ever again to mount such an armored force— that was the decisive clash, fatally weakening the *Wehrmacht* for the engagements to come. Stalin sometimes called the struggle "the Great Patriotic War," though officially he liked to call it the "Fatherland War," harking back to the epic struggle against Napoleon in 1812 and the title by which that conflict had gone down in Russian history. "If the Soviets harbored any doubts about their ability to win the war before the battle of Kursk," historian Michael J. Lyons declared, "they had none afterward." A. J. P. Taylor unequivocally stated that Kursk proved to be "the decisive battle of the war."

Whatever the turning point, or points, may have been, by late summer of 1943 the Soviets boasted a manpower advantage of four to one over the Germans. They were also the recipients of large amounts of lend-lease material from the United States, were cranking out more and more war materials themselves, and were gaining increasing strength in their battle with the German air force. For the Nazi invaders, the situation could only become worse. "Short of a miracle," as one military historian wrote, "there was no way the Germans were going to stem the tide of military power massing to the eastward."[13]

The Germans faced an army "of a kind never before seen in modern warfare," wrote A. J. P. Taylor. "At the head came the elite forces, often honoured with the name of Guards divisions: tanks, artillery, rockets, men of high professional competence and technique. Once a breakthrough had been achieved, the inexhaustible mass of infantry followed like a barbarian horde on the march." According to Taylor, the Russian infantry could advance for as long as three weeks "without receiving supplies, and when the Germans tried to cut their lines of communication, they found that there were none to be cut." These brutal Soviet forces "slaughtered the German infantry, pillaged the towns and villages through which they passed, and raped the women. . . . After the infantry came another elite corps: the military police, who restored order, shot the worst offenders out of hand, and drove the infantry forward to fresh assaults."[14]

Nevertheless, Stalin and the Soviets, despite the war going in their favor, became increasingly suspicious of Anglo-American motivations. From the time America entered the war until the invasion of Normandy two and a half years later, the Soviet Union shouldered the bulk of the fighting against the Germans. Continually Stalin urged the United States and Great Britain to provide relief for the Russians by opening a major second front in Western Europe. In May 1942, Roosevelt promised V. M. Molotov, the Soviet foreign minister, that a second front would be established within a year. Instead, the Anglo-American partners attacked the Germans in North Africa in the fall of 1942. Next they invaded Sicily and then Italy, both in 1943.

Good reasons could be cited for all three Mediterranean moves, but Stalin feared that his allies, for their own benefit, sought to prolong the horrendous struggle on the Eastern Front and weaken severely both the Germans and the Russians. To Stalin, the North African, Sicilian, and Italian invasions constituted little more than a very minor sideshow to the big show on the Eastern Front. He suspected, too, that the Western Allies might even go behind his back, achieve a settlement with Germany, and maybe enlist German aid—a move that might well thwart Stalin's ambitions for Soviet security and territorial gain. Thus, by mid- to late 1943, Stalin repeatedly, adamantly, called for an immediate cross-channel invasion of Europe that would compel the Germans to pull forces from the Russian front in order to meet the Western threat.

Increasingly—and interestingly—American military and government leaders also believed a cross-channel invasion must be undertaken soon in order to guarantee, among other considerations, that Russia remained in the war. Further delaying the second front, they thought, might drive the Soviets, who were continuing to bear the brunt of the casualties and that by a wide margin, out of the conflict. "There can be no doubt," wrote Gerhard Weinberg, "that during the period May to September, 1943, the British and American governments were very much concerned about the possibility of a separate peace [between the Soviet Union and Germany]." Their concern was strengthened, continued Weinberg, "by the withdrawal of Soviet ambassadors from London and Washington at the end of June" and by intercepted Japanese telegrams indicating "there was great pressure from Tokyo" to bring the Soviets and the Germans together once more.

The First World War had seen the Russians, as they suffered awful losses, make a separate peace with Germany. History just might repeat itself. If that should happen again, freeing Nazi Germany to redeploy all its might on the Western and Mediterranean fronts, the result would be, in the words of no less a figure than General Dwight D. Eisenhower, "the blackest day in history."[15]

Yet, a Soviet compromise with the Germans, after the incredible slaughter of 1941–43, seemed highly unlikely to some observers. Lord Beaverbrook said in 1943, "The Russian dead stand in the way. You don't cross over that graveyard with ease." So one might suppose. Russian casualties in World War I, terrible though they were, pale in comparison with the millions of dead, maimed, and wounded suffered in World War II. Perhaps the great Soviet marshals Georgi Zhukov and Ivan Koniev, despite their intense rivalry for military power and glory, symbolized the attitude of many Russians, for in one respect at least, observed Cornelius Ryan, "they saw eye to eye: they could not forgive Nazi atrocities. For Germans they had neither mercy nor remorse."

Undoubtedly, there were masses of Soviets who bitterly hated Germans and hated them to the depth of their being. They would never have initiated any kind of a settlement with the enemy. But they, of course, were not the decision makers. No great imaginative power is required to conceive of the callous, coldly calculating Uncle Joe, his hands long stained with the blood of untold numbers of his own people, ignoring the millions of Soviet sacrifices on the altar of Mars—if the strength of the nation (not to forget Stalin's personal power and stature) might rest in the balance, as he evaluated that balance. Stalin did not trust his Western allies. He was surprised by the resurgence of the German war machine following Stalingrad, which clearly foreshadowed many more months of horrendous fighting, even if the Russians obviously possessed the greater strength. Thus, an acceptable accommodation with the Nazis well might have been to Stalin's liking.

After all, the Soviet casualties, whatever their magnitude, could be "spun" to the renown of Stalin whichever path he pursued. He could wage an uncompromising war of vengeance on the barbaric German until the enemy's utter desolation should be achieved, thus paying back in full measure, and more than full measure, the suffering and destruction that the Nazi had visited upon the Russian; or, he could achieve a settlement with the Reich that would guarantee, at the least, Soviet possession of the Ukraine with its vast resources and dominance of much, if not all, of a Polish buffer state, together with the strategic territories on the Baltic. This latter course would save hundreds of thousands of Soviet lives by halting the fighting, but this would come only after the world clearly recognized the triumph of the Stalinist state, which had successfully defended itself against a powerful invader whom many initially appraised as invincible.

If a peace between the Reich and the Soviet Union resulted in the Americans and the British fighting Germany and Japan by themselves, that prospect, to quote Gerhard Weinberg again, "was not necessarily so sad from Moscow's point of view." Regardless of the outcome of such a struggle, both sides would be significantly weaker, while the Soviets, declared Weinberg, "would be secure and in a stronger position than before 1941." Additionally, if the possibility of a separate peace on the Eastern Front should make the British and American governments more open to "political concessions to the Soviet Union, or to strike earlier against Germany in the West, that would be all to the good" of the Russians, concluded Weinberg, "even if no such peace actually came about."

However, a Soviet settlement with Germany, regardless of what the premier of the Soviet Union might have been willing to consider in mid-1943, was not about to happen. While some Germans apparently favored treating with Stalin, Adolf Hitler, as we now know, was never willing to negotiate with the Russian leader. Thus the Fascist-Communist tango, at best awkwardly performed in its early, ill-fated measures prior to Hitler's treacherous assault upon his partner in 1941, was not to be resumed. Even Stalin himself, by late 1943, probably no longer contemplated, or had any interest in, negotiations with the Reich, whatever Hitler's thoughts might have been in the war's later stages.[16]

At last both the Americans and the British had agreed to an invasion of Europe, scheduled for the late spring of 1944. Once Stalin became convinced that Roosevelt and Churchill actually were committed to launching the cross-channel assault in the first half of 1944, he agreed, for the first time, to a summit meeting of "the Big Three." They met in Tehran in late November and December of 1943. Stalin promised a great Soviet offensive to coincide with the Anglo-American landings in Normandy. True to his word, when the Allies invaded on June 6, 1944, Stalin mounted a massive offensive that ultimately carried the Red Armies westward, spanning from north to south, into East Prussia, Warsaw, and Budapest. He had also promised at Tehran to enter the war against Japan after victory in Europe.

At the same time, it must be emphasized that dealing with Stalin and the Russian leaders became ever more difficult in the wake of continuing Soviet triumphs. Such problems, however, seemed only to challenge the American leaders, some of them, to even greater efforts of cooperation. The Americans, as will become increasingly evident in the pages to follow, kept their eyes firmly fixed on the major prize they sought: air bases in far-eastern Russia and Soviet entry into the war against Japan.

For example, in mid-December 1944, less than six months before the end of the European war, General A. E. Antonov, chief of the Red Army General Staff, announced to General Deane that Soviet forces "would need all the air and naval bases in the Maritime Provinces" and that, therefore, American air and naval forces "will be unable to operate from there." General Deane later admitted that he "staggered a bit" under that blow, which was "in direct contradiction to promises that Stalin had given us on six separate occasions." The U.S. Chiefs of Staff soon sent a protest, which Deane said he delivered to Antonov, while Averell Harriman, U.S. ambassador to the Soviet Union, protested to Stalin. Their efforts were to no avail.

"There was a ray of light, however," declared Deane. He referred to the new Boeing B-29 Superfortress bombers, which were then coming into full production. Because of their exceptionally long range, the B-29s "could operate from bases far north of Vladivostok, perhaps near the mouth of the Amur River." Thus, Deane stated, "we decided to accept the decision on the Maritime Provinces," and instead, the Americans would seek bases "farther to the north for our B-29s, when we met at the Yalta Conference." With Yalta, the timeline moves to early February 1945. This proposal likewise came to nothing. "In the spring of 1945 I began to suspect," wrote Deane in a striking word choice for so late a date, "that the importance of the concessions we were receiving or hoped to receive from the Soviet Union was being reduced to practically nothing."[17]

★ ★ ★

During the fall of 1943, as the powerful Red Army was securing a death grip on the *Wehrmacht,* the USAAF simultaneously experienced the darkest days of the heavy-bomber offensive. Missions to Munster, Regensburg, and Schweinfurt became the most costly American raids of the war. The near-disastrous losses, unacceptable at any time, proved especially disturbing as the cross-channel invasion of Nazi-occupied Europe, anticipated for the spring of 1944, drew closer. If the Western Allies were going to gain air superiority over the continent, the single most significant factor clearly entailed the buildup of large numbers of long-range fighter planes, flown by well-trained, combat-experienced pilots. They were charged with both protecting the big bombers and, above all, destroying the German interceptors.

Also, General Henry H. Arnold, commanding general of the Army Air Forces, along with other influential Americans, believed that air bases in the Soviet Union could be helpful. Whenever the Eighth and Fifteenth Air Forces flew missions deep into Germany and German-controlled territory in Eastern Europe, the flights could be shortened considerably, and the timeframe for attacks by enemy fighters, too, if U.S. planes could land in Soviet-controlled territory on the first leg of a shuttle mission. Refueling and rearming at Soviet bases, the Americans could again strike German targets, either the same or new ones, on the way back to their English or Mediterranean bases. They might sometimes assist the Russians as well, possibly bombing targets of special value to the Red Army's westward advance. The shuttle missions, in the optimistic musings of some Americans, might even contribute to more cooperation and understanding between the United States and the Soviets.

Another factor of major significance motivated important Americans, particularly those who were working in Moscow. Ambassador Harriman and General Deane, head of the recently established United States Military Mission (USMM), which had been set up to work closely with the ambassador, believed that air bases in western Russia for shuttle missions against Germany would establish a strong precedent, as well as a good working relationship, later in the war, for U.S. air bases in the Soviet Far East. From there heavy bomber strikes could be launched against Japan.

For Harriman, Deane, and others, shuttle missions against Germany, while desirable for their own sake, were actually viewed as a means to an end—a far more important end, as they conceived the matter. In the hope of attaining those strategic bases from which to bomb Japan, Harriman and Deane endured a great deal of ongoing abuse from the Soviets. "As long as we attached importance to these ventures," stated Deane in his memoir, "we hesitated to take a firm, tough attitude toward Russia for fear that we would lose whatever concessions had been granted."[18]

As for the Soviets, they obviously were whipping the Germans, but as long as lend-lease material remained desirable, plus the establishment of a second front in France, Stalin felt compelled to make periodic concessions to the United States—even though sometimes nothing more than words were ever intended. Among these gestures was a secret agreement to cooperate in "Operation Frantic," the code name for a shuttle-bombing collaboration employing Russian air bases. At the Tehran conference, Ambassador Harriman discussed the proposal in some detail with Stalin, who seemed in favor of the plan, according to Harriman.

With Stalin's approval, the Soviet foreign minister, V. M. Molotov, along with representatives of the Russian army, next met with Harriman and Deane, who fully explained the American concept for shuttle missions. The Russians "agreed in principle" to the operation. Harriman and Deane were greatly encouraged. They had not learned, as Glen Infield pointed out, that approval "in principle" did not mean the same thing to the Soviets that it did to the Americans. "Agreement" did not necessarily mean action, and "in principle" usually entailed specifics quite different from the U.S. proposals. And always, whatever happened, or did not happen, came down from Uncle Joe.

Harriman informed the Russians, as recommended by the USAAF, that six air bases would be necessary, along with twenty-one hundred Americans to operate the bases and maintain and arm the airplanes. The Russians, however, after the passage of what seemed to the Americans an inordinate amount of time, approved only three bases and twelve hundred American personnel to man them. The Soviets also wanted to select targets, control flight operations, and provide weather information—all on a schedule devised by them. On these and other matters, realistic compromises had to be worked out, all of which consumed yet more time. A number of Americans, understandably, were convinced that the Soviets were purposely complicating and delaying the project.

One of the greatest difficulties centered around Stalin's pronounced suspicions that American capitalists would use the "Frantic" operation as a ruse to sneak agents into the Soviet Union. Not until late March 1944, and only after much American frustration, did an agreement materialize whereby U.S. personnel, stationed in Russia for "Operation Frantic," might enter the country on group visas. This procedure never worked smoothly, but it seemed to be the only solution that the Russians were going to accept. Another aspect of Stalin's thinking that most Americans failed to perceive at the time—and that because they were focused on the United States and the Soviet Union striving as allies to assist each other against the German foe—was that Stalin did not intend for either his own people, or the Eastern Europeans whom he planned to dominate, to think that the Soviets needed any help whatsoever from the USAAF to win the war.[19]

Through April and May, both major and minor problems continued to plague the American attempts to set up the shuttle missions. "Even getting the Soviets to advance their own preference for bombing targets of value to their army brought one delay after another," wrote George Menzel. The Russians were, however, continued Menzel, "quick to reject American suggestions as to targets." In spite of all the difficulties, whether Soviet-instigated or otherwise, the project slowly went forward. At last, on June 2, 1944, the first shuttle mission, called "Frantic Joe," was launched.

For the initial effort, General Carl Spaatz had hoped to target German aircraft production at the Heinkel plants in Riga, Latvia, and Mielec, Poland. Claiming that these targets were unacceptable because they lay within the Soviet "sphere of operations," Lieutenant General N. V. Slavin of the Red Army wanted a strike in the Bucharest-Brasov-Debrecin-Budapest area. General Deane protested that such targets could just as readily be attacked from Italy without continuing on to Russia. Slavin became angry. Clearly, he had no intention either to reconsider Spaatz's target selection or to entertain a compromise target. For Slavin it seemed to be his way or no way. Deane then not only recommended that the United States accept the Russian target but also optimistically expressed his belief that, once started, the Frantic operations "will meet with great enthusiasm [by the Russians] and we will be allowed a great deal more freedom of action, not only in the selection of targets, but on all other questions."[20]

Led by General Ira Eaker, then commanding Allied air forces in the Mediterranean, the mission was flown by 130 B-17s, escorted by 70 P-51 fighters. Successfully bombing their target in Debrecin, Hungary, all but one of the Fortresses, together with 64 of the fighters, flew on to land at the Russian bases of Piryatin, Mirgorod, and Poltava. The bomber carrying General Eaker, known as "Yankee Doodle II," was the first B-17 to touch down at Poltava, where a big reception and celebration soon got underway.

Ambassador Harriman, accompanied by his daughter Kathy and General Deane, had flown in from Moscow. "For an American on the field below [the B-17s circling to land] it was a thrill beyond description," wrote General Deane. Several other American officers were on hand for the occasion as well, and both American and Soviet journalists covered the cooperative effort. The Russians, too, sent in some important military men to welcome the Americans, most notably Lieutenant General

Slavin. Amusingly, at least in retrospect, General Slavin missed the ceremony because he had decided to take a nap and no one remembered to wake him. The roar of Flying Fortresses roused the Soviet general, but the American guards detailed to secure the landing area refused to permit Slavin to join the other Russians who were already engaged in receiving the U.S. dignitaries. Slavin was furious. When he finally got the opportunity, he vented his anger on the presiding Russian officer, who was Slavin's inferior in rank, proceeding to curse and berate him at length. Some Americans could hardly refrain from cracking a smile. General Deane said that he "spent the rest of the day trying to shoulder the blame and pacifying Slavin."

Otherwise, the welcoming festivities went satisfactorily, leaving American officials optimistic about the future of U.S.-Soviet cooperation. Bad weather, however, prevented General Eaker's planes from returning to Foggia, Italy, for over a week. Eaker grew increasingly nervous, having decided that the Russian antiaircraft defenses were inadequate—the guns too few and of too small caliber. Also, the Russians had no radar-directed, night-fighter aircraft, and most of their firemen were woefully equipped. Informed that German reconnaissance activity in the area had increased in recent days, Eaker concluded that his aircraft were in serious danger. The general was greatly relieved when the bombers eventually took off from the Soviet bases. General Eaker's fears, unfortunately, proved well founded, which became destructively evident within only a few days.

On June 21, the Eighth Air Force launched the ill-fated "Frantic II," the second shuttle mission, during which they bombed an oil refinery at Ruhland, south of Berlin. One hundred thirty-seven Fortresses participated, escorted by sixty-three Mustangs, and afterward the planes headed east for the Russian bases, where they landed with notable U.S. and Soviet fanfare again marking the occasion. Since the Poltava base was rather small, the B-17s were parked close together, presenting a juicy target should enemy bombers strike. And at thirty minutes past midnight, precisely 0030 hours, the Germans attacked. First dropping flares to light up the base, HE 111s and JU 88s relentlessly pounded the American aircraft. *Luftwaffe* reports indicate that the German flyers were surprised upon finding such an easy target.

Russian antiaircraft fire, what little there was, had virtually no effect. Neither the Americans on the ground nor the Germans in their bombers spotted a single Russian fighter aloft to oppose the *Luftwaffe*. Although the enemy attack persisted for some time and included a second wave of aircraft, no Russian defenders ever appeared in the Poltava skies. While it is true that the Russians possessed no radar to assist their fighter planes at night, they did have pilots well trained in attacking enemy bombers illuminated by searchlights, and of searchlights Poltava had no shortage. Also, both formidable Lavochkin Russian fighter planes and the renowned Stormovik aircraft were based within striking distance of Poltava. These planes were capable of wreaking havoc on the German bombers. Yet they remained on the ground. The damage to U.S. aircraft would have been even greater had not a German navigational error spared another shuttle base that the *Luftwaffe* attempted to target.

Martin Bowman penned a vivid account of the destruction: "For two hours the German pilots made run after run, picking off aircraft one after the other, the heavy caliber shells of their machine-guns exploding and adding to the general chaos and noise. Ammunition dumps . . . and the fuel dump, containing 450,000 gallons of fuel, exploded in an angry orange mushroom of flame and debris. . . . Skeletal remains of the Fortresses were clustered around the airfield like carcasses. Some were only a collection of engines and twisted propellers which marked the spot where once bombers had stood." American Mustangs, some of which had landed at the other shuttle bases, were refused permission by the Russians to take off and attack the German marauders. As noted in the previous chapter, all but two of the seventy-two B-17s on the field at Poltava were either destroyed or heavily damaged; well over half of them were smashed and burned beyond repair. Fourteen P-51s were destroyed. Not one German bomber was lost.[21]

Glenn Infield's detailed analysis, in his thought-provoking book *The Poltava Affair*, presents a plausible thesis that the Russians not only allowed the disastrous attack to continue without attempting either to stop it or strike back at the German bombers but also very possibly, subtly, had assisted the *Luftwaffe*, making it easy for the Germans to gain pertinent information about the location of the American bombers.[22]

Understandably, the Poltava raid caused some Americans to re-think the future of the shuttle-bombing project. General Spaatz, over-all commander of American strategic bombers in Europe, declined to commit any more heavy bombers until further consideration of the shuttle-bombing operation. Two more missions were flown in July, in-volving only fighters (P-51s) and fighter-bombers (P-38s). Then, prob-ably feeling a bit of pressure because he knew the president, General Arnold, and other high-ranking political, military, and diplomatic fig-ures were determined that Frantic go forward, Spaatz took a calcu-lated risk in August. He sent Eighth Air Force B-17s, escorted by P-51s, into the Soviet bases once more, after striking the Focke-wulfe plant in Poland.[23]

While the mission succeeded without incident, Americans, both air-men and ground personnel, detected a much cooler attitude on the part of the Russians than had existed back in the spring. Furthermore, reports of disturbing incidents involving Americans and Soviets at the shuttle bases, some of them nasty and violent, became more frequent. Nevertheless, optimistic American thinking persisted, with Roosevelt and other powerful figures convinced that the Poltava raid had simply been a most unfortunate incident. The Soviets—and Uncle Joe in par-ticular, they believed—were making a sincere effort to cooperate with the Americans. General Deane even interpreted the Poltava tragedy as a sort of "blessing in disguise" that would enhance Soviet-American rela-tions by causing the presumably embarrassed and regretful Russians to become more receptive to American interests and requests.

In fact, Deane and Harriman still hoped to expand the Frantic operation, despite their earlier rebuff, presenting their new proposal to Slavin and Molotov, respectively. Not only was the Russian general disturbed at the thought of more American military personnel coming into the Soviet Union, but he also obviously thought there were already too many. He thus countered Deane's proposal with a request that the United States reduce the size of the Frantic operation. As for the for-eign minister, Molotov bluntly told Harriman that the Russian bases had only been granted to the Americans through the summer. When Harriman angrily responded that they had been approved until the end of the war, Molotov, in condescending, dismissive fashion, declared that the whole operation was under review by Stalin. He had nothing more to say.[24]

★ ★ ★

Meanwhile, during August and September 1944, the desperate and tragic Polish uprising against the Germans in Warsaw served clearly to reveal, yet again, the callous brutality of Joseph Stalin. The Polish issue stood front and center in Uncle Joe's calculations for Soviet security and power after the war. As previously noted, Stalin had no intention ever of accepting the Polish government-in-exile in London, which both the British and the Americans supported. Stalin's resolve on this issue became even more hardened after the London Poles called for an international investigation of the Katyn Forest massacre of thousands of Poles—the discovery of which had been announced to the world by the Germans. Time would show that the killings had been perpetrated by the Soviets. (However, in fairness, it should be noted that the Katyn massacre was but the proverbial "drop in the bucket" when compared with the millions of Poles killed by the Nazis.) Thus, when the Red Army took the Polish city of Lublin, located in close proximity to Warsaw, a Polish National Committee of Liberation was there established as a Soviet puppet regime, composed of Communists and Socialists, in late July 1944.

By this time the Red Army, advancing upon Warsaw, inspired the Polish underground forces (which, it should be noted, were loyal to the Polish government-in-exile) to rise against the Germans whom they supposed would be evacuating the city shortly. Soviet radio actually called upon the Poles to help drive out the German invader. On August 1, the animated Poles, forty thousand strong and hoping to liberate their capital themselves, rose to successfully reclaim more than half of the city—briefly.

Disaster followed. The Germans did not leave, while the Red Army's drive first slowed and then stopped its advance just short of the Vistula River. The Russian guns, frequently heard in recent days, went strangely silent. Russian aircraft, often seen in Warsaw skies for some time, disappeared. The Germans counterattacked with demonic fury.

Stukas dive-bombed the city day after day. German tanks blasted buildings into rubble. The Germans deployed savages to murder, rape, and loot, as well as regular army units to systematically destroy the insurgents and the city block by block.

Soviet apologists would later claim that the Russian forces had been held back by the strength of the *Wehrmacht*. But as Weinberg correctly stated in his excellent history, "The argument that the Germans were blunting the Red Army offensive so that help could not be provided by the Soviet Union will not hold up when nearby offensive operations are examined." Indeed. The Soviets somehow managed to advance both north and south of Warsaw. The truth is that the Red Army not only stood down while the Germans smashed the Polish uprising, but the despicable Stalin also denied permission for several weeks for American or British planes, seeking to drop supplies to the Poles, to land at Soviet bases.[25]

The Soviet dictator relented only when the Germans were clearly winning, and any help for the insurgents was too little and too late. The city of Warsaw "virtually ceased to exist," wrote Stalin biographer Isaac Deutscher, as perhaps 250,000 died, while the stocky little dictator's heartless stance "sent a shudder of horror through the Allied countries." Deutscher concluded that Stalin "was moved by that unscrupulous rancour and insensible spite of which he had given so much proof during the great purges."[26]

After Poltava and Warsaw, American-Soviet cooperation became ever more strained, exacerbated further within a few weeks by a most unfortunate USAAF mistake. Near Nis, Yugoslavia, American P-38s bombed and strafed a Russian column, thought to be German, and killed a general, two other officers, and several enlisted men. The Fifteenth Air Force believed this terrible incident might never have occurred if the Soviets had been more inclined to work out practical arrangements with their U.S. ally. Nevertheless, the damage had been done, and the Russians then forbade Americans to overfly their military zones without clearance.[27]

By January 1945, the future of American-Soviet relations, viewed realistically, was anything but encouraging. The Soviets had closed two of the three shuttle bases, with only Eastern Command headquarters at

Poltava still operated by American personnel, who had been reduced to a total of two hundred. ("Eastern Command headquarters," in view of the involuntary downsizing, seems a rather grand title that might more appropriately be couched in quotation marks.) Frantic operations clearly were a thing of the past. "The ruthless ambitions of Stalin and the men around him," as Glen Infield observed, "became more and more evident" as the winter wore on.

Aggravating, harassing, and unpredictable restrictions were placed upon Americans in Russia. In his book, George Menzel summarized several of the problems: "American flights would be grounded without a reason given, American rescue teams were not permitted to service American aircraft known to have made forced landings in Poland, and the American practice of removing sick and wounded air crew members from Poltava to Teheran for better care was halted by the Russians."[28]

The Red Air Force sometimes shot down an American plane. No doubt at times the Russians made a mistake; at other times they did not. Surviving crew members occasionally found themselves treated by the Soviets as if they were prisoners of war. When the Russian forces over-ran German prisoner-of-war camps that held U.S. prisoners, they might delay, or even refuse, to return them to U.S. military authorities—always denying any such action, of course. Occasionally, they failed even to notify American authorities of such prisoners, just as they had neglected for weeks to cable Poltava about the safety of Myron King and his crew. Yet the Soviets expected—demanded, in fact—the immediate return of their own troops freed by the U.S. Army from German imprisonment. Relations between the Allies were further aggravated by Soviet espionage in the West. Perhaps the tension created thereby would have been even worse if the Allies had realized the full extent to which Soviet spies were operating. And General A. E. Antonov had told General Deane, as early as mid-December 1944, that no American air forces would be permitted to operate from bases in the Soviet Far East.[29]

Still, in spite of the myriad frustrations and mistreatment of Americans, in spite of figurative slaps in the face time and again, General Deane and Ambassador Harriman continued their quest for Soviet-American cooperation, still seeking those elusive far-eastern Soviet bases and above all, Soviet entry into the war against Japan. For Myron King, their quest became a snare.

12 ★ Orchestrating a Court-Martial

"It has always been my view that the Americans intended to find Myron guilty in order to appease the Russians," said navigator Richard Lowe, who served as a witness at the Moscow court-martial of Myron King, in a telephone conversation sixty-two years after the event. A careful review of the extant, pertinent documents strongly supports Lowe's observation.[1]

In late March 1945, American-Soviet wartime relations arguably reached an all-time low. While some Americans did not, and could not, have realized the full extent of Stalin's dissatisfaction and paranoia, they knew the situation was not good. Many factors were involved, one of which directly related to Myron King. On Friday, March 30, General A. E. Antonov, chief of the Red Army General Staff, penned a letter to General Deane, head of the USMM in Moscow, complaining of "a number of instances when crews of American airplanes and individual military personnel of the American Army rudely violated the order established by the Command of the Red Army in territory occupied by the Soviet troops, and did not live up to elementary rules of a relationship between friendly nations."[2]

General Antonov then described three instances of alleged violations. One of these involved King and his crew. According to Antonov, "On 5 February, 1945, an American B-17 airplane, Lieutenant Myron King commander of the plane, made a landing at Kuflevo (Poland) where, without the knowledge of the Soviet military command, he took a civilian in the plane for the purpose of taking him to England." Continuing his inaccurate and misleading account, Antonov said King's plane made a second landing "where the person taken on the plane gave himself first of all as a member of the crew of the plane, with the name Jack Smith, and the crew covered him." Next claiming that King acknowledged planning to take the man to England, Antonov stated that "this civilian person admitted that the name Jack Smith was fictitious and that actually he was a Pole." According to Soviet information, asserted Antonov, the man "is a terrorist-saboteur, brought into Poland from London."[3]

The second event related by the Russian general involved an American B-24 of the Fifteenth Air Force, commanded by First Lieutenant Donald R. Bridge, which landed at Mielec, Poland, on March 22 because it was running low on fuel after a bombing mission. Two days later, the bomber having been refueled, Bridge and his crew took off and flew to Italy after being ordered by the base commander not to leave the airfield without Russian permission; this departure occurred even though control signals (red flares) forbidding the flight were fired as the Liberator turned and began its takeoff run. General Antonov charged that "these actions of the American crew called forth extreme indignation and perplexity on the part of the personnel of the Red Army Air Force." Furthermore, he even claimed that "a Soviet Engineer-Captain" by the name of Melamedov "was so indignant and put out by this instance that on the very same day he shot himself."[4]

The final example cited by Antonov concerned U.S. Army lieutenant colonel James D. Wilmeth, who had been working in Moscow with General Deane for several weeks at the USMM. In February, as described by Antonov, Wilmeth "was permitted to make the trip from Moscow to Lublin to get acquainted on the spot with the former prisoners of war—Americans." At the end of what the Russian general termed "the established period" of Wilmeth's visit in Lublin, which was declared by Antonov to have been March 11, Wilmeth "refused to leave for Moscow, with the excuse that he did not have instructions from General Deane to return to Moscow, and that he did not consider it necessary for him to hold to the established time of the visit in Lublin." According to Deane's later admission, Wilmeth several times had refused to leave when "invited" to do so.[5]

Lieutenant Colonel Wilmeth's apparent defiance of the Soviets, in not leaving Lublin at "the established time," constituted, in Antonov's perception, "a rude violation of the elementary rights of our friendly mutual relationship." The Russian obviously viewed the matter as on a par with the Bridge and King incidents. The surprising—even incredible—thing about the Wilmeth incident is that General Deane, who decided to move against King with court-martial proceedings in Moscow, then selected the lieutenant colonel to head the prosecution as trial judge advocate in the King case and this in spite of Antonov's complaint against him and the fact that Wilmeth was not a lawyer.

As for the March 30 Antonov communiqué to Deane, the Soviet general closed in a somewhat awkwardly expressed but demanding manner: "I am obliged to remind you that the obligation assumed by you on a strict observance by American military personnel of the order established by the Command of the Red Army on territory occupied by Soviet troops, with regrets, is not being carried out." Clearly, the general expected some kind of action on the part of Deane. "I request you to take the necessary measures to keep us from a repetition of such instances of rude violation of the order established by the Command of the Red Army on territory occupied by Soviet troops," he wrote. "Please inform me on the measures taken by you."[6]

Meanwhile, at the U.S. Embassy in Moscow, on the same day that Antonov was framing his complaints against King, Bridge, and Wilmeth—which was also the same day that the Russians were grounding all American aircraft in Soviet-controlled territory—General Deane and his British counterpart, Admiral Earnest R. Archer, awaited confirmation that their countries' respective ambassadors to the Soviet Union, Averell Harriman and Sir Archibald Clark-Kerr, had succeeded in arranging for a meeting with Stalin on the next day. They would be delivering a top-level cable to the Soviet leader. It had come from General Dwight Eisenhower to inform Stalin of Ike's proposal for "joining hands with your forces" along the Erfurt-Leipzig-Dresden axis, where the American commander aimed "to make my main effort." This would be approximately one hundred miles south of Berlin. Before finalizing his plans, however, Eisenhower believed it "most important" that they be coordinated with Soviet actions, thus perfecting "the liaison between our advancing forces." The Soviets had almost reached the gates of Berlin, and Eisenhower had no intention of contesting the Red Army for its possession—much to the consternation of both Winston Churchill and Bernard Montgomery, the latter having breezily expressed his intention of moving on the capital of the Reich "by autobahn . . . I hope."[7]

In late afternoon on Saturday, March 31, Deane, Harriman, Archer, and Clark-Kerr met with the Soviet leader at the Kremlin to deliver Ike's message. It was the first time that the supreme commander of Allied forces in the West had communicated directly with Stalin. Eisenhower believed that immediate attention at the highest military level was imperative in order to avoid an accidental clash of arms as Anglo-American and Soviet forces approached each other. (And, by way of procedural clarification, all American communication with Stalin went through the U.S. Embassy.) The Soviet premier, upon hearing Eisenhower's message, complimented the Anglo-American strategy outlined by the American general and declared unequivocally that the American commander's proposed "main effort" was a good plan. Although noncommittal about his own strategy, Stalin promised to reply to Eisenhower within twenty-four hours, as soon as he could meet with his military staff.[8]

Actually, what the Soviet leader really thought was that Eisenhower was lying, that the British and Americans intended to race the Russians for the Nazi capital. Through his spies, Stalin knew that two Allied Airborne divisions were being quickly prepared for a drop on Berlin. (It should be noted that such readiness of airborne forces involved only Allied contingency plans, and constituted a fairly routine procedure.) Possibly also, Stalin knew of Montgomery's blustery posturing—his anticipated autobahn excursion to the Reich capital. After all, the British field marshal had freely spoken of Berlin as the ultimate objective of the Allies, and clearly he had in mind the Western Allies. Furthermore, the Russian leader could not believe that Ike, who did once call Berlin "the main prize" (although the German army was always his prime objective), would not be interested in possessing the capital city.

Stalin's paranoia did the rest. Shortly after his Allied guests were gone, Stalin was on the phone, ordering Marshals Zhukov and Koniev to fly to Moscow at once, for an urgent meeting the next day, April 1. "The little allies [*soyuznichki*]," he would tell his commanders on that Easter Sunday, "intend to get to Berlin ahead of the Red Army." The mission for his marshals— and top priority it was—would be to see that the Red Army got there first.[9]

Stalin had become riled about another matter as well. He accused the United States and Great Britain of making a deal with the Germans "behind the back of the Soviet Union" when the Germans attempted to surrender their forces in northern Italy and the Allied commanders had refused Stalin's request for the presence of a Russian observer. On this matter Uncle Joe vented his anger in a fiery letter to President Roosevelt, declaring that he could not understand why the Soviets had been "excluded" from the negotiations and claiming that "the Germans have already taken advantage of the talks with the Allied Command to move three divisions from Northern Italy to the Soviet front." The Soviet leader seemed even more irritated in an insulting note to Roosevelt on April 3. He was "sure" that Anglo-American and German negotiations had "ended in an agreement with the Germans, whereby the German Commander on the Western Front, Marshal [Albert] Kesselring, is to open the front to the Anglo-American troops and let them move east, while the British and Americans have promised, in exchange, to ease the armistice terms for the Germans." Proceeding next to blame the British as the primary instigators of "this unpleasant matter," Stalin then concluded, "And so what we have at the moment is that the Germans on the Western Front have, in fact, ceased the war against Britain and America. At the same time, they continue the war against Russia, the Ally of Britain and the U.S.A. Clearly this situation cannot help preserve and promote trust between our countries."[10]

President Roosevelt obviously was taken aback by the Stalin communiqué. "I have received with astonishment your message of April 3," declared the president in the opening sentence of his response. After attempting to soothe and assure the Soviet leader that he would never "have entered into an agreement with the enemy without first obtaining your full agreement," FDR closed with the following: "Frankly, I cannot avoid a feeling of bitter resentment toward your informers, whoever they are, for such vile misrepresentations of my actions or those of my trusted subordinates."[11]

And then there was Poland—perennial Poland, or so it must sometimes have seemed. Over many months the exasperating Polish issues, particularly involving that unfortunate nation's postwar frontiers and the character of its government, had troubled the relations of the Western powers and the Soviet Union. But at Yalta, some of the British and especially the Americans, meeting in the resort palace built by Nicholas II, the last tsar, came to believe that somehow "the dawn of the new day we had all been praying for" (to quote Harry Hopkins's effervescent appraisal of the supposed achievements of the conference) had at last broken through the seemingly impenetrable gloom of Soviet intransigence.[12]

The Big Three had accepted a United Nations format, a general policy for democratic institutions in Eastern Europe, and, above all, a specific compromise policy for Poland (a subject that consumed more time at the conference than any other). They had agreed upon a postwar plan of government for Germany; and finally, the Soviets (secretly promised the recovery of Far East territories lost in the Russo-Japanese conflict of 1904–5) would enter the war against Japan once Germany had fallen. The Western powers imagined themselves on the verge of succeeding in the grand work—peace, freedom, security—that Woodrow Wilson had envisioned at the end of the Great War. The mood of some Americans bordered on euphoria. The Russians had been "reasonable and farseeing," to again quote Hopkins, and there seemed to be no doubt in the minds of "the President or any of us that we could . . . get along with them peacefully for as far into the future as any of us could imagine." Hopkins's single reservation, ironically, involved what would result "if anything should happen to Stalin." FDR's trusted adviser added, "We felt sure that we could count on him to be reasonable and sensible and understanding."[13]

Within weeks such words came to seem not only naïve but asinine. Less than one month after the alleged unity of Yalta, Stalin had thrown out the government of Rumania and established Rumania's Communist chief as prime minister of the country. Poland was gone, too, the promised free elections never taking place. "Contemptuously," observed Cornelius Ryan, "Stalin seemed to have turned his back on the very heart of the Yalta Pact, which stated that the Allied powers would assist 'peoples liberated from the dominion of Nazi Germany . . . to create democratic institutions of their own choice.'" All of Soviet-occupied Eastern Europe appeared on the brink of Communist domination. During the last days of March, Roosevelt apparently awakened to the reality of Uncle Joe's ruthless territorial designs. When yet another disturbing message arrived from Averell Harriman relating to the disappointing developments in Poland, the president reputedly pounded the arms of his wheelchair and, in near rage, cried out, "Averell is right! We can't do business with Stalin! He has broken every one of the promises he made at Yalta!" It was said that FDR repeated the words again and again.[14]

By early April, realistically speaking, Poland and Eastern Europe were hopelessly lost in the Soviet-Communist sphere. What the Americans still wanted—and that desperately, and in spite of all the problems—was Soviet entry into the war against Japan. Top-level U.S. military advisers continued to tell President Roosevelt that America needed Russian help. They projected that the war in the Pacific would last another year and a half—even with Soviet assistance. Within only a few months, such estimates would prove strikingly inaccurate. Japan was far weaker than most "experts" had thought. The devastating fire raids of the B-29 Super Fortresses, for example, reduced highly flammable Japanese cities to ashes, resulting in hundreds of thousands of deaths, losses comparable to the destruction wreaked by the atomic bombs. Coupled with the U.S. submarine campaign and the Soviet entry into the Pacific war, highlighted by an impressive offensive in Manchuria, the Empire of the Rising Sun fell much sooner than had been anticipated. No one, of course, could have predicted such a result.[15]

Consequently, Roosevelt, Harriman, Deane, and others strove continually to pacify Stalin to the end of insuring Soviet assistance in bringing down Japan. Thus, in the strange twists of fate, the Polish-Soviet experience of Myron King and his crew came to assume an unlikely magnitude. Evidently, around mid-April, the King saga became a subject of discussion at a meeting between General Deane and General

N. V. Slavin, assistant to the chief of staff of the Red Army General Staff. At approximately the same time, Marshal Stalin brought up the King incident to Ambassador Harriman, claiming that American aircraft were coming into Soviet territory for "ulterior purposes," such as getting in touch with the Polish underground. Stalin made reference to a U.S. aircraft landing on a pretext of engine trouble, and then, as the American translator for Harriman testified, the Soviet dictator declared the Americans "immediately flew off with a Pole on board." Quite possibly, General Antonov would never have written his March 30 letter to General Deane, citing King's, Bridge's, and Wilmeth's alleged transgressions, except with the approval and likely the initiative of Uncle Joe. All of this may well have been a Soviet "offensive" to counter and deflect American questions and concerns about how U.S. ex-POWs and downed flyers were being treated by the Russians. The chances are, from the American perspective, that the King episode would have been relegated to the "much-ado-about-nothing" category had it not been for the U.S. determination to pull Russia into the Pacific War, whatever the price of Soviet participation.[16]

★ ★ ★

It is a curious fact, and significant, that even before General Antonov penned his complaints about King, Bridge, and Wilmeth, General Deane had cabled Colonel Thomas K. Hampton at Poltava in a message classified "TOP SECRET," instructing that "charges be drawn against 1st Lieutenant M. L. King . . . without delay and the charges and specifications be radioed to me as soon as drawn." Furthermore, Deane said he was appointing Lieutenant Colonel Wilmeth "as investigating officer to investigate charges after I have seen them." On the same day, March 27, Deane sent another TOP SECRET cable to Hampton, inscribed "for Wilmeth's eyes only" and informing Wilmeth that "I directed Hampton to prefer charges against 1st Lieutenant Myron L. King. You will be appointed investigating officer to investigate charges when I direct you to do so in later communication."

Deane's messages of March 27 are remarkable, particularly when analyzed in the context of Colonel Hampton's cable from Poltava to the

USMM on the previous day. Hampton had stated that, according to the Soviet commander at Poltava, the Russians in Moscow were denying flight clearance for the B-17, piloted by King, to leave Soviet territory: "He says the reason for delay should be known to us, and that the Fortress will not be cleared. . . . [Soviet General] Kovalev's reference to reason for delay [is] *not understood* [emphasis added]. . . . This is the B-17 that was in Poland for 7 weeks unreported." Probably, General Deane, who earlier asked Hampton for more information on King's long stay behind Soviet lines, already knew something of Soviet displeasure about the episode, and that from the Russians in Moscow, before he received the preceding cable from Hampton or the March 30 letter from General Antonov. After all, Deane did not get his requested information from Hampton until March 28. Yet he had already decided to bring charges against King—and had elevated the matter to TOP SECRET.[17]

Equally intriguing in evaluating General Deane's role in the enigmatic developments that led to the court-martial of Myron King are the communiqués between Deane and his chosen investigator, Lieutenant Colonel James Wilmeth. On March 30, Deane cabled Hampton and Wilmeth, instructing that Hampton's charge and specification against King, which of course Hampton had drawn up at the request of Deane, be amended to read as follows: "Charge: Violation of 96th Article of War. Specification: In that First Lieutenant Myron L. King, 0-828453, 614 Bomb Squadron, 401 Bomb Group, while operating an American aircraft in Poland under the auspices of the Red Air Force of the Soviet Union, did at Szczuczyn, Poland, on or about February 5, 1945, willfully conceal from the Soviet authorities that he had transported as stowaway Polish subject from Warsaw, Poland to Szczuczyn, Poland, and did hereby bring discredit on the military service of the U.S." Wilmeth responded that the charge "willful concealment" would be difficult to substantiate, with the trial probably ending in acquittal. He thought "failure to disclose" provided a stronger case for conviction.

Seemingly "reading between the lines" as to what might be prompting Deane's actions, Wilmeth advised, "If trial is needed for political reasons only, then try as charge stands. If King must be punished, then the charges must be able to stand without necessity of Soviet testimony, which, I assume, is neither desirable nor forthcoming." He proceeded to suggest, although again prefacing his advice with the qualifier "if King must be punished," the points that he thought should be emphasized by the prosecution.[18]

"There is no question of trying King for political reasons," shot back General Deane, apparently intent on squelching any such talk or thought—and regardless of the reality. Rather, he declared, King was to be tried for an offense "which brought discredit on the Military service of the United States, and which has hampered our operations and for which he would deserve punishment. If your investigation indicates that there is sufficient basis for bringing him to trial, I authorize you to change the specification in any way that you think would contribute to the best ends of justice and submit such changes to me for approval."[19]

Wilmeth's answering cable probably surprised Deane. Certainly it was not what the general had been seeking from him. "My recommendation is to withdraw the charges," wrote Wilmeth. While acknowledging that he was not in a position to evaluate all the ramifications of the King case, Wilmeth argued that "from a purely practical viewpoint," a trial would consume the time of many officers and men "whose services are more urgently needed in other occupations. To use this time in forcing a pilot's own crew to convict him of a deed in which all were involved and the consequences of which could not be foreseen at the time of commission does not serve the interests of the Government as well as to get the unified crew back into service at the earliest opportunity." Some might think Wilmeth had a strong, well-expressed point.[20]

General Deane responded briefly and pointedly: "Recommendation contained in your T- 3439 April 3 disapproved. Charges should read 'Discredit of Service,' and Lt. King should be brought to trial before a General Court. Request that you request Col. Hampton to recommend composition of Court to me."

And so it was a done deal. Two days later, Deane cabled Hampton that a "General Court Martial [was] being appointed to meet in Moscow. It will include officers from the Mission and two or three air officers from the list recommended by you. Wilmeth will be designated as the Trial Judge Advocate. Request that you inform him."[21]

It was about this time—within a couple of days at the very latest—that Lieutenant Colonel Wilmeth learned that among several incidents generating Soviet displeasure with American servicemen in territory under Soviet control was Wilmeth's own failure, more than once, to leave Lublin when requested to do so by the Soviets. Without a doubt, based on several cables between the USMM and Poltava, dated April 9 and 10, this matter was weighing on Wilmeth's mind.

On April 10, Deane sent to Wilmeth a very interesting and striking message, particularly when viewed in the context of the court-martial proceedings he was orchestrating against King. He sought to reassure Wilmeth that in making a complaint about him, "I feel that [the Soviets] are seizing on this incident and exaggerating the importance they attach to it because of the overall situation, both political and military." (Might not the same have been said of the King case?) As for Wilmeth, in more than one communiqué, he expressed his "regret that I allowed an issue to develop," and understandably, he was very grateful, declaring his "deep appreciation" for Deane's strong support. Deane's choice of Wilmeth as trial judge advocate for the King court-martial must have been pleasing to the general. He now had strong reason to believe he could rely on his man. Wilmeth's own self-interest, to a greater degree than before the Lublin episode, was obviously dependent upon Deane's influence and good will toward him.[22]

General Deane, a veteran of World War I and a career military man, rendered significant service to the United States Army over a period of many years. Of that fact there is no doubt. His service in Russia, which constituted a difficult assignment, generally was commendable. But his handling of the King case—unless there are unknown and pertinent facts that might shed a different light on the matter should they ever be recovered—does not appear to be among his finest moments.

Of the three Americans cited by General Antonov in his March 30 letter of complaint to General Deane, Lieutenant Bridge of the USAAF would face a court-martial in Italy, while Lieutenant King would be tried, not in Poltava, but in Moscow—within sight of the Kremlin. General Deane even informed General Slavin that the King court-martial was to take place in Moscow rather than Poltava because, in essence, the USAAF personnel in Poltava could not be trusted to render a just verdict. While Deane's explanation to Slavin about the change of venue for the King trial was not couched in such specific words, the meaning of his message was clearly to that effect. As for the third American who had drawn the ire of the Red Army's General Antonov, Lieutenant Colonel James Wilmeth of the U.S. Army, West Point class of 1934, General Deane appointed him trial judge advocate of the King court-martial. Myron King obviously needed a defense attorney—a good one.[23]

13 ★ Moscow—The Visit of a Lifetime

EARLY ON SUNDAY MORNING, MARCH 18, 1945—THE SAME DAY THAT
Myron King and his crew, after being detained for weeks by the Russians, flew from Lida to Poltava—Second Lieutenant Leon Dolin, a navigator on a B-17 of the 487th Bomb Group, Eighth Air Force, took off
from his base in Lavenham, England, on a bombing mission to Berlin.
A graduate of New York University Law School, Dolin had been admitted to the New York bar in 1943, shortly before he entered the USAAF.
He and King had never met, but their paths were about to cross in an
unlikely manner.

"We were hit badly . . . on March 18, and we headed east," Dolin
wrote, "pursued by one Messerschmitt who put a few more holes in the
plane" before leaving. Once across the Oder River and over Russian-controlled territory, the crew bailed out. Two Russian planes appeared
and "made a pass at us hanging in our chutes." A little later Dolin
learned that two members of his crew were killed, apparently by the
Russians. "The Russians would not let us see the bodies," he said.

"I had been picked up by a Mongolian Infantry outfit. They spoke
no human tongue," declared the navigator. "I am your friend [which
the American crews had been taught to say in Russian] meant nothing
to the Mongolians. They proceeded to beat the crap out of me," continued Dolin as he recounted his exasperating, terrifying experience,
"and prepared to shoot me, until a Russian officer in a tank showed

up." The Russian tanker's fortuitous appearance saved Dolin's life. Dolin was then taken to the Russian officer's headquarters, where "all was friendly." Two days later, he and the remainder of his crew were flown to Lublin, where he met Lieutenant Colonel James Wilmeth and Lieutenant Colonel Curtis Kingsbury.[1]

Quickly the plot thickened. Wilmeth and Kingsbury were there, stated Dolin, "theoretically to contact all the American Ex-POWs who were in Poland" and give them shots. Lieutenant Colonel Kingsbury was with the Army Medical Corps, and Wilmeth assisted him. "Actually," Dolin declared, "they were clearly there to gather intelligence." The lieutenant said that "there were reports on their desks concerning Red Army Units, armaments, morale, etc." (Perhaps this explains why Wilmeth, if he had not yet gained all the information he sought, did not leave Lublin by the timetable the Russians established.) Within a few days, Lieutenant Dolin and the other members of his crew were transferred to Poltava and there "waited to ship out." Wilmeth and Kingsbury also arrived in Poltava.[2]

"About April 10 or 11," Dolin said, he was "called into a private room where Wilmeth and Kingsbury were sitting together. No one else was present." One of them asked Dolin if he was a lawyer. Upon hearing his affirmation of law school at NYU and admittance to the New York bar, they asked if he had any trial experience. Of course, he did not, having immediately thereafter gone into the USAAF. Next they asked if he knew a Lieutenant King, and upon learning that he had never met King, they inquired if Dolin had any objection to being assistant defense counsel to Kingsbury. "I was told that I was the only American lawyer in Russia and was needed for a Court Martial in Moscow. Nothing important; just wanted to have at least one lawyer there. Nothing else."[3]

Such was the manner in which King acquired a lawyer—commendably a man who seemed both to know his business and to take his duty as assistant defense counsel seriously. Unfortunately, as just noted, Dolin lacked any trial experience. "A day or two later," as Dolin recalled, "we were off to Moscow. There I met King, Sweeney, and two others of the crew, the navigator and engineer." Dolin said he there received access to the pertinent documents concerning the trial. His memory of this procedure is both intriguing and revealing: "I was given the orders, specs, a copy of the U.S. Army Articles of War and permission to read (but no copies) all the correspondence and reports on the case. These were available to me in the U.S. Embassy. I could get no copies, *nor make notes* [emphasis added]. They were marked 'Secret' and were not allowed before the court." Of Lieutenant Colonel Kingsbury, Dolin remarked that "he had made no attempt to read these reports and wouldn't listen to me when I told him about them. A Great Defense Counsel." Myron King affirmed that he had not a single conference with Kingsbury, even though he was in Moscow for a week before the court-martial got underway.[4]

It should be remembered that General Deane had requested Colonel Thomas Hampton to recommend personnel for the composition of the court in the King trial. Hampton had named Lieutenant Colonel M. L. Alexander of the USAAF to be the defense counsel. In fact, Curtis Kingsbury, the doctor with the U.S. Army Medical Corps, was not to be found on the list of personnel suggested by Hampton. But when Deane approved the ten-man court, Alexander was not among the chosen group, and Curtis Kingsbury had been named defense counsel for King. Of course, as noted earlier, James Wilmeth, who had worked with Kingsbury at Lublin, was the trial judge advocate. And those two, Wilmeth and Kingsbury, had lined up Lieutenant Dolin, the only lawyer involved in the entire proceedings, as subordinate to Kingsbury on the defense team.

The Wilmeth-Kingsbury relationship strikes one as a bit of "a strange alliance," to borrow the title of Deane's memoirs, and just possibly might be viewed as a conflict of interest—that is, if one were concerned with a fair and impartial verdict. Of the ten-member court orchestrated by Deane, only three were Air Corps men, with one of those, Lieutenant Dolin, the assistant defense counsel. Of the six voting members, therefore, only two were Air Corps personnel. One well might conclude that the court had been stacked against King. He thought so and believed further that interservice bias against the USAAF had been an issue.[5]

The voting members of the court were Colonel Moses W. Pettigrew, president of the court, and five others: Lieutenant Colonel Francis W. Crandall, Lieutenant Colonel Harry W. Robb, Major John J. Light,

Major Richard E. Conner, and Major Kern C. Hayes. Major Hayes was the "law member," which meant that he had the responsibility to rule on questions of law during the proceedings, including motions made by counsel. But Hayes was not a lawyer; apparently, his only qualification for the job was that he had more general court-martial experience than anyone else available. Lieutenant Dolin said that when the trial started, "I pointed out that the Court was improperly constituted because the law member, Major Hayes, was not a lawyer. He had one year of law school; had dropped out and gone into the army." Dolin's objection was denied, and Dolin recalled that "I was then told by Kingsbury, a doctor and lead counsel, to shut up, cause no trouble, and everything would be o.k."[6]

Others composing the court were Lieutenant Colonel James D. Wilmeth, trial judge advocate; First Lieutenant Serge J. Dankevich, assistant trial judge advocate; Lieutenant Colonel Curtis B. Kingsbury, defense counsel; and Second Lieutenant Leon Dolin, assistant defense counsel. The three men from the USAAF were Robb (who King said had been irritated by this assignment because it had delayed his anticipated return to Italy), Conner, and Dolin.[7]

The trial took place on April 25 and 26, 1945, at the U.S. ambassador's residence, Spaso House, which is located on Mokhavaya Street, a rather short distance from the Kremlin. King, in fact, was billeted in Spaso House, while Lowe, Sweeney, and Pavlas, as Lowe remembered, were quartered at the Red Cross. Spaso House was a large and elaborate mansion constructed before the 1917 revolution; it had been serving as the ambassador's residence since the early 1930s.

The place was quite interesting to a person with King's artistic taste and knowledge. He admired the splendid detail of the great rooms: the moldings, the medallions, the chandeliers, the expansive use of marble, and the impressive columns and capitals. Particularly he remembered the living room and the ballroom. In the ballroom, he recalled, "every piece of furniture, the chairs, the tables, the sideboards—everything—was faced in gold leaf. Everything, except one table. It was gold leaf also, except that the top was black onyx. The onyx was about an inch thick, and there was a spray of Talisman roses inlaid in that black onyx. Every leaf and petal had maybe thirty different pieces of semiprecious stones." He then declared, "Of all the inlaid marble work I have ever seen, whether in a mansion or a museum, nothing has matched that piece of work." Incidentally, Spaso House was featured in one of the 1988 issues of *Architectural Digest*. It is unfortunate that a person of King's interests could not have explored and absorbed the nuances of the exquisite Spaso House under more desirable circumstances.[8]

When the trial got underway, King was arraigned upon the charge of violating the 96th U.S. Army Article of War. Specifically, the charge read:

In that 1st Lieutenant Myron L. King, 401st Bomb Group, 614 Bomb Squadron, did, in Poland, on or about 5 February, 1945, while, as Senior Pilot, operating an American aircraft under the auspices of the Soviet Army, transport, without proper authority, an alien from near Warsaw to Szczuczyn, and did, thereafter, until such alien was removed by Soviet authorities on or about 6 February, 1945, permit this alien to wear U.S. Army flying clothes, and to associate himself with the American aircraft's crew under the name "Jack Smith," known to be an alias, thereby bringing discredit on the military service of the United States.[9]

The next page of the trial transcript records that King entered a plea of "not guilty to the specification and charge." Significantly, the transcript does not contain either the opening statement of the trial judge advocate (although it is noted that he did make one), or the opening statement of the defense counsel (also noted that one was made), both obviously essential for a true record of the proceedings. In fact, Lieutenant Dolin said that when the trial started, "I immediately asked for a change of venue because of the obvious outside pressure." Not only was his motion denied, but it, too, does not appear in the trial transcript.[10]

Furthermore, in examining the introductory pages of the transcript, one observes that Colonel Thomas K. Hampton is named as the "accuser" of King, and he is said to have "investigated the matters" set forth in the charges. Attesting thereto and signing an affidavit confirming Hampton's role as the investigator of the King case was a Captain George Fisher. Apparently, a bit of awkwardness was avoided by not listing General Deane's chosen man, James Wilmeth, as the investigator since he was, of course, serving as trial judge advocate. Perhaps it should be noted that Lieutenant Colonel Wilmeth's "investigation" left something to be desired, as he neglected to interview five of the Maiden's nine crew members. After all, those men had spent as much time with "Jack Smith" at Szczuczyn as did King, Sweeney, Lowe, and Pavlas.[11]

Following five pages of miscellaneous introductory matter, the transcript's next seventeen pages detail the testimony of the first witness called by the prosecution, Second Lieutenant William J. Sweeney. To a remarkable degree, Sweeney's testimony paralleled King's story, as well as that of Lowe and Pavlas, who were called to testify after the copilot. In essence, there simply were no material inconsistencies to be found in their testimonies. Sweeney recounted how, on February 5 at Kuflevo, a Russian General's C-47 landed and immediately taxied up beside the B-17. When Sweeney deplaned from the nose hatch of the bomber and approached the general, the man called Jack Smith was present and acting as interpreter between Sweeney and the general. Neither Sweeney nor King, who came up momentarily, had ever seen Jack Smith before that occasion and naturally assumed that the man, since he acted as interpreter, had arrived with the general's party. Indeed, if he was not with the general's party, his appearance at that particular moment and his role as an interpreter posed a peculiar conundrum: who was he and why was he there?

Sweeney next described what he termed a "hectic time" and "a very dangerous takeoff." His testimony, undeniably clear to any open-minded person, confirms that Jack Smith was, beyond doubt, a stowaway on the Maiden and that his late discovery on board by Pavlas negated any possibility of transferring him to the general's transport, which was at the head of the runway about to begin its takeoff roll. "It seemed only ordinary courtesy to bring along the General's interpreter," Sweeney said, knowing that they too would be landing where the General landed—if they managed to take off.

When Sweeney and the others did discover, at five thousand feet, that he was not the man they had supposed him to be, "we couldn't throw him out," declared Sweeney, who added, "So we took him on to Szczuczyn." That was where the general had decided to land—presumably because, as a non-pilot, he did not like to fly after dark—rather than continue on to Lida, the place he had told King and Sweeney would be their destination. Sweeney also said that he and King, in keeping with accepted American procedures as they understood them, decided to take Jack Smith on to Poltava, which they hoped to reach later that night after refueling, and turn him over to the American authorities at the base. Of course, as matters developed, they were not able to refuel at Szczuczyn; did not see the Russian General again that night; found that the Russians had billeted Jack Smith with their crew; and would be detained for weeks by the Russians at Szczuczyn.[12]

Neither Lowe nor Pavlas was questioned as extensively as was Sweeney. In particular, the prosecution attempted to get Sweeney, Lowe, and Pavlas to state that they knew that Jack Smith was not the real name of the man in question and that he was of Polish nationality. All three men seem to have been wise to Wilmeth's game, however. While they did not think he was an American, none of the three ever indicated that they thought Jack Smith was a Pole. After Sweeney, Lowe, and Pavlas had all testified and were excused from the witness stand, it was clear that no shred of evidence had emerged to indicate that Jack Smith was smuggled on board the Maiden. Nor was there an indication that King and the "skeleton crew" ever had any intention other than surrendering him to the American authorities at Poltava, where they hoped to fly later that night, or on the following day at the latest. No witness, in fact, ever provided even indirect evidence that Jack Smith was anything but a stowaway on the plane.[13]

The next witnesses for the prosecution, following Sweeney, Lowe, and Pavlas, introduced Russian General Antonov's March 30 letter to General Deane. It was in that letter, as previously detailed, that the Russian levied complaints against Lieutenants King and Bridge—and Lieutenant Colonel Wilmeth as well. This led to revealing exchanges between the prosecution and the defense, particularly involving Dolin in his capacity as assistant defense counsel. The prosecution's witnesses in this matter were, first, Major Howard W. Taylor and, second, Captain Henry H. Ware. Major Taylor, U.S. Army, served as the aide-de-camp to General Deane and also as deputy chief of staff for the USMM. He was present merely to identify the letter from Antonov to Deane, which, of course, was in the Russian language. In short order, Captain Ware was called by the prosecution and sworn in to testify. Captain Ware, also of the U.S. Army and attached to the USMM, described himself as the "official interpreter for General Deane" and said that he translated "most of the official Russian documents" that came to Deane's attention.[14]

As the authenticity of Antonov's letter and the translation thereof had been established through the testimony of Taylor and Ware, the prosecution wanted then to introduce the translated copy (the original translation being in the records of the USMM) into the court-martial records. To this the defense objected. Lieutenant Dolin pointed out that "we have had no notice of what the letter contains; no means of knowing whether this letter is derogatory." The defense also questioned "the phraseology in the letter as translated from the Russian meaning to English," which might have resulted in "a more severe form inadvertently used in translation." Another reason for the objection "is that the locale of this court has been changed for a distance of 500 miles for the convenience of the Russians to appear here. They have been requested to be here by the Commanding General of the Mission to give, as properly should be given, their own testimony. If they wish to absent themselves, then this type of testimony should properly be excluded." The objections of the defense were overruled by the law member, Major Hayes, and the Antonov letter was marked Exhibit Number 2 for the Prosecution.[15]

At that point, the trial judge advocate, quite strikingly, began to read excerpts to the court from General Antonov's letter. But Wilmeth chose not to indicate which parts were read and which were not. It seems rather likely that, at the least, he would have omitted the portions critical of his own conduct. He quickly found himself challenged by the defense, whose objection seemed to indicate that Wilmeth had not included the portion of Antonov's letter that concerned him. "Objection is made to the omission of parts of that letter," reads the trial transcript, "based on the fact that the displeasure, if any, shown by this General is based on a number of instances, not just the one before the court." Thus, the rights of the accused, continued Dolin, "are affected injuriously by the reading of these excerpts."[16]

There is no record of the law member ruling on this objection, only that Wilmeth then replied that the court had the entire letter before it. "The other cases mentioned in the letter do not form a part of this trial," he said. Thus, he somewhat cleverly avoided reading into the transcript Russian criticism of his own conduct, which, as George Menzel pointed out, "would have been shared by Lieutenant Colonel Kingsbury, the defense counsel, who was a part of Wilmeth's team at Lublin." Might this have been one of the several occasions when, according to Dolin, Kingsbury told him to "sit down and shut up"?[17]

Not only is there no ruling in the trial transcript on the defense's objection to the reading of selected excerpts from Antonov's letter, but there is also no record therein of the portions that Wilmeth read—yet more instances of the surprising omissions that occur throughout the transcript. After this episode about Antonov's letter, Captain Ware was again called to testify. Questioned whether, as General Deane's interpreter, he had been present "upon occasions at which Soviet official reaction was expressed to the alleged act of Lieutenant King," the captain replied in the affirmative. Particularly, he recalled being present at a meeting between General Deane and General Slavin who, as previously noted, was the assistant to the chief of staff (General Antonov) of the Red Army's General Staff. At that meeting, testified Ware, "General Slavin said that as a result of recently occurred incidents it was necessary for the Soviet General Staff to take protective action to protect themselves against the recurrence of such alleged acts [as that of King]." When asked how many incidents caused Slavin's reaction, Ware said he could name only four. However, he said, "there were implied to be many others, which were not given to us at that time."[18]

Lieutenant Dolin objected to the introduction of such "hearsay evidence," especially with it coming from a meeting that occurred about mid-April, more than two months after King's alleged misconduct, and when "we are in a locale where this testimony can be properly given. We are 200 yards from the Kremlin." He also asked Captain Ware if he had ever heard of the expression "Slavinism," indicating anti-American attitudes characterizing the Russian general Slavin. Ware answered that he had not, even though Dolin then brought out that Ware had spent several years in Russia. Obviously, Dolin, from comments in a 1992 letter, was quite skeptical about the veracity of Ware's response to his "Slavinism" question.

The president of the court then asked Ware whether General Slavin attempted to establish "any degree of seriousness" among the various offenses to which he referred. Ware claimed the King offense "was given particular stress." When questioned further about the other alleged violations by Americans in Russia and Russian-controlled territory, Captain Ware—who, it should be noted, never mentioned the Wilmeth case—clearly confused the Bridge and Morris Shenderoff cases. (The latter will be explained shortly.) Ware mentioned one other case, but failed to recall a name, while painting only a brief and vague account of the alleged instance. Altogether, the captain's testimony left something to be desired. In fact, the prosecution saw fit to acknowledge to the court that Ware was confused about the Bridge and Shenderoff cases.[19]

The next witness for the prosecution was Edward Page Jr., a resident of Spaso House and second secretary of the American Embassy, who described his official duties as an "Interpreter for the Ambassador, and at times general political work." Asked if he had attended any meetings where official Soviet reaction was expressed to King's alleged violation of the order established by the Red Army, Page said that he did and gave the date as April 15. The defense objected to this "hearsay" evidence, contending that it was being given long after the alleged incident and that other events "could have caused or affected the reaction of the Soviets." The objection was overruled, and Page proceeded to read to the court from the notes he said he made at the time of the meeting.

Present upon the occasion of the meeting were the American ambassador, Marshal Stalin, and various interpreters, according to Page. "Marshal Stalin," he said, "stated that it appeared American aircraft were coming into Soviet controlled territory for ulterior purposes." Page further said that Stalin "more or less defined the acts," claiming the American aircraft "were dropping supplies, wireless sets, and getting in touch with the Polish underground." When Ambassador Harriman asked for facts in these cases, Stalin replied that the facts "would be forthcoming later," adding that General Deane "had undoubtedly informed the Ambassador of the case of an airplane coming down on a pretext of engine trouble, had received the help and hospitality of the Russians, and then had immediately flown off with a Pole on board."[20]

Lieutenant Dolin, at this point, made a pertinent observation for the defense, stating that Stalin's primary concern, according to Page's notes, related to "anxiety and worry . . . that our [American] aircraft were dropping supplies and getting in touch with the underground." That concern, declared Dolin, "does not involve the case here. We have no proof that King was ever in touch with the underground."

Responding for the prosecution, James Wilmeth stated that his purpose, in examining Page, was "to bring out that Marshal Stalin took note of this case, the circumstances of which indicate it was Lieutenant King's case, and that his reaction to it was extremely unfavorable." Major Conner, USAAF, spoke up immediately: "I would like to know whether [Stalin] was definitely referring to that incident, whether you have proof that it was this incident that he was referring to. Whether Marshal Stalin mentioned the name of Lieutenant King when he said 'you know of the incident where an aircraft came down and took away a Pole.' Did he or did he not mention Lt. King's name?"

Page admitted, "No, he did not." Further questioning of Page brought out that Stalin did not give the identification number of the aircraft or specify where the alleged incident took place. And Page had no idea, not even an approximation, because Stalin gave no other examples, of "how many incidents did form the basis of the unfavorable comment of Marshal Stalin." In summation, Page's impression of the major cause of Stalin's anger had to do with "the general subject of assistance to the underground."[21]

★ ★ ★

After the court took a brief recess, all personnel were back in their seats by 3:00 p.m., at which time the prosecution called upon Rear Admiral Clarence E. Olsen, U.S. Navy, USMM. Olsen was then acting as head of the USMM in the absence of General Deane, who had left Moscow for Washington, D.C., before the court-martial began. In the course of his testimony, Olsen mentioned other incidents, in addition to the King case, which allegedly led to Soviet displeasure. When requested to expound upon these, he brought up the unfortunate Morris I. Shenderoff.

Shenderoff may have been—he claimed to be—a U.S. citizen, born in Cleveland, Ohio, in 1912, the son of an immigrant building contractor who became a naturalized citizen in 1921. This information, and much more, Shenderoff volunteered on an extensive background interrogation report for American authorities in Italy when he arrived March 22, 1945, on a B-24 flying from a Russian-controlled Hungarian airfield. Shenderoff claimed the pilot of that Liberator, having listened to his story, encouraged him to stow away for a flight to the American base in Bari, Italy.

Morris Shenderoff's story was that his father returned to Russia for a visit in the mid-1920s, but stayed on, and the immediate family, including Morris, afterward joined him. He stated that the Soviets executed his father in 1936, claiming the man was a spy. The son's attempts to return to the United States proved unsuccessful, and in the crisis of the 1941 German attack on Russia, he was conscripted into the Russian army. Wounded and run over by a tank, according to his account, Shenderoff was transferred to the Red Air Force, becoming a maintenance man for Soviet airplanes. In that capacity he contacted the pilots of a B-24 that had made an emergency landing at the base where he was stationed. When the repaired bomber returned to Italy, Shenderoff was on board.[22]

The Russians were not pleased. When word from the United States came through at the USMM in Moscow that Shenderoff was not an American citizen, the Americans at the USMM complied with the Soviet demand for Shenderoff's return to their custody. On April 12, having been flown to Moscow from Bari, Italy, in an American plane, Shenderoff was immediately turned over to the Russians. Myron King had heard of Shenderoff before his name came up during the court-martial. According to King, a story had apparently circulated among the U.S. personnel in the Russian capital that Shenderoff had been executed by the Soviets on the same day that he arrived in Moscow. That was not the only thing that King heard about the Shenderoff case: allegedly, a "deal" had been arranged whereby the United States gave the Russians Shenderoff in return for a clearance (American planes still being grounded) that enabled Averell Harriman to fly from Moscow in time to attend the initial United Nations conference at San Francisco.[23]

Whatever the truth about Shenderoff may have been, it is not difficult to believe that the Russians shot the man. For that matter, one might perhaps be a trifle naïve in ruling out a deal by the Americans for a flight clearance. After all, even though American aircraft were grounded, Ambassador Harriman somehow managed to gain permission to leave Moscow on an American plane—and more than likely General Deane flew with Harriman. In this context, one might note that the U.S. review of Shenderoff's claim to American citizenship, and the denial thereof, had been accomplished in a remarkably short time frame.

When the defense questioned Admiral Olsen about still other incidents that might have ignited Soviet displeasure, particularly involving the American base at Poltava at the time of the Yalta Conference in early February, the admiral was compelled to admit and describe an incident involving Colonel Thomas K. Hampton, commander of the U.S. forces at Poltava. Hampton, flying from the Crimea to Poltava, was refused permission to land until cleared by Moscow. After circling the field several times, and never receiving clearance, the colonel landed anyway. Then he was told, when requesting permission from Moscow to return to the Crimea, that he could not take off. However, because of his duties in making preparations for the upcoming conference of the Big Three at Yalta, Colonel Hampton simply took off without clearance.[24]

The trial transcript provides ample evidence of a multiplicity of incidents involving American military personnel that aggravated the Soviets. One well might observe that the Soviets, over a period of time, had been both extremely sensitive and uncooperative to the point of provoking several of the incidents about which they complained. But that fact was really of no consequence, since the Americans in Russia had no choice except to get along with the Soviets as best they could. And thus it seems that Myron King was the man chosen to suffer for the "sins" of others (to borrow Lieutenant Colonel James Wilmeth's word when he earlier, penitently, expressed to General Deane his regret for "my sin" in overstaying his "established" time, set by the Russians, for visiting Lublin). The prosecution, throughout the court-martial, attempted to demonstrate time and again, directly as well as indirectly, that the grounding of all U.S. aircraft in Soviet-controlled territory resulted from Russian irritation over the King incident.

Actually, the weight of evidence presented leads to a quite different conclusion: that no one incident triggered the Soviet action; rather, a cumulative effect probably best explains the grounding of American planes. After all, the King incident occurred nearly two months before the grounding took place. If any single event did bring on the Soviet action, it just might have been something entirely apart from any of the incidents mentioned or discussed at the King trial. It was possibly something of which the Americans were not even aware—for example, the paranoid Stalin's belief that Eisenhower had lied to him and that the Anglo-American forces intended a campaign to take Berlin before the Russians could enter the German capital. This, as noted earlier, occurred at the very time of the Soviet action in grounding the aircraft. Yet, when all things are considered, the buildup of multiple events displeasing to the Soviets offers the most rational explanation.

Admiral Olsen concluded his testimony with the opinion that "it was an accumulation of events which brought about the [Soviet] reaction which resulted in the grounding of everybody. . . . In my opinion the [King] case was apparently inflated, blown-up, and misrepresented to Marshal Stalin; so that he reacted and caused other reverberations down the line. We have obtained or been given no other incidents relating to Poles."[25]

Of course, no one at the court-martial ever established that Jack Smith was a Pole. There was only the Soviet claim that he was "a Polish terrorist-saboteur." In fact, the Soviets, though they promised to do so, never furnished the Americans with any concrete information to substantiate their several charges against U.S. military personnel—most notably and importantly, the charge of dropping supplies to the Polish anti-Communist underground. They did nothing regarding that matter except make allegations.

The admiral being excused, the prosecution recalled to the stand Major Howard Taylor. He was asked first about the case of Lieutenant Bridge. Essentially, he knew nothing about it but did say that a cable had come in from Italy that very morning stating that a report would be forwarded to the USMM at a later date. (Bridge was tried and found guilty of violating the 96th Article of War, and when, later in 1945, a U.S. Congressman attempted to have the case reopened, the U.S. Army rejected any reconsideration of the matter.)[26]

Next Taylor was questioned about the Shenderoff case. The major did make an interesting observation in this connection about the role of General Deane: "The first I knew of the Shenderoff case was when General Slavin, I think it was, brought it to General Deane's attention. . . . General Deane sent a cable off to Italy about the matter. . . . General Deane said the Soviets wanted the man returned right away and to please get him here." Possibly the most striking thing about Taylor's return testimony concerned the grounding of American aircraft. According to Taylor, the Russians never issued any oral or written order to American personnel that banned U.S. flights. They simply stopped granting flight clearances at the end of March. Nor were Americans ever told specifically that the ban was lifted. The Russians just began granting clearances once again at some time about three weeks, or a little more, into April. Apparently, no Soviet official ever admitted that a grounding had taken place.[27]

After Taylor finished his testimony and withdrew, the prosecution made a closing statement and rested. That statement is not found in the trial transcript. The defense then, in the person of Lieutenant Leon Dolin, moved for a "finding of not guilty as to the Specification and Charge, on the ground that the prosecution has failed to present sufficient evidence to support a finding of guilty as to the Specification and Charge." His motion being denied, Dolin proceeded to make an opening statement that, as noted above, was not included in the trial transcript. Next Dolin called to the stand, as his first witness, Myron King.[28]

★ ★ ★

King then proceeded to tell his story "as I had reviewed it with him," said Dolin in his later account of the proceedings. "Kingsbury," added Dolin, "never talked to him." King's account is straightforward. He wasted no words, gave a complete account, and resisted any temptation to evade, exaggerate, or misrepresent. When questioned, he was articulate and managed to avoid saying anything that might inadvertently have proved embarrassing to his case. Overall, King acquitted himself quite well.[29]

His testimony plainly indicated that Jack Smith was a stowaway on the Maiden. Clearly, too, the stowaway took the coat for altitude flying from the B-17's emergency bag because he was cold. In any case, this could not have constituted the wearing of a "duly prescribed [military] uniform" illegally permitted by King, as alleged by the prosecution, since the coat bore no form of rank or unit insignia. Furthermore, King had nothing to do with allowing the man to wear it anyway, as the stowaway donned the clothing while King was busy flying the plane. Because the weather was very cold when they landed at Szczuczyn, King saw no reason to order the man to take off the coat.

Equally clear, as confirmed by both Sweeney and Lowe, the quartering of Jack Smith with the King Crew at Szczuczyn had been arranged by the Russians. Obviously, too, the long sojourn of the King Crew in Szczuczyn and Lida was engineered by the Russians. King's testimony conveys that his actions throughout the ordeal were essentially reasonable and understandable. The idea that he was attempting to smuggle a Polish "terrorist-saboteur" out of Russian-controlled territory, when one examines all of the evidence, is ludicrous.[30]

Following King's testimony, the defense called Lieutenant Colonel Wilmeth to the stand. Referring back to Admiral Olsen's testimony that "a number of instances besides Lt. King's" had aggravated the Soviets, the defense asked Wilmeth if he could tell the court, based upon the information he had gathered while in Lublin, the approximate number of American airplanes "which have landed behind the Russian lines in recent months." Prefacing his answer by cautioning that "this is hearsay evidence," the lieutenant colonel responded, "The opinion I received from hearing others talk [both in Lublin and Poltava] was to the effect that there were some 50 combat planes down behind the Soviet lines." The defense then made the obvious point that, with all these American combat crews passing through the Russian lines, there had been many possibilities for "annoyances to have sprung up in high Soviet headquarters." The implication was that far too much emphasis was being placed upon the King case.[31]

When the defense rested after the testimony of Wilmeth, the court recalled Major Howard Taylor, who was questioned by the president, Colonel Moses Pettigrew. Taylor, since his previous testimony, had been able to establish the precise dates when American aircraft were grounded, which he said was from March 31 through April 23; the planes based at Poltava, he added, "have never been released." Attesting again to the mysterious ways of Soviet operations, Taylor remarked, "The Russians aren't the type of people who come out and say it was because of this, that we take such action."

Along with the questions and comments of Lieutenant Colonel Francis W. Crandall, the most significant aspect of Taylor's reappearance before the court related to and seemed to confirm "that a number of Russian airplanes had been shot down by American Fortresses." The date when this occurred, assuming that it did occur, not being precisely established, Crandall's impression was that "the ban [on American flights] was imposed for that reason." Crandall wanted to know if that unfortunate event happened "just before the ban was imposed, or whether it was after." Taylor proved unable to answer that question and was excused from the stand. By then it was 6:30 p.m., and the court adjourned until the next day.[32]

★ ★ ★

The court-martial proceedings resumed at 11:05 a.m. on April 26, with the transcript record indicating that all of the court personnel, the prosecution, and the defense "who were present at the close of the previous session in this case" were present at that time. Ernest Pavlas was called back for further questioning. The court wanted more information about his contact with Jack Smith. The implication was that Pavlas, when he found Jack Smith on board the B-17, must have told King more than he earlier reported. This matter was belabored. The law member, in fact, charged, "You hardly made a special trip forward for the purpose of telling [King] that the passenger had an uncle in England. Exactly what did you tell him?" Pavlas responded, quite appropriately, "I am under oath and that is exactly what I told him."[33]

After Pavlas was excused from further interrogation, the president of the court requested that the trial judge advocate read to the court the testimony of Admiral Olsen. As nothing more was recorded about this reading, one is left to speculate about the reason for Pettigrew's action; after all, the court had listened to Olsen's testimony on the previous day. Captain Henry H. Ware was then recalled to the stand. His questioning uncovered nothing of substance that in any way contributed to the case for King's guilt. James Wilmeth was recalled next and asked about his role in the investigation of the King case: first his investigation at Poltava and then a second, or continuing, investigation after he returned to Moscow. An effort was made to clarify the trial judge advocate's stand, first in recommending against a court-martial, and afterward, when it became clear that King would be tried, recommending two different approaches, dependent upon whether the trial was "necessary for political reasons" or "if it was intended to punish [King]."[34]

The most interesting testimony, and probably the most significant, on the second and last day of the court-martial came when Major Howard R. Taylor was recalled. Asked if General Deane had replied to General Antonov's March 30 letter, Taylor stated that Deane wrote a reply to the Russian general on the very next day. Colonel Pettigrew at once asked Taylor to tell the court "the gist of that letter." Taylor said that Deane told Antonov the King case was already being investigated by the Americans. Furthermore, in Taylor's words, General Deane "said he had issued instructions that Lieutenant King should be brought to trial by court-martial, and asked the Soviets if they would have a Soviet officer come, or be represented in some way during the trial. *General Deane made the statement in this letter that he did not think there was any excuse for Lt. King's conduct* [emphasis added]."

This is strikingly indicative that King did not receive a fair trial. All members of the court knew at this point—if not before, as some of them probably did—that Deane considered King guilty, or, at the least, that Deane had put that view before the Russians. And Deane was the commanding general of the USMM in Moscow, superior to all who composed the court. The ugly specter of possible command pressure thus reared its head. This alone would be enough to invalidate a verdict of guilty.

In testimony that took up three pages of transcript, Taylor was also asked if the Soviets ever replied to Deane's invitation "that they have witnesses or representatives at the trial." The major responded that at a meeting of Deane and General Slavin on April 4, Slavin "said he thought it would be quite out of order to have Soviets as witnesses in a purely American case." In a very interesting commentary on Russian procedures, Taylor related that Slavin had implied "that the requirement for testimony of eye-witnesses would be an insult to General Antonov, who had already given General Deane an official letter—that is the letter of 30 March, which outlined the whole thing." But, of course, that letter provided no evidence, only charges. And no evidence, despite the promise, ever came from the Soviets.[35]

When Major Taylor was excused from the stand, the testimony of King from the previous day was read to the court at the request of President Pettigrew. Then followed oral arguments by the defense and the prosecution. Years later, Lieutenant Dolin said, "In summation, I tried to point out all the problems [with the case of the prosecution]. Kingsbury said nothing." Although no credible evidence had been presented to support the charges against King, the court found him guilty. His punishment was to be reprimanded and to forfeit $100 per month of his pay for six months. "After the sentence," recalled Dolin, "I felt lousy because King felt lousy. He wanted to make the Air Corps a career, and this would destroy it. At that point, Pettigrew came over and thanked me for the good job I had done. He then told me: 'Don't worry. When this gets back to Washington for review, it will be set aside. I am making such a recommendation.' I told this to King and he seemed to feel better." Dolin then added that "the case was so obviously staged for Stalin's benefit that I could see no other result." Years later, King described the whole affair as simply "a big farce."

George Menzel recorded that in all of his research in the King court-martial file and other files examined in Washington, D.C., he never found such a recommendation from Pettigrew. This does not necessarily mean that Pettigrew never wrote the promised recommendation; certainly someone could have removed it from the records of the court martial. It should also be noted that the court, having declared King guilty, then formulated a petition, signed by every member of the court, not just the voting members, recommending clemency for King because of his youth and his lack of intention to violate any army regulations.[36]

★ ★ ★

When the court-martial was over, the Americans at the USMM moved to get King out of Moscow as quickly as possible—the very next morning, in fact. Up to that time, according to King, he, along with Sweeney, Lowe and Pavlas, had been free to roam about the city, although always in the company of a Russian interpreter. King said they never trusted the Russian, believing that the man was reporting to the Soviets on the activities and conversations of the Americans. After the court-martial, however, their situation was quite different. The U.S. military arranged, with marked secrecy, to transport King and the others from the Soviet capital at once.[37]

King said that Brigadier Generals William L. Ritchie and Frank N. Roberts of the USMM feared that the Russians might consider the sentence King had received as too lenient. They were concerned that the Soviets might spirit him away to administer their own punishment, and that was why they wanted to get him out of Russia so quickly. King said that the brigadiers formulated a closely run schedule to fly him out the next morning. He described how General Ritchie sneaked him out the back door of the embassy and into a waiting car. They proceeded at once to pick up Sweeney, Lowe, Pavlas and Dolin, who had been prepared for the clandestine departure, and rapidly headed for the airfield where a C-47 waited to fly them to Poltava. Ritchie swore them to secrecy about everything that had happened. Dolin said that when he asked why, he was told the case "was sensitive and should remain so till King was in the U.S.A." King recalled that as they approached the plane, Ritchie said good bye, telling them that as soon as the car stopped, they should board the aircraft immediately. As quickly as they were aboard, the door was closed and the transport took off.[38]

There was reason to be concerned. If the Soviets had been dealing with a man charged with attempting to secret away a Polish anti-Communist agent, it is not difficult to imagine the penalty they likely would have exacted. Almost certainly, it would have been more severe than the sentence King received. Judging from all we know about Soviet methods, the punishment well might have been death.

14 ★ Back to England, Home to the United States

AFTER A ONE-NIGHT STAY IN POLTAVA, KING AND HIS CREW, EXCEPT FOR tail gunner George Atkinson, who had been involved in a traffic accident (and whose situation will be explained shortly), left for England under orders to depart on April 28. The Maiden had been ferried back to Deenethorpe several days before, and thus King and the others flew as passengers on Air Transport Command (ATC). King was feeling a little better. "I just wanted to get out of Russia," he said. "I thought that the minute I got back home, back in the U.S., it would all be set right. But it didn't turn out that way." Meanwhile, the crew got in some sightseeing. The ATC did not fly at night; consequently, the journey took a week, with stopovers at Teheran, Cairo, Athens, Naples, Marseilles, and Paris. King has a picture of himself with several of the crew and other "tourists" who flew on the ATC plane, taken in front of an Egyptian Pyramid.[1]

About the same time that King arrived back in England, General Deane, having returned to Moscow following his trip to the United States, signed a document approving Myron King's court-martial sentence. He also signed a letter of reprimand, called for as a part of the sentence. The harsh tone of the letter is quite striking—and perhaps a bit surprising. It would be difficult to improve upon George Menzel's summation: "It is a particularly strong letter in light of the trial transcript and in consideration of the unanimously signed plea for clemency by the Court Martial members and officers." Menzel went so far as to say that the letter "raises a serious question whether Deane ever really reviewed the proceedings . . . before preparing the letter, or whether he personally prepared it." Indeed, one has to wonder. When Deane wrote his memoirs shortly after the war and referred briefly to the King case, he clearly knew little about it (the most charitable interpretation of his words), remarking that "one [American] crew attempted to smuggle a discontented Polish citizen out of Poland by disguising him in an American uniform."[2]

General Deane's letter of reprimand, in its entirety, reads as follows:

To: First Lieutenant Myron L. King, 401 Bomb Group, 614 Squadron
Subject: Reprimand

1. *On 3 February, 1945, having sought sanctuary for your aircraft and crew in a foreign country, you came under the jurisdiction of the military forces of an ally. Subsequently you transported an unauthorized foreigner to another airfield within the jurisdiction of this ally. Upon arrival, you failed to check the identity of this unauthorized person and did not report him to the proper authorities. You further aggravated this situation by allowing this person to be associated with your crew and to wear U.S. flying clothing, and by otherwise indicating that he was a member of your crew, thus attempting to deceive the military authorities of our ally, until he was sought out and apprehended by them.*

2. *This foreigner, transported and covered by you, was alleged by our ally to be an agent dangerous to their interests. As a result of your misguided and reprehensible actions, our ally assumed that representatives of the U.S. Army were engaged in activities with an ulterior purpose. So seriously were these events received that they were brought to the attention of our Ambassador by the Chief of State of our ally.*

3. *Your abuse of the hospitality and sanctuary offered you by our ally is totally inexcusable.*

4. *Your actions in this case have demonstrated a deplorable lack of judgment and common sense on your part, and have brought discredit upon your organization and upon the Military Service of the United States.*

5. *A copy of this reprimand will be filed with your record.*

John R. Deane, Major General, U.S. Army Commanding General, U.S. Military Mission.[3]

Meanwhile, George Atkinson found himself in serious trouble. As a result, he would not get out of Russia until well into June, and for a while it seemed that he might be there much longer. After King left for Moscow along with the rest of the skeleton crew, which took off from Kuflevo, Sergeant Atkinson volunteered to assist American personnel at Poltava. The Americans were ferrying U.S. Army trucks from the Poltava airfield to a depot warehouse several miles distant, where the vehicles were presented to the Russians rather than being shipped back to the United States. On the face of it, the duty seemed innocent enough. The reality, for Atkinson, proved something else again. On April 19, Atkinson was driving one truck while towing another that had been disabled; the latter was steered by Lieutenant Martin R. Schlau.

Slowing to a speed of about ten miles per hour, according to the account of both Atkinson and Schlau, they crossed some railroad tracks. Immediately afterward, within approximately fifty feet, maybe less, they came upon a parked Russian truck that extended into the road for five or six feet. Atkinson managed to safely skirt the Soviet vehicle, but Schlau clipped the left rear of the unoccupied Russian truck, which, unfortunately, did not have its brakes engaged. The Russian vehicle then rolled forward, off the road, and ran over a Russian woman who chanced to be standing in its path, killing her.

Both the American military and the NKVD (the Soviet internal security police, later replaced by the better-known, infamous KGB) investigated the incident. The Russians claimed the two Americans did not have a towing chain that met their specifications, were exceeding the speed limit, and that the brakes on both American trucks did not work. Although the U.S. investigation (and there were four American witnesses of the accident) indicated that Atkinson could not have been driving faster than fifteen miles per hour, that the brakes on both trucks worked satisfactorily, and that no Americans seemed to know anything about Soviet regulations for a towing chain, the American authorities nevertheless recommended paying twenty-three thousand rubles (nearly two thousand dollars) to the fourteen-year-old daughter of the woman who died—and that before Atkinson and Schlau were brought to trial.

Subsequently charged with manslaughter, the two young airmen were tried, without benefit of legal advice, before a Soviet court presided over by a woman major in the Russian army. Atkinson said the memory of that woman was forever etched in his memory—and that certainly was not a compliment. He also said that both he and Schlau were declared guilty and sentenced to two years of hard labor. "I really believed my government would have let this nineteen-year-old hang," commented the tail-gunner several decades after the event. Then suddenly, inexplicably, a few days after they were sentenced, the case was reopened, and their sentences were suspended.

They were placed on probation, and fined 25 percent of their pay for twelve months. The fine had to be paid before they could leave Russia. Atkinson, to raise the money, had to draw against his future pay. He had no idea—and apparently never did—as to why the original verdict was overturned. Possibly some influential person—American, or maybe even Russian—intervened and convinced high-ranking Soviets (Moscow was involved) that the court had exceeded any rational standard of punishment.

Whatever the explanation may have been, Atkinson, like King, just wanted out of Russia. On about June 18, he at last left Poltava on an ATC flight. Atkinson also felt that he had been deserted by his crew—left alone in Russia while his fate was decided. Myron King said that when he left Poltava, his understanding of the matter was that Atkinson had not been at fault in the accident, which apparently was the truth, and the case soon would be cleared up. In any case, King had orders to leave Poltava immediately, as did the other members of the crew, and could not have stayed longer even if he so wished.[4]

★ ★ ★

Myron arrived back at Deenethorpe just in time for the big victory celebration: VE Day (Victory in Europe). The date was May 8, and it was obviously a memorable occasion. Thousands of flares, rockets, and mortars were set off. In the afternoon, a large number of the men gathered at the control tower to hear an appropriate address by the commanding officer of the 401st, Lieutenant Colonel William T. Seawell. Religious services followed—Catholic, Jewish, and Protestant—for all who cared to attend. More fireworks followed after nightfall, with ample quantities of beer made available for any who desired it, as of course many did.[5]

King and the crew wanted to visit the Maiden, naturally, and Myron soon painted "Mission to Moscow" on the side of the fuselage nose. Richard Lowe saved a photograph of Patsy DeVito, Robert Pyne, Ernest Pavlas, and Myron and himself standing beside the plane, with "Mission to Moscow" appearing just above their heads. "Why couldn't they," King asked as he reflected on the fate of the Maiden, "have set that plane aside until they found out a little more about it? That plane—it was history. That B-17 should have been preserved. There was no one B-17 that had as much to do, that was as much involved, I mean, with the initial stages of the Cold War as that plane. Also, it had survived thirty-five missions, and it got back to the United States. But they scrapped it."[6]

In the days that followed, King flew several "missions" with a skeleton crew into Austria, evacuating recently liberated prisoners of war. He said it was satisfying work. He also piloted some observation trips to German targets that the 401st had bombed. These sightseeing excursions carried ground personnel of the 401st in order for them to witness firsthand the destruction wrought by the bombers and crews that they had supported in various ways. These flights were conducted at low altitude and were interesting to the bomber crews, as well as to their passengers.[7]

But going home soon occupied the thoughts of everyone at Deenethorpe. Dubbed "Operation Home Run," the evacuation of the base that had been the home of the 401st Bomb Group for approximately a year and a half, necessitated a great deal of work. Moving several thousand men and all their equipment, and this at the same time many other bases located in close proximity were also closing down, required much planning, cooperation, and labor. Some planes flew home with their regular crews and carried passengers as well. Other crews, for whatever reasons, were broken up for the journey to the United States. Such was the fate of the King Crew: the enlisted men returned home by ship, as did many of Deenethorpe's non-officer corps, while the officers flew as passengers on bombers. By the last days of May and the first days of June, everyone was heading home. Many of the departing

Americans' English friends came in from the villages and the countryside to express their appreciation for the immense contribution of "the Yanks" and to wish them "the best" as they returned to the States.

Myron King said the bomber on which he came home was scheduled to make a landing at an airfield near the British coast, prior to heading for the Azores. He does not recall the reason for that stop. What he does remember, understandably, was that the pilot missed the location of the field and they found themselves out over the ocean. Turning back toward land, the pilot finally located an airstrip and landed, although he was not at the assigned destination. Then, when he tried to take off (King did note that they were at a fighter base that had a relatively short runway for a bomber), "that pilot got off on the grass, hit a vent pipe, and knocked three or four feet off the end of the wing." Thus, they were delayed for some time while getting the wing repaired. By that time, King said his confidence in that pilot was "not much." Nevertheless, wanting to get home as soon as possible, he stuck with the man. They flew an unusual route, first to the Azores, then turning back to the north, through Newfoundland, and finally into the United States at Bangor, Maine.[8]

Richard Lowe and William Sweeney came back home together as passengers in a B-24 Liberator. Like Myron, they too had some anxious moments while attempting to get out of England. Lowe told both King and George Menzel that the bomber they flew on experienced five aborted attempts to take off, as various mechanical problems plagued the plane. At last it got into the air, and from that point on, thankfully, all essential parts functioned well enough to get them to the United States.[9]

Certainly it is not surprising that when King arrived back in the United States, a high priority, probably the very highest, was to see Eleanor Goodpasture again. He had sent her a wire from Moscow, assuring her he was safe and ignoring the reason for his presence there. He told her he was "having a wonderful time in Moscow." Throwing in a little play on words, King said he was "painting Red town." Perhaps most important, he told her, "Still have hopes for June. All my love. M.K."[10]

Indeed, he did get back into the United States in June. Perhaps he even had hopes, initially, of getting married that month. Soon he and

Eleanor were planning their wedding, which occurred just one day before the Japanese surrendered, which meant that Myron would not be facing a deployment to the Pacific theater—wonderful news, obviously. They were married on August 13, 1945, with Eleanor's father, B. C. Goodpasture, a well-known Nashville minister, presiding at the ceremony.

15 ★ Vindicated—Finally

RETURNING FROM THEIR HONEYMOON, MYRON AND ELEANOR PROCEEDED to "get on with their lives," to employ that popular cliché describing the millions of veterans who were readjusting to civilian life in those postwar years. Utilizing the G.I. Bill, King soon went back to college. He studied at George Peabody College (today a part of Vanderbilt University) and also at Vanderbilt, as well as at the old University of Tennessee at Nashville (later merged with Tennessee State University). In 1948, he earned a bachelor's degree in art from George Peabody.[1]

That same year, he opened a business in Nashville. For $550 he purchased land on Thompson Lane near its intersection with Nolensville Pike and established a small shop, which he called "Lyzon Art Gallery." King specialized in the sale of original art, as well as modern furniture that he designed and crafted. Through the years his business expanded, growing in both size and quality. Myron seemed to have a keen ability to identify artistic talent, with some artists such as Will Edmondson, Red Grooms, and MALVA rising to international fame. Eventually, Lyzon would offer many of their paintings for auction through Sotheby's of London. King also developed a profitable framing business for prints and original works. Lyzon Art Gallery enabled him to work successfully in a field in which he had both talent and passion.[2]

Taking the long view, perhaps it was just as well that his "Mission to Moscow" had eliminated the possibility of a career in the Air Force. But the choice should have been King's to make. Instead, the U.S. military, because of the court-martial verdict, slammed shut that career door. As for his experiences in Soviet-controlled Poland and Russia, King came home anxious to share with people what the Russian leaders were really like, to tell them of the looming threat to peace posed by the Soviet Union. He soon discovered that his message fell upon deaf ears. People did not want to hear about new foreign problems or more challenges. They had just won a great, but costly, victory over vicious enemies bent on world domination. Americans seemed determined to savor their peace—and that, they hoped, for many prosperous years to come.

Worse for King, he realized that most people who did listen to him just did not believe what he told them. They reasoned that surely the Soviets, America's recent ally in the monumental struggle to defeat Nazi Germany, could not be emerging, even if they were Communists, as America's enemy. Worse still, King sensed that some people might be concluding that he was "flak happy," as he expressed it, employing the then-common description for an airman whose mind had been detrimentally affected by prolonged, close exposure to the bursting shells from antiaircraft guns. Soon, therefore, King stopped telling his story.[3]

Not until the Iron Curtain descended upon Eastern Europe and the Soviets blockaded Berlin while also acquiring "the Bomb"—to mention only the most dramatic events—would Americans at last awaken to the fact that the Cold War was upon them. Then King's assessment took on credibility. But by that time, he seldom engaged the topic. His experiences in Soviet-controlled territory, however, weighed heavily on his mind—above all, the way he had been, in essence, "railroaded" by the U.S. Army in the court-martial proceedings.

Anticipating, as he had been led to believe, particularly by Colonel Moses W. Pettigrew, the president of the court in Moscow, that "all would be set right" once he arrived back in the United States, King discovered that suddenly no one in the Army seemed to know anything about what went on in Moscow. Nor did anyone seem to care. And all the proceedings had been classified as SECRET. All Myron possessed was his copy of the trial transcript. It was also a classified document, but fortunately it had been mailed to him at Deenethorpe back in May 1945, as required by law. (And, yes, he also had the stern letter of reprimand from General Deane.) An ex–first lieutenant in the USAAF, King concluded, stood no chance of being heard—unless he could find a powerful champion for his cause.[4]

Naturally, King wondered what, precisely, had driven the U.S. Army to a position of total silence on the issue. All he could do was speculate. Maybe the army, due to ever-increasing tension between the United States and the Soviet Union and fully aware that King had been dealt a grave injustice by his own countrymen, had concluded that any public knowledge of the case just might arouse a sympathetic American outcry, thereby further fueling the wrath of Stalin's regime. Actually that scenario seemed farfetched to King, because he found it difficult to believe that his case could possibly engender a significant reaction from either the Americans or the Soviets. A much more likely explanation, he supposed, was that the army did not want to embarrass the career colonels and generals at the USMM who treated King so shabbily. Better to sacrifice a little lieutenant who, after all, had been neither career military nor U.S. Army—only a lowly USAAF personage and now a civilian. Never mind that he had risked his life on twenty combat missions over Nazi-occupied Europe, while some of those officers sat at a desk. King realized, of course, that he could muse as much as he might, but he had no hard evidence that he could bring to bear on the question. Also, even if he were right in supposing the latter explanation to be the more plausible and reasonable, what possible good was that to him? He had to find some way to get his case reconsidered. The task seemed herculean.[5]

Then, in 1947, a major event occurred—a development without which King possibly would never have been able to get his case reopened. It was also a highly significant development for the betterment of the U.S. military forces. The air force was officially separated from the army, with the United States Air Force (USAF) becoming a full-fledged department equal in standing to the army. Decisive for King's hopes was a provision hammered out in 1950, which stated that all court-martial cases tried after the attack on Pearl Harbor, December 7, 1941, and involving an accused who was a member of the Army Air Forces, would henceforth be the responsibility of the USAF, rather than the army. For King, to treat with the USAF certainly appeared to be an advantage over the days when the army brass sometimes responded to its air wing as if it were a troublesome, unappreciated, and even undesirable stepchild. But King still needed the support of a powerful personage if he hoped to get results. He had to find someone with major clout in the U.S. government, someone who could demand attention for his cause.

Unlikely though it might seem, but consistent with several incredible truths of King's experience, the answer was right beside him: his wife. Eleanor came up with what proved to be the crucial contact. Eleanor's close friend Emma Ruth Fox, with whom she had grown up, had a sister named Miriam, who worked in the office of U.S. Senator Pat McCarran of Nevada, then serving as chairman of the Senate Judiciary Committee and as the senior member of the Appropriations Committee. Miriam, in fact, managed the senator's Washington office. Obviously, she was in a position to bring King's case to the senator's attention. After hearing King's story, the senator, according to Myron, said "it is unbelievable that anything like this could have happened." The important thing was that McCarran believed it had happened, and that it must be corrected. And through this contact, King's case came to the attention of the man who would play the single most important role in bringing about a reversal of the court-martial verdict.[6]

This was Lieutenant Colonel John A. Doolan, USAF, an attorney at the Pentagon and an air force liaison officer to the U.S. Senate. Beyond doubt, Doolan at once became fascinated by King's case. Apparently—and fortunately for King, who deserved a bit of good luck—it became a pet project for the colonel during 1951. He analyzed the trial transcript provided by King, the only document available, due to the cloak of secrecy, with which he could work. That transcript, however, proved more than sufficient, and Doolan would afterward write of the court-martial: "This is the worst miscarriage of justice I have ever witnessed. To say that a multitude of ignorant practitioners destroys a court is charity to those involved in this scandal."[7]

Finally, it was as if an impenetrable fog of legal entanglement promised to lift, with the anticipation that a few traces of blue sky might soon appear upon King's military horizon. Colonel Doolan pursued his work with a vengeance, and that is hardly an overstatement. Perhaps, too, it should be noted that King's case received some unexpected and widely circulated publicity. In mid-summer of 1951, the nationally syndicated, right-wing Hearst columnist Westbrook Pegler devoted an entire column to the King issue. Where he obtained his information he did not say, probably to the surprise of no one.

Pegler's politics and controversial style had earned him many enemies, but others found him interesting and stimulating. Most important, people read his columns, both friends and foes. Wherever he got his information about the King case, he seemed to have a firm grasp of the basic story. Pegler presented a hard-hitting account, sympathetic to King, of a young man who served his country honorably and bravely in the air war, only to be unjustly treated by his own nation's army. Pegler claimed that King feared justice would never be rendered. The columnist's biting summation was that the case "has been smothered all this time out of the obsequiousness of certain Americans toward the Russians, and later out of a determination, for obvious reasons, to conceal the facts from the American public."[8]

Such sympathy might warm King's heart, but the real "mover and shaker" in whom King now placed his hopes was Colonel Doolan. He would not be disappointed. Even to this author, a Ph.D. in history with no legal training (other than a college course in business law) a careful study of the trial transcript revealed a gross miscarriage of justice. To a man of Doolan's training and experience, the analysis of King's court-martial could only have been an exasperating procedure. On July 30, 1951, Doolan forwarded his appeal on behalf of King to the judge advocate general of the USAF, Major General Reginald C. Harmon. His review document was almost as long, eighty-eight pages, as the trial transcript, which he proceeded to rip apart. When Doolan had finished, the court-martial verdict had been revealed, without a doubt, as an asinine piece of work.

In a damning "Specification of Errors," Doolan listed and convincingly elaborated at length upon ten points, some of which, even standing alone, would demand that the verdict of guilty be overturned. Their cumulative weight was overwhelming. Doolan probably hoped to convince the Air Force JAG that a new trial would be a waste of time and money and that the ridiculous verdict should simply be reversed by the authority of the JAG. The ten errors specified were as follows:

I. *The accused was not adequately and fairly apprised of the nature of the offense intended to be charged against him.*

II. *The Specification is fatally defective in that it alleges more than one offense.*

III. *The facts under the circumstances alleged in the Specification are insufficient to constitute Conduct to the Prejudice of Good Order and Military Discipline or Conduct to the Discredit of the Military Service of the United States.*

IV. *The Specification as found proved by the Court fails to allege facts sufficient to support the charge.*

V. *The findings are based on an error of law materially prejudicial to the substantial rights of the accused.*

VI. *The evidence is insufficient to support the findings of guilty of the Charge and Specification.*

VII. *The findings of the Court are contrary to the weight of the evidence.*

VIII. *The accused has been, by the deficiency of the record, deprived of the right to have the complete proceedings at his trial reviewed in an appellate capacity as provided by the Articles of War.*

IX. *The unanimous recommendation to clemency by the members of the Court constitutes a finding that the accused is not guilty of the charge preferred.*

X. *The members of the Court by their conduct failed to render to the accused a fair and impartial trial.*[9]

Colonel Doolan had done an excellent job for King, crafting thorough and irrefutable arguments—conclusive evidence for any open-minded legal analyst—that the verdict against King was unjust and must be overturned. In a final, thoughtful, summary paragraph, Doolan wrote:

The proceedings fail to exhibit any offense to any person or thing connected with the military service. The accused acted from necessity and was wholly free from wrong or blame in occasioning or producing the necessity which required his action. There is no evidence in the record which reflects adversely on the accused. The conditions under which the trial was held created a mental atmosphere in which reason could not function. The errors of law set forth in this brief are so plainly violative of the fundamental principle of military law and justice that the accused cannot be said to have had a fair trial. Irrespective of the question whether the accused's guilt of the offense charged was established by such portions of the evidence as were competent, he ought not to stand convicted of and be punished for any offense as the result of a trial conducted as was the one under consideration.

Following the foregoing conclusion, Colonel Doolan submitted, as the last page of his petition on behalf of King, a "PRAYER FOR RELIEF," which reads as follows:

1. *That the Judge Advocate General of the Air Force allow oral argument upon this petition.*
2. *That the Judge Advocate General of the Air Force cause such additional investigation to be made and such additional evidence to be secured as he may deem appropriate.*
3. *That Petitioner herein, as indicated in this brief, has been by the deficiency of the record of trial or proceedings, deprived of the right to have the complete proceedings at his trial reviewed in an appellate capacity as provided by the Articles of War. It is requested that the Judge Advocate General of the Air Force obtain the deficient parts of the record and furnish copies thereof to Petitioner herein in order that he may have a complete copy of the record as provided by the Articles of War in order to adequately present his case on oral argument upon this petition.*
4. *That the Judge Advocate General of the Air Force grant a new trial or vacate the sentence adjudged in Petitioner's general court-martial and restore all rights, privileges and property affected by such sentence.*

Clearly, Major General Harmon found Doolan's work convincing. Not only did he determine that a new trial for King would not be required, but he also decided there was no need for King or any witnesses to appear before him for an oral hearing. The JAG's four-and-one-half-page, single-spaced opinion and evaluation of King's case concluded with the following statement: "Therefore, good cause for relief within the provisions of Section 12, Act of 5 May, 1950 (formerly Article of War 53) having been established, the findings of guilty and the sentence are vacated, and all rights, privileges, and property of which accused has been deprived by virtue of the findings and sentence so vacated will be restored."[10]

General Harmon's action was dated January 11, 1952, and Colonel Doolan's letter to King informing him of the decision and enclosing a copy of all pertinent documents bore the date of January 17, 1952. At long last, King had been vindicated. Of course, life was then going well for him, but the good news from the air force was a source of deep personal satisfaction. After the passage of nearly seven years, finally, all had been "set right"—or more precisely, as right as it could be set after the passage of so much time. Notable too, and surely pleasing both to King and his attorney, Colonel Doolan's cover letter revealed that he never had to play what he obviously considered an "ace in the hole," apparently holding it back just in case he might need to strengthen his hand at a last, crucial moment. "In addition to the foregoing," he told King in reference to the ten specifications of errors, "I was prepared, upon oral hearing before the Judge Advocate General of the Air Force, to submit, among additional specification of errors, the fact that you were denied a fair trial because the record in your case shows that at the close of the trial a Major Taylor was called as a witness by the Court, and upon examination by the President of the Court, testified in effect that General Deane, who ordered your court-martial trial, was of the opinion that you were guilty."

Colonel Doolan had well chosen his reserve ammunition. He possessed a blockbusting salvo should it become necessary. "Further," he continued to inform King, "that the record indicates that General Deane, who ordered your court-martial, was the accuser or prosecutor in your case, and acted as reviewing authority; therefore, you were denied a fair and impartial review of your case as provided by the Articles of War." But, as noted above, Doolan had built a compelling case for a redress of King's grievances and never needed his reserve arguments.

Doolan concluded by telling King that he was "getting this letter off in a hurry, so that you will know the official decision and opinion in your case." He promised King that "as soon as I have time, I will write to you in more detail," and then closed, "With kind personal regards to you and your wife."[11]

Epilogue

NEVER AGAIN AFTER THEIR EXPERIENCES IN THE SOVIET UNION WOULD King and all his crew be united. When tail gunner Atkinson finally got away from Poltava, most if not all of the crew had already departed from England for the United States. The Soviet experience would cast a long shadow over the ensuing years, subtly detrimental to the crew's closeness to one another. After the weeks of detention by the Soviets—the apprehension, inevitable tension, and uncertainty of their eventual fate—there seemed little inclination to call up the memory of that perilous time. Some years, at the least, needed to pass. Perhaps there were members of the crew who would never have been interested in a reunion. Very possibly Sergeant Atkinson, for one, never got beyond a gnawing resentment that his crew, as he saw it, had abandoned him; he may also have believed that U.S. authorities had inexcusably refused to support him against the Soviets.

Of course, as the years came and went, there were the usual demands, often consuming demands, upon men in their twenties, thirties, and forties as they strove to succeed in their chosen careers. King and his crew obviously were not immune to such pressures, which always make difficult the maintenance of relationships from younger days. Obviously, too, as people mature, some find little interest in the acquaintances and events of their younger years. Even if the war left King and the others with the most all-consuming memories and emotions of their lives—which likely it did—they still would never be motivated to come together again as a crew.

There were occasional contacts between a few of the men. King and Sweeney visited each other. On one occasion, Myron, Eleanor, and their children visited with the Sweeneys in New York. King and Lowe also saw each other a few times. In fact, Lowe visited King at his Nashville home in the fall of 2006, shortly after work began on this book. King said that Phil Reinoehl had sometimes stopped by Lyzon to see him when he traveled between Indiana and Florida. He also recalled that Lowe and Sweeney had gotten together. Reinoehl had some contact with Lowe. Perhaps there were a few other contacts between crew members as the years passed. Now most of the men are deceased, and there will never be a reunion. That seems a bit sad, when one reflects upon the unique event the crew had shared.

★ ★ ★

The significance of King's war experience, in addition to being a rattling good adventure, lies in its stark relevance—for yesterday, today, and tomorrow. Robert E. Lee's classic summation, as he observed the slaughter at Fredericksburg, rises to mind, still ringing true across the ages: "It is well that war is so terrible, lest we should grow too fond of it." King and his crew had embarked upon "the glorious thing called war," as have thousands of men before and since: with youthful spirit and anticipation, keen to know that grand event in comparison with which, if Patton is to be believed, all other human endeavors pale. Also, they believed that the cause for which they fought was just. Hitler and his Nazi regime must be destroyed; so, too, the empire of Japan. They went to war with flair, buzzing with their new B-17 selected sites in Nashville, Chattanooga, Philadelphia, and Long Island. They arrived in England, somewhat shaken to be sure by the storm through which they had passed, yet primed to get on with the great task at hand.

Right from the first, however, during that raid on Bohlen of November 30, 1944, they confronted the horror of war as they flew one of the costliest missions of the conflict. B-17s went down all around them, some exploding in big balls of fire and smoke. Others spiraled downward, out of control, part of a wing or tail shot away, trailing fire and smoke as they fell. "Our position made it so we could see the planes ahead of us and the ones behind us," said King. "They were just all over the target, you see, going down all around us. I was in shock." And Phil Reinoehl remembered, "I saw planes go down out of the group ahead of us. The sky was black [with flak] . . . and I was never so scared in all of my life as I was when we started over the target."[1]

The reality of war had struck to the depth of their being, never to be erased. And the terrible thing would continue. Later, in 1945, when Warsaw came into view, the sight proved dreadful. "We crisscrossed the city and were horrified at what we encountered," King related. "I had seen heavily damaged cities, but nothing like Warsaw. Sometimes there was a wall or two and a chimney still standing. Many times there was nothing left but rubble. When we found the airport, the runways had been totally bombed out, and the adjacent fields plowed up into trenches."[2]

For most of the crew, it would seem reasonable to conclude, any fondness for war had been permanently leavened by the horrors of the awful, sometimes unspeakable experience. But they did not shrink from their job, carrying out what had to be done with workmanlike dedication and efficiency. When it was all over, they came back home and conducted their lives, not as heroes, but as men who simply did their duty.

★ ★ ★

In brief, summary reflection: Perhaps, if the court-martial had never occurred, Myron King would have pursued a career in the United States Air Force. Perhaps he would have become a commercial airline pilot. Perhaps he would have done exactly what he did. All in all, King deserved commendation for the reasonable, responsible manner in which he conducted himself throughout the long ordeal when he and his crew were under Soviet control. Instead, he received condemnation and that at the hands of fellow Americans who, like him, wore the uniform of their country. The positive aspect is that he at last was vindicated. The shame is that seven years passed before the record was corrected. If not for high-powered support from a U.S. senator, it is sad to say that vindication likely would never have occurred. This author offers one last, if biased, thought: King deserved a Distinguished Flying Cross for getting that B-17 into the air at Kuflevo. *That* was quite a feat.

Notes

Prologue

1. The location and description of the air base known as Station 128 is taken from the information provided for a large display model depicting the field (runways, buildings, planes, and so on) at the Mighty Eighth Air Force Museum in Pooler, Georgia, a suburb of Savannah. Also helpful is John N. Smith, *Deenethorpe,* Airfield Focus No. 37 (Peterborough, UK, 1998), 3–4, and the map on the back cover. Airmen usually spoke of a "Bomb Group" rather than the formal "Bombardment Group" employed in the first paragraph. Thus, Bomb Group will be used henceforth throughout the text.

2. Thomas Parrish, ed., *Simon and Schuster Encyclopedia of World War II,* s.v. "Hermann Göring" (New York, 1978), 243. William L. Shirer, *The Rise and Fall of the Third Reich* (New York, 1960), 517. Walter J. Boyne, *Clash of Wings: World War II in the Air* (New York, 1994), 299. I. C. B. Dear, ed., *The Oxford Companion to World War II,* s.v. "Reichsmarschall Hermann Göring" (New York, 1995), 490.

3. George H. Menzel, *Portrait of a Flying Lady: The Stories of Those She Flew With in Battle* (Paducah, KY, 1994), 129. Bill Schiller, ed., *401st Bomb Group: "The Best Damn Outfit in the USAAF"* (Paducah, KY, 2000), 98. Roger A. Freeman, *The Mighty Eighth: A History of the Units, Men and Machines of the U.S. 8th Air Force* (Osceola, WI, 1991), 113. Vic Maslen, *614th Bombardment Squadron (H) Squadron History, 401st Bombardment Group (H)* (Tampa, FL, n.d.), 110, 127. Vic Maslen, "401st Bombardment Group (H): The Deenethorpe Diary; Flying Control Log Books," Book 3 (Oct. 1, 1944–June 4, 1945), 38, Library and Archives, Mighty Eighth Air Force Museum, Savannah, GA. Martin W. Bowman, *Castles in the Air: The Story of the B-17 Flying Fortresses of the U.S. 8th Air Force* (Wellingborough, Northamptonshire, UK, 1984), 183. Donald L. Miller, *Masters of the Air: America's Bomber Boys Who Fought the Air*

War Against Nazi Germany (New York, 2006), 420. Conrad C. Crane, *Bombs, Cities, and Civilians: American Airpower Strategy in World War II* (Lawrence, KS, 1993), 105–8. The quotation from Tooey Spaatz is found in Miller, p. 420; Eisenhower is quoted in Crane, p. 106.

4. Maslen, "Deenethorpe Diary," 75. Myron L. King, interview with author, Nashville, TN, Jan. 22, 2007. Roger A. Freeman, *Mighty Eighth War Manual* (London, 1984), 12, 13.

5. Freeman, *Mighty Eighth War Manual,* 13.

6. Freeman, *Mighty Eighth War Manual,* 13. Maslen, "Deenethorpe Diary," 75. Menzel, *Portrait,* 130. Robert A. Hand Sr., *Last Raid* (Johnson City, TN, 2006), 10. Myron King interview, Jan. 22, 2007.

7. Freeman, *Mighty Eighth War Manual,* 10, 15.

8. Freeman, *Mighty Eighth War Manual,* 15.

9. Freeman, *Mighty Eighth War Manual,* 16.

10. Maslen, *614th Squadron History,* 128, 114, 122, 123, 124. Menzel, *Portrait,* 9.

11. Maslen, "Deenethorpe Diary," 75. Freeman, *Mighty Eighth War Manual,* 17, 15.

12. Maslen, *614th Squadron History,* 127, 128. Maslen, "Deenethorpe Diary," 75. Runway-length information is taken from the Station 128 display model at the Mighty Eighth Air Force Museum.

13. Freeman, *Mighty Eighth War Manual,* 17. Myron King interview, Sept. 18, 2006. Maslen, *614th Squadron History,* 110, 127, 128.

14. Freeman, *Mighty Eighth War Manual,* 18. Hand, *Last Raid,* 14.

15. Myron King interview, Jan. 5, 2007. Freeman, *Mighty Eighth War Manual,* 19.

16. Maslen, *614th Squadron History,* 127. Menzel, *Portrait,* 129, 244. Myron King interview, Jan. 5, 2007. For further explanation of the design of the combat box, see Thomas M. Coffey, *Iron Eagle: The Turbulent Life of General Curtis LeMay* (New York, 1986), 28–59.

17. Myron King interview, Oct. 5, 2006.

18. Menzel, *Portrait,* 130, 131.

19. Maslen, *614th Squadron History,* 127. Menzel, *Portrait,* 130. Crane, *Bombs, Cities, and Civilians,* 108. Roger A. Freeman, *The Mighty Eighth War Diary* (London, 1981), 433. Schiller, ed., *401st Bomb Group,* 112.

20. Myron King interview, Sept. 18, 2006.

21. Myron King interview, Oct. 5, 2006.

22. Myron King interview, Oct. 5, 2006.

23. Myron King interview, Oct. 5, 2006.

24. Myron King interview, Apr. 30, 2007. Roger A. Freeman, *The Mighty Eighth in Color* (Stillwater, MN, 1992), 141.

25. Myron King interviews, Apr. 30, 2007, Oct. 5, 2006.

1. A Passion for Flying

1. General James H. "Jimmy" Doolittle, with Carroll V. Glines, *I Could Never Be So Lucky Again* (New York, 1992), 170, 167–69, 96–99.

2. Myron King interview, Jan. 5, 2007. Mary S. Lovell, *The Sound of Wings: The Life of Amelia Earhart* (New York, 1989), 176–95.

3. Louise McPhetridge Thaden, *High, Wide, and Frightened* (1938; repr. Fayetteville, AR, 2004), 75–90, vii, 109–22.

4. Ron King (Myron's son), interview with author, Nashville, Feb. 8, 2007. Myron King interview, Feb. 15, 2007.

5. Robert Wohl, *The Spectacle of Flight: Aviation and the Western Imagination, 1920–1950* (New Haven, Connecticut, 2005), 19. Myron King interview, Jan. 5, 2007.

6. Myron King interview, Jan. 5, 2007. Notes written by King on page 297 of his personal copy of Edward Jablonski, *Flying Fortress: The Illustrated Biography of the B-17s and the Men Who Flew Them* (New York, 1965). Tony Wood and Bill Gunston, *Hitler's Luftwaffe: A Pictorial History and Technical Encyclopedia of Hitler's Air Power in World War II* (New York, no date), 133. Kenneth Munson, *German War Birds: From World War I to NATO Ally* (Dorset, England, 1986), 134. Bruce Bissonette, *The Wichita 4: Cessna, Moellendick, Beech & Stearman* (Destin, Florida, 1999), 78–84, 88–102. Bill Yenne, *The Pictorial History of American Aircraft* (New York, 1988), 28–30, 42. Sally Van Wagenen Keil, *Those Wonderful Women in Their Flying Machines: The Unknown Heroines of World War II* (New York, 1979), 43–44, 46. Leslie Haynsworth and David Toomey, *Amelia Earhart's Daughters: The Wild and Glorious Story of American Women Aviators from World War II to the Dawn of the Space Age* (New York, 1998), 19–20.

7. Myron King interview, Jan. 5, 2007.

8. Myron King interviews, Sept. 18, 2006, Oct. 5, 2006, Jan. 5, 2007.

9. Myron King interview, Jan. 5, 2007.

10. Myron King interview, Jan. 5, 2007.

11. Jablonski, *Flying Fortress*, xx–xxii. Martin W. Bowman, *Combat Legend: B-17 Flying Fortress* (Shrewsbury, UK, 2002), 6–7. Dan Patterson and Paul Perkins, *The Lady: Boeing B-17 Flying Fortress* (Charlottesville, VA, 1993), 10.

12. Bowman, *Combat Legend*, 9–10.

13. Jablonski, *Flying Fortress*, 11. Bowman, *Combat Legend*, 10.

14. Bowman, *Combat Legend*, 10–11.

15. Jablonski, *Flying Fortress*, 18–19.

16. Jablonski, *Flying Fortress*, 22–24, 309.

17. Frederick Lewis Allen, *Since Yesterday: The Nineteen-Thirties in America, September 3, 1929 to September 3, 1939* (New York, 1961), 272.

2. And Then There Was a War On

1. Myron King interview, Oct. 5, 2006. Warren M. Bodie and Jeffrey L. Ethell, *World War II War Eagles: Global War in Original Color* (Hiawassee, GA, 1998), 43–44. Bodie and Ethell state that, in 1944 alone, more than twenty-three thousand people were killed while attempting to learn to fly a military airplane, a figure that seems strikingly high. Unquestionably many lives were lost.

2. Myron King interview, Oct. 5, 2006.

3. Bodie and Ethell, *World War II War Eagles,* 80, 44, 73. Myron King interview, Oct. 5, 2006.

4. Edward Jablonski, *Air War: Outraged Skies* (New York, 1971), 40.

5. Myron King interview, Oct. 5, 2006. Eleanor Goodpasture King, interview with author, Nashville, Sept. 5, 2007.

6. Myron King interview, Feb. 15, 2007. Bodie and Ethell, *World War II War Eagles,* 70. Myron King interview, Oct. 5, 2006.

7. Jablonski, *Flying Fortress,* 37, 33–34. Roger Freeman, "Flying Fortress," in *The Great Book of World War II Airplanes* (New York, 1984), 148.

8. Patterson and Perkins, *The Lady,* 11, 13. Bowman, *Combat Legend,* 15. Freeman, "Flying Fortress," 132.

9. Freeman, "Flying Fortress," 141, 147, 132. Patterson and Perkins, *The Lady,* 13. Stephen L. McFarland and Wesley P. Newton, *To Command the Sky: The Battle for Air Superiority over Germany, 1942–1944* (Washington, DC, 1991), 96. Morgan quoted in Miller, *Masters of the Air,* 85.

10. Freeman, "Flying Fortress," 132. Myron King interview, Oct. 5, 2006.

11. Myron King interviews, Oct. 5, 2006, Apr. 30, 2007.

12. Myron King interview, Oct. 5, 2006. Starr Smith, *Jimmy Stewart: Bomber Pilot* (St. Paul, MN, 2005), 67.

13. Myron King interview, Jan. 5, 2007.

14. Myron King interview, Feb. 15, 2007.

15. Myron King interview, Feb. 15, 2007. Menzel, *Portrait,* 123.

16. Richard I. Lowe to author, letter, Mar. 2007. Myron King interview, Oct. 5, 2006. Menzel, *Portrait,* 123.

17. Patterson and Perkins, *The Lady,* 17. Myron King interview, Feb. 15, 2007.

18. Patterson and Perkins, *The Lady,* 19. Richard A. Reinoehl, "Overseas Diary," in possession of Richard A. Reinoehl, Brazil, IN. Schiller, ed., *401st Bomb Group,* 166.

19. Patterson and Perkins, *The Lady,* 16, 17. Myron King interview, Feb. 15, 2007.

20. Menzel, *Portrait,* 124. Patterson and Perkins, *The Lady,* 19.

21. Myron King interview, Jan. 5, 2007. Menzel, *Portrait,* 124.

22. Myron King interview, Feb. 15, 2007.

23. Myron King interview, Feb. 15, 2007.

24. Lowe to author, letter, Mar. 2007.

25. Myron King interview, Apr. 30, 2007. Lowe to author, letters, Mar. 2007, Sept. 2007. Richard A. Reinoehl to author, letter, June 2007.

3. From Savannah to Northamptonshire

1. Myron King interview, Oct. 5, 2006.

2. Myron King interview, Oct. 5, 2006.

3. Myron King interview, Oct. 5, 2006.

4. Myron King interview, Oct. 5, 2006. Reinoehl, "Diary," Oct. 23, 1944.

5. Myron King interview, Oct. 5, 2006.

6. Myron King interview, Oct. 5, 2006. Reinoehl, "Diary," Oct. 23, 1944.

7. Myron King interview, Oct. 5, 2006. Reinoehl, "Diary," Oct. 25, 1944.

8. Reinoehl, "Diary," Oct. 25–Nov. 7, 1944.

9. Myron King interview, Oct. 5, 2006.

10. Reinoehl to author, letter, Feb. 2007. Myron King interviews, Oct. 5, 2006, Oct. 19, 2006.

11. Myron King interview, Oct. 5, 2006, Oct. 19, 2006.

12. Myron King interview, Oct. 5, 2006. Lowe, letter to author, Mar., 2007.

13. Reinoehl, "Diary," Nov. 8–10, 1944. Lowe, letter to author, Mar., 2007.

4. Concerning Those Who Went Before

1. Freeman, *The Mighty Eighth: A History*, 12. Smith, *Jimmy Stewart*, 93. John Fleischman, "In the Footsteps of the Mighty Eighth," *Air and Space Smithsonian Magazine* (Feb.–Mar. 2007): 62–69. On July 4, six American crews, flying American-made, twin-engine Douglas Bostons, the British version of the A-20, and a light-bomber, had participated in a raid on enemy airfields in Holland. See Boyne, *Clash of Wings*, 304.

2. James L. Stokesbury, *A Short History of World War II* (New York, 1980), 281.

3. Walter J. Boyne, *Clash of Wings: World War II in the Air* (New York, 1994), 282–90.

4. Boyne, *Clash of Wings*, 285–90. Stokesbury, *World War II*, 276. See also Tami Davis Biddle, *Rhetoric and Reality in Air Warfare* (Princeton, NJ, 2002).

5. Doolittle, *I Could Never Be So Lucky Again*, 349.

6. Boyne, *Clash of Wings*, 285–86. Miller, *Masters of the Air*, 109.

7. Boyne, *Clash of Wings*, 286. Miller, *Masters of the Air*, 11.

8. McFarland and Newton, *To Command the Sky*, 127–28. Jablonski, *Flying Fortress*, 131.

9. McFarland and Newton, *To Command the Sky*, 128–29. Miller, *Masters of the Air*, 7. Smith, *Jimmy Stewart*, 104.

10. Doolittle, *I Could Never Be So Lucky Again*, 349–50.

11. Boyne, *Clash of Wings*, 284.

12. McFarland and Newton, *To Command the Sky*, 6–7. Michael S. Sherry, *The Rise of American Air Power: The Creation of Armageddon* (New Haven, CT, 1987), 120. Jorg Friedrich, *The Fire: The Bombing of Germany, 1940–1945* (New York, 2002), 51. Wesley Frank Craven and James Lea Cate, *The Army Air Forces in World War II*, 5 vols. (Washington, DC, 1983), vol. 3: 9.

13. Doolittle, *I Could Never Be So Lucky Again*, 353, 352.

14. Doolittle, *I Could Never Be So Lucky Again*, 354.

15. McFarland and Newton, *To Command the Sky*, 57, 167. Doolittle, *I Could Never Be So Lucky Again*, 352–53.

16. Doolittle quoted in McFarland and Newton, *To Command the Sky*, 160–61.

17. Adolf Galland, *The First and the Last: The Rise and Fall of the German Fighter Forces, 1938–1945* (New York, 1954), 273–78. Doolittle, *I Could Never Be So Lucky Again*, 366.

18. Boyne, *Clash of Wings*, 336–37. Doolittle, *I Could Never Be So Lucky Again*, 367.

19. Doolittle, *I Could Never Be So Lucky Again*, 367. Boyne, *Clash of Wings*, 337–38.

5. Into the Thick of It

1. Reinoehl, "Diary," Nov. 10–11, 1944. Craven and Cate, *The Army Air Forces* 3: 92.

2. Myron King interview, Apr. 30, 2007. Craven and Cate, *The Army Air Forces* 3: 84, 87, 89. Menzel, *Portrait*, 40.

3. Schiller, ed., *401st Bomb Group*, 8.

4. Freeman, *The Mighty Eighth: A History*, 154–55, 110. Michael L. Gibson, *Aviation in Northamptonshire: An Illustrated History* (Northampton, UK, 1982), 161.

5. Smith, *Deenethorpe*, 3, 5, 6. Schiller, ed., *401st Bomb Group*, 10.

6. Smith, *Deenethorpe*, 6. Schiller, ed., *401st Bomb Group*, 10–11, 78–80.

7. Menzel, *Portrait*, 1, 4, 8.

8. Myron King interview, Oct. 19, 2006. Reinoehl, "Diary," Nov. 13, 14, 16, 19, 20, 21, 22, 23, 24, 26, and 27, 1944. Myron King interview, Apr. 30, 2007.

9. Maslen, *614th Squadron History*, 107, 108. Schiller, ed., *401st Bomb Group*, 95. Jablonski, *Flying Fortress*, 146. Menzel, *Portrait*, 92. Miller, *Masters of the Air*, 260, 313.

10. Maslen, "Deenethorpe Diary," 35. Lowe to author, letter, Mar. 2007. Richard I. Lowe to George Menzel, letter, Sept. 1991 (copy provided to author by Lowe). Reinoehl, "Diary," Mission #1, Nov. 30, 1944. Maslen, *614th Squadron History*, 108.

11. Maslen, "Deenethorpe Diary," 35.

12. Maslen, "Deenethorpe Diary," 35. Jablonski, *Flying Fortress,* 311. Menzel, *Portrait,* 93.

13. Reinoehl, "Diary," Mission #1, Nov. 30, 1944.

14. Myron King interview, Oct. 19, 2006. Reinoehl Diary, Mission #1, Nov. 30, 1944.

15. Myron King interview, Oct. 19, 2006. Freeman, *The Mighty Eighth: A History,* 181.

16. Myron King interview, Oct. 19, 2006. Menzel, *Portrait,* 93.

17. Myron King interviews, Oct. 5, 2006, Jan. 5, 2007.

18. Freeman, *The Mighty Eighth: A History,* 181. Schiller, ed., *401st Bomb Group,* 15. Maslen, *614th Squadron History,* 107.

6. Berlin, Bad Weather, and "the Bulge"

1. Maslen, *614th Squadron History,* 110.

2. Maslen, "Deenethorpe Diary," 38. Reinoehl, "Diary," Mission #2, Dec. 5, 1944.

3. Menzel, *Portrait,* 95. Maslen, *614th Squadron History,* 110.

4. Hand, *Last Raid,* 11. Reinoehl, "Diary," Mission #2, Dec. 5, 1944. Alkire quoted in Miller, *Masters of the Air,* 11.

5. Maslen, *614th Squadron History,* 110. Reinoehl, "Diary," Mission #2, Dec. 5, 1944.

6. Maslen, "Deenethorpe Diary," 39.

7. Schiller, ed., *401st Bomb Group,* 24. Maslen, *614th Squadron History,* 110.

8. Menzel, *Portrait,* 95. Maslen, *614th Squadron History,* 111. Schiller, ed., *401st Bomb Group,* 35. Myron King interview, Oct. 19, 2006.

9. Myron King interview, Oct. 19, 2006. Reinoehl, "Diary," Mission #3, Dec. 6, 1944. Maslen, *614th Squadron History,* 111. Freeman, *Mighty Eighth War Diary,* 392.

10. Reinoehl, "Diary," Mission #3, Dec. 6, 1944. Maslen, "Deenethorpe Diary," 40.

11. Bowman, *Castles in the Air,* 176. Lowe to author, letter, Sept. 2007. Freeman, *The Mighty Eighth: A History,* 183.

12. Lowe to author, letter, Mar. 2007. Myron King interview, July 9, 2007.

13. Lowe to author, letter, Sept., 2007. Maslen, *614th Squadron History,* 111. Reinoehl, "Diary," Missions #4 and 5, Dec. 11 and 12, 1944. Menzel, *Portrait,* 96.

14. Maslen, *614th Squadron History,* 112. Maslen, "Deenethorpe Diary," 44. Reinoehl, "Diary," Mission #6, Dec. 15, 1944.

15. Myron King interview, Oct. 5, 2006.

16. Lowe to author, letter, Mar. 2007. Reinoehl to author, letter, June 2007.

17. Myron King interviews, Apr. 30, 2007, July 9, 2007.

18. Myron King interviews, Oct. 5, 2006, July 9, 2007.

19. Myron King interview, Oct. 5, 2006.

20. James Lee McDonough and Richard S. Gardner, *Sky Riders: History of the 327/401 Glider Infantry* (Nashville, TN, 1980), 90–91.

21. Freeman, *Mighty Eighth War Diary*, 403. Myron King interview, Jan. 22, 2007. Lowe to author, letter, Sept. 2007.

22. Maslen, "Deenethorpe Diary," 47–48.

23. Menzel, *Portrait*, 99.

24. Myron King interview, Jan. 22, 2007. George Menzel, ed., *Poop From Group* (401st Bomb Group Association newsletter), no. 90, Mar. 1996, 11–12.

25. Smith, *Deenethorpe*, 18–19.

7. From Christmas Eve to Berlin Again

1. Maslen, *614th Squadron History*, 113. Freeman, *Mighty Eighth War Diary*, 403. Menzel, *Portrait*, 100. Reinoehl, "Diary," Mission #7, Dec. 24, 1944.

2. Myron King interview, Oct. 5, 2006.

3. Maslen, *614th Squadron History*, 113. Maslen, "Deenethorpe Diary," 51.

4. Freeman, *Mighty Eighth War Diary*, 403.

5. Myron King interview, Oct. 5, 2006. Freeman, *Mighty Eighth War Diary*, 403–4.

6. Freeman, *Mighty Eighth War Diary*, 400, 404. Myron King interview, Oct. 5, 2006.

7. Reinoehl, "Diary," Mission #7, Dec. 24, 1944. Maslen, *614th Squadron History*, 113. Myron King interview, Oct. 5, 2006.

8. Maslen, "Deenethorpe Diary," 51.

9. Myron King interview, Oct. 5, 2006.

10. James H. Hayes, "Rita Hayworth's Role in the Battle of the Bulge," *Los Angeles Times*, undated clipping in author's possession.

11. Maslen, "Deenethorpe Diary," 52. Maslen, *614th Squadron History*, 114. Menzel, *Portrait*, 103.

12. Reinoehl, "Diary," Mission #8, Dec. 27, 1944. Maslen, "Deenethorpe Diary," 52. Maslen, *614th Squadron History*, 114. Menzel, *Portrait*, 103.

13. Maslen, *614th Squadron History*, 114. Menzel, *Portrait*, 103.

14. Reinoehl, "Diary," Mission #8, Dec. 27, 1944. Maslen, "Deenethorpe Diary," 53. Menzel, *Portrait*, 103.

15. Maslen, *614th Squadron History*, 115, 120, 125. Menzel, *Portrait*, 111–14. Schiller, ed., *401st Bomb Group*, 35.

16. Maslen, *614th Squadron History*, 116. Menzel, *Portrait*, 116–18.

17. Maslen, *614th Squadron History*, 118.

18. Maslen, *614th Squadron History*, 120–25. Reinoehl, "Diary," Mission #16, Jan. 21, 1945.

19. Maslen, "Deenethorpe Diary," 67, 68. Maslen, *614th Squadron History*, 123. Reinoehl, "Diary," Mission #16, Jan. 21, 1945.

20. Maslen, *614th Squadron History*, 123. Myron King interview, July 9, 2007. Reinoehl, "Diary," Mission #16, Jan. 21, 1945.

21. Maslen, *614th Squadron History*, 124. Maslen, "Deenethorpe Diary," 71.

22. Maslen, *614th Squadron History*, 124. Reinoehl, "Diary," Mission #18, Jan. 28, 1944. Maslen, "Deenethorpe Diary," 71.

23. Schiller, ed., *401st Bomb Group*, 16. Smith, "Deenethorpe," 18, 19. The Doolittle quotation is from Schiller.

24. Myron King interviews, Jan. 5, 2007; Feb. 15, 2007.

25. Schiller, ed., *401st Bomb Group*, 16.

26. Freeman, *The Mighty Eighth: A History*, 208.

8. Behind Russian Lines

1. Schiller, ed., *401st Bomb Group*, 16. The latest German figures on the number of civilians killed on February 3, 1945, are much lower than the American. See Jorg Friedrich, *The Fire: The Bombing of Germany, 1940–1945* (New York, 2002), 310. Myron King interview, Feb. 15, 2007.

2. Myron King interviews, Oct. 5, 2006, Feb. 15, 2007.

3. Myron King interview, Oct. 5, 2006.

4. *The Gatefold Book of World War II Warplanes* (New York and London, 1995), s.v. "Aircraft Number 21," n.p. Myron King interview, Oct. 5, 2006.

5. Myron King interview, Oct. 5, 2006. Lowe to George Menzel, letter, Sept. 16, 1991 (copy provided to the author by Lowe, 2007).

6. Myron King interview, July 9, 2007. Lowe to author, letter, Mar. 2007. Also, Lowe to author, letter, Sept. 2007, and Lowe to Menzel, letter, Sept. 16, 1991.

7. Myron King interview, Oct. 5, 2006.

8. Reinoehl, "Diary," Feb. 3, 1945. Menzel, *Portrait,* 139. Myron King interview, Oct. 5, 2006.

9. Myron King interview, Oct. 5, 2006.

10. Myron L. King testimony, Record of Trial by General Court-martial of Myron L. King, Apr. 25–26, 1945, at the American Embassy, Moscow, U.S.S.R (Spaso House), 65–66. A copy of the trial transcript was provided to the author by Myron King and is hereafter referred to as "King trial transcript."

9. A Bizarre Affair

1. Myron King interview, Oct. 5, 2006.

2. William J. Sweeney testimony, King trial transcript, 6–7.

3. Sweeney testimony, King trial transcript, 7. Myron King interview, Oct. 5, 2006.

4. Sweeney testimony, King trial transcript, 7, 15. Myron King interview, Oct. 5, 2006.

5. Sweeney testimony, King trial transcript, 7, 18, 19. Richard I. Lowe testimony, King trial transcript, 27.

6. Freeman, "Flying Fortress," 132. Myron King interview, Oct. 5, 2006. King testimony, King trial transcript, 65.

7. Myron King interview, Oct. 5, 2006. Bowman, *Combat Legend*, 77.

8. Myron King interview, Oct. 5, 2006.

9. Sisson to George Menzel, letter, quoted in Menzel, *Portrait,* 57.

10. Myron King interview, Oct. 5, 2006.

11. Myron King interview, Oct. 5, 2006.

12. Ernest S. Pavlas testimony, King trial transcript, 31. King testimony, King trial transcript, 67. Myron King interview, Oct. 5, 2006.

13. King testimony, King trial transcript, 66–67. Myron King interview, Oct. 5, 2006.

14. Sweeney testimony, King trial transcript, 14, 18. King testimony, King trial transcript, 67.

15. Sweeney testimony, King trial transcript, 12, 13, 15, 18. Lowe testimony, King trial transcript, 25. King testimony, King trial transcript, 67.

16. Myron King interview, Oct. 5, 2006.

17. King testimony, King trial transcript, 67. Myron King interview, Oct. 5, 2006.

18. King testimony, King trial transcript, 67. Sweeney testimony, King trial transcript, 8. Pavlas testimony, King trial transcript, 32.

19. King testimony, King trial transcript, 67. Myron King interviews, Oct. 19, 2006, Oct. 17, 2007. Reinoehl to author, letter, Nov. 9, 2007.

20. King testimony, King trial transcript, 68. Myron King interview, Oct. 19, 2006. Sweeney testimony, King trial transcript, 13.

21. Myron King interview, Oct. 19, 2006.

22. Myron King interview, Oct. 5, 2006. Richard I. Lowe, telephone conversation with author, Nov. 5, 2007.

23. Myron King interviews, Oct. 5, 2006, Oct. 17, 2007.

24. Information on Szczuczyn came from an exhibit at the National World War II Museum, New Orleans, on loan from the Holocaust Museum, Houston, from September 27, 2008, to January 11, 2009. The author visited the exhibit on October 9, 2008. Information also came from Louis D. Levine, ed., *Lives Remembered: A Shtetl Through a Photographer's Eye* (New York, 2002), 32–33. Sweeney testimony, King trial transcript, 8, 16.

25. Myron King interview, Oct. 19, 2006. Reinoehl to author, letter, Nov. 9, 2007.

26. Menzel, *Portrait,* 143.

27. Eleanor Goodpasture King interview, Sept. 5, 2007. Mrs. King also provided a copy of the Fellows letter for my use.

10. The Russian Adventure Darkens

1. King testimony, King trial transcript, 69.
2. King testimony, King trial transcript, 70. Myron King interview, Oct. 5, 2006.
3. King testimony, King trial transcript, 70.
4. King testimony, King trial transcript, 70.
5. Reinoehl, "Diary," Feb. 7, 1945. Myron King interview, Oct. 5, 2006.
6. Myron King interview, Oct. 5, 2006.
7. Reinoehl, "Diary," various entries, Feb.–Mar. 1945. Myron King interview, Oct. 5, 2006.
8. Myron King interview, Oct. 5, 2006.
9. Lowe to author, letter, Mar. 2007. Myron King interview, Oct. 5, 2006.
10. Lowe to Menzel, letter, Sept. 16, 1991. Reinoehl, "Diary," Feb. 22, 23, 1945.
11. Valerie Moolman, *Women Aloft,* The Epic of Flight (Alexandria, VA, 1981), 157–71. Myron King interview, Jan. 22, 2007. *Wings of the Red Star: The Flying Tank, The Ilyushin IL-2 Stormovik,* television documentary shown on the Military Channel, May 2, 2007.
12. Myron King interview, Jan. 22, 2007.
13. Myron King interview, Jan. 22, 2007.
14. Myron King interview, Oct. 19, 2006.
15. Myron King interview, Oct. 19, 2006.
16. Testimony of Sweeney, King trial transcript, 13.
17. Myron King interview, Jan. 22, 2007. Reinoehl, "Diary," Mar. 9, 1945.
18. Myron King interview, Jan. 22, 2007.
19. Myron King interview, Oct. 19, 2006. Lowe to author, letter, Sept. 2007.
20. Glen B. Infield, *The Poltava Affair: A Russian Warning; An American Tragedy* (New York, 1973), 33. Myron King interview, Oct. 19, 2006.
21. Freeman, *The Mighty Eighth: A History,* 158. Infield, *Poltava Affair,* 160, 162, 230–32.
22. Myron King interview, Oct. 5, 2006.
23. Myron King interview, Oct. 5, 2006.
24. Reinoehl, "Diary," Mar. 18, 19, 1945. Myron King interview, Nov. 7, 2007.
25. Myron King interview, Oct. 5, 2006.
26. Myron King interview, Oct. 5, 2006. Myron King interview, Sept. 5, 2007. Menzel, *Portrait,* 168, 169.

11. The Eagle and the Bear

1. William Faulkner, *Requiem for a Nun* (New York, 1951), 92.

2. Robert B. Morris, ed., *Encyclopedia of American History* (New York, 1961), 772. Robert Ergang, *Europe in Our Time: 1914 to the Present* (New York, 1958), 176–77. Isaac Deutscher, *Stalin: A Political Biography* (New York, 1960), 1–26.

3. Ergang, *Europe in Our Time*, 177. Howard Jones, *The Course of American Diplomacy: From the Revolution to the Present* (Chicago, 1988), 342–45. Jerald A. Combs, *The History of American Foreign Policy* (New York, 1986), 228–30.

4. Combs, *American Foreign Policy*, 229–30. Deutscher, *Stalin*, 410.

5. Deutscher, *Stalin*, 410, 376. John R. Deane, *The Strange Alliance: The Story of Our Efforts at Wartime Co-operation with Russia* (New York, 1947), 48.

6. Cornelius Ryan, *The Last Battle* (New York, 1966), 150. John Toland, *The Last 100 Days* (New York, 1965), 91, 44.

7. Ryan, *The Last Battle*, 151. Thomas A. Bailey, *Probing America's Past: A Critical Examination of Major Myths and Misconceptions*, 2 vols. (New York, 1973), 2: 734. Combs, *American Foreign Policy*, 303. Toland, *The Last 100 Days*, 91.

8. Ryan, *The Last Battle*, 149–50.

9. Glen B. Infield, *The Poltava Affair: A Russian Warning; An American Tragedy* (New York, 1973), xi.

10. Jones, *American Diplomacy*, 436. William Faulkner, *Intruder in the Dust* (New York, 1948), 194.

11. Deutscher, *Stalin*, 464. Robert E. Sherwood, *Roosevelt and Hopkins: An Intimate History* (New York, 1948), 339–43. The Stalin quotation appears in both sources, with Deutscher citing Sherwood.

12. Menzel, *Portrait*, 146. Infield, *Poltava Affair*, 3.

13. John Keegan, *The Second World War* (New York, 1989), 451. For summary and analysis of the war on the Russian front, see pages 173–208, and 450–76, of Keegan's book. See also Gerhard L. Weinberg, *A World At Arms: A Global History of World War II* (New York, 1994), 264–99, 447–68, 601–15. Also helpful is Albert Seaton's work *The Russo-German War 1941–45* (New York, 1971). Deutscher, *Stalin*, 530, notes the significance of "Fatherland War" in the mind of Stalin. Michael J. Lyons, *World War II: A Short History* (Englewood Cliffs, NJ, 1994), 249. A. J. P. Taylor, *The Second World War: An Illustrated History* (New York, 1975), 179. James L. Stokesbury, *A Short History of World War II* (New York, 1980), 242.

14. Taylor, *The Second World War*, 180.

15. Robert H. Ferrell, *American Diplomacy: The Twentieth Century* (New York, 1988), 208. Weinberg, *A World At Arms*, 610. Eisenhower quoted in Jones, *American Diplomacy*, 439.

16. Beaverbrook quoted in Taylor, *The Second World War*, 218. Ryan, *The Last Battle*, 240. Weinberg, *A World At Arms*, 609–10.

17. Deane, *The Strange Alliance*, 259, 262.

18. Infield, *Poltava Affair*, 1–14. Menzel, *Portrait*, 148–49. Deane, *The Strange Alliance*, 262.

19. Infield, *Poltava Affair*, xi–xiv.

20. Menzel, *Portrait*, 153. Infield, *Poltava Affair*, 53, 56, 57.

21. Jablonski, *Flying Fortress*, 237, 238, 242, 217. Deane, *The Strange Alliance*, 119, 121. Bowman, *Castles in the Air*, 154. Infield, *Poltava Affair*, 67–83.

22. Infield, *Poltava Affair*, 140–69.

23. Infield, *Poltava Affair*, 178–81. Menzel, *Portrait*, 156–57.

24. Infield, *Poltava Affair*, 207–8. Menzel, *Portrait*, 156–57.

25. Weinberg, *A World At Arms*, 711, for the quotation. See also pp. 708–11, 732–34.

26. Deutscher, *Stalin*, 523, 524.

27. Weinberg, *A World At Arms*, 735. Freeman, *The Mighty Eighth: A History*, 237.

28. Infield, *Poltava*, 237. Menzel, *Portrait*, 160. See also Deane, *The Strange Alliance*, 123, which fully supports Menzel's summation.

29. Weinberg, *A World At Arms*, 737. Infield, *Poltava*, 226–40. Menzel, *Portrait*, 160–61.

12. Orchestrating a Court-Martial

1. Richard Lowe, telephone conversation with author, Nov. 5, 2007. In essence, Lowe expressed the same sentiment to George Menzel in a letter of September 16, 1991, in which he wrote, "I do not remember all the details about the trial. However, it is my firm belief that the Americans were determined to find Myron guilty to appease the Russians."

2. King trial transcript, Prosecution Exhibit #2, copy of letter addressed to Major General John R. Deane, U.S. Army, from General Antonov, dated Mar. 30, 1945; introduced on p. 38 of the King trial transcript; translated from the Russian by Captain Henry H. Ware, U.S. Army, official interpreter for General Deane.

3. King trial transcript, Prosecution Exhibit #2.

4. King trial transcript, Prosecution Exhibit #2.

5. King trial transcript, Prosecution Exhibit #2. Deane, *The Strange Alliance*, 196.

6. King trial transcript, Prosecution Exhibit #2.

7. Ryan, *The Last Battle*, 211–12, 126. Stokesbury, *World War II*, 360. Taylor, *The Second World War*, 220.

8. Ryan, *The Last Battle*, 236.

9. Ryan, *The Last Battle*, 236, 242. Stephen E. Ambrose, *Eisenhower and Berlin, 1945: The Decision to Halt at the Elbe* (New York, 1967), 60. Taylor, *The Second World War*, 221.

10. Stalin quoted in Stewart Richardson, ed., *The Secret History of World War II: The Ultra-Secret Wartime Cables of Roosevelt, Stalin and Churchill* (New York, 1986), 255, 263, 264. Combs, *American Foreign Policy,* 311.

11. Roosevelt quoted in Richardson, ed., *Secret History,* 264–66.

12. Hopkins quoted in Jones, *American Diplomacy,* 456.

13. Ferrell, *American Diplomacy,* 219. Hopkins quoted in Jones, *American Diplomacy,* 456.

14. Ryan, *The Last Battle,* 150–51.

15. Ferrell, *American Diplomacy,* 225, 226.

16. Testimony of Captain Henry H. Ware and Edward Page Jr., King trial transcript, 39–45.

17. Cable, USMM to Poltava (Deane to Hampton) M-23527, Mar. 27, 1945. Cable, USMM to Poltava (Deane to Wilmeth, "for Wilmeth's eyes only"), Mar. 27, 1945. Cable, USMM to Poltava (Edmund W. Hill to Hampton) M-23331, Mar. 21, 1945. Cable, Poltava to USMM (Hampton to Hill) T-3274, Mar. 26, 1945. Cable, Poltava to USMM (Hampton to Hill) T-3322, Mar. 28, 1945. All cables relating to the King case are in the National Archives, Washington, DC, Record Group 334.

18. Cable, USMM to Poltava (Deane to Hampton and Wilmeth) M-23549, Mar. 30, 1945. Cable, Poltava to USMM (Wilmeth to Hill, for Deane) T-3388, Mar. 31, 1945, and T-3405, Apr. 1, 1945.

19. Cable, USMM to Poltava (Deane to Wilmeth) M-23599, Apr. 2, 1945.

20. Cable, Poltava to USMM (Wilmeth to Deane) T-3439, Apr. 3, 1945.

21. Cable, USMM to Poltava (Deane to Wilmeth) M-23641, Apr. 4, 1945. Cable, USMM to Poltava (Deane to Hampton) M-23713, Apr. 6, 1945.

22. Various exchanges between Poltava and the USMM, Apr. 9 and 10, 1945, some in the National Archives and some at the U.S. Air Force Historical Research Center, Maxwell Air Force Base, AL.

23. Menzel, *Portrait,* 178.

13. Moscow—The Visit of a Lifetime

1. Leon Dolin to George Menzel, letter, July 21, 1992 (provided to author by Menzel).

2. Dolin to Menzel, letter, July 21, 1992.

3. Dolin to Menzel, letter, July 21, 1922.

4. Dolin to Menzel, letter, July 21, 1992. Myron King interview, Oct. 19, 2006.

5. Cable, Poltava to USMM (Hampton to Deane) T-3457, Apr. 4, 1945. Listing of the court members, King trial transcript, 2. Myron King interviews, Oct. 19, 2006, Nov. 7, 2007.

6. King trial transcript, 2. Dolin letter, July 21, 1992.

7. King trial transcript, 2. Myron King interview, Oct. 19, 2006.

8. Myron King interview, Oct. 19, 2006.

9. King trial transcript, 4.

10. King trial transcript, 1–5. Lieutenant Colonel John A. Doolan, United States Air Force, Petition on behalf of a New Trial for Myron King, to the Judge Advocate General of the USAF, July 30, 1951, and containing 88 pages of SPECIFICATION OF ERRORS in the King Court Martial, 79 (copy furnished to author by George Menzel). Dolin to Menzel, letter, July 21, 1992.

11. King trial transcript, 2–5.

12. King trial transcript, 6–22.

13. King trial transcript, 6–34.

14. King trial transcript, 35, 36.

15. King trial transcript, 37, 38.

16. King trial transcript, 38.

17. King trial transcript, 38. Menzel, *Portrait,* 177. Dolin to Menzel, letter, July 21, 1992.

18. King trial transcript, 39–42.

19. King trial transcript, 39–43. Dolin to Menzel, letter, July 21, 1992.

20. King trial transcript, 44–45.

21. King trial transcript, 46–48.

22. Menzel, *Portrait,* 180.

23. Myron King interview, Oct. 19, 2006.

24. King trial transcript, 53–54.

25. King trial transcript, 59.

26. King trial transcript, 61. Menzel, *Portrait,* 177.

27. King trial transcript, 62–63.

28. King trial transcript, 63.

29. King trial transcript, 64–81. Dolin to Menzel, letter, July 21, 1992.

30. King trial transcript, 64–81.

31. King trial transcript, 81–83.

32. King trial transcript, 83–86.

33. King trial transcript, 88.

34. King trial transcript, 89–95.

35. King trial transcript, 95–98.

36. King trial transcript, 98. Dolin to Menzel, letter, July 21, 1992. Menzel, *Portrait,* 188. Myron King interview, Oct. 19, 2006.

37. Myron King interview, Oct. 19, 2006.

38. Myron King interview, Oct. 19, 2006. Dolin to Menzel, letter, July 21, 1992.

14. Back to England, Home to the United States

1. Myron King interview, Oct. 19, 2006.

2. Menzel, *Portrait*, 190. Deane, *Strange Alliance*, 123.

3. USMM official letter of reprimand to First Lieutenant Myron L. King from Major General John R. Deane, May 10, 1945, Record Group 334, National Archives, Washington, DC (copy provided to author by Myron L. King).

4. The story of Atkinson's ordeal is primarily based on and summarized from the account presented by George Menzel in his *Portrait of a Flying Lady*, 193–201. Also helpful were King's comments to me on October 19, 2006. Perhaps it should be noted that Glenn Infield (*The Poltava Affair*, 222), relates how Brigadier General William L. Ritchie dramatically saved "an American lieutenant" who had "accidentally killed a Russian woman in an automobile accident near Poltava." However, Infield offered no documentation as to the lieutenant's identity and made no mention of two Americans being involved. Infield may have been writing of another accident. Otherwise, if he refers to Atkinson and Schlau, his account is certainly not complete.

5. Maslen, *614th Squadron History,* 161. Myron King interview, Oct. 19, 2006.

6. Myron King interview, Oct. 19, 2006.

7. Myron King interview, Oct. 19, 2006. Menzel, *Portrait,* 203.

8. Myron King interview, Nov. 7, 2007.

9. Myron King interview, Nov. 7, 2007. Menzel, *Portrait,* 204.

10. Myron King interview, Sept. 5, 2007.

15. Vindicated—Finally

1. Myron King interview, Sept. 5, 2007.

2. Myron King interview, Nov. 7, 2007. Ron King interview, Sept. 5, 2007.

3. Myron King interview, Oct. 19, 2006.

4. Myron King interview, Oct. 19, 2006. Also, King spoke of this subject in several subsequent interviews.

5. Myron King interview, Oct. 19, 2006.

6. Myron King interview, Oct. 5, 2006.

7. The quotation from Doolan's letter came from a copy in Myron King's possession; King brought it to my attention during the interview of October 5, 2006.

8. Westbrook Pegler, "As Pegler Sees It," *Savannah Morning News,* July 6, 1951 (summation and quotation taken from a copy of the column in the possession of Myron King).

9. Copy of the Petition for A New Trial under Section 12 of the Uniform Code of Military Justice, on behalf of accused Myron L. King, submitted to

the Judge Advocate General, Department of the Air Force, by Lieutenant Colonel John A. Doolan, USAF, together with an 88-page SPECIFICATION OF ERRORS and detailed, substantiating argumentation concerning the Court Martial of King. The copy was sent to King by Doolan. George Menzel provided a copy for my use.

10. The quotation from Harmon was taken from the copy of the major general's decision that Doolan mailed to King immediately after the lieutenant colonel acquired a copy of the document.

11. From Doolan's cover letter to King, Jan. 17, 1952.

Epilogue

1. Myron King interview, Oct. 19, 2006. Reinoehl, "Diary," Mission #1, Nov. 30, 1944.

2. Myron King interview, Oct. 5, 2006.

Bibliography

Official Records and Communications

Letter of Major General Reginald C. Harmon, JAG, USAF, overturning the
verdict of the King court-martial, Jan. 11, 1952. Copy in possession of
Myron L. King.

Petition on behalf of a New Trial for Myron L. King, to the Judge Advocate
General of the United States Air Force, July 30, 1951, by Lieutenant
Colonel John A. Doolan, USAF, and containing 88 pages of SPECIFICA-
TION OF ERRORS in the King Court Martial. Copy provided to the author
by George Menzel.

Record of Trial by General Court Martial of Myron L. King, April 25–26,
1945, at the American Embassy, Moscow, U.S.S.R. (Spaso House). Copy
provided to the author by Myron L. King.

United States Military Mission cables to and from Moscow and Poltava, re-
lating to the King court-martial, National Archives, Washington, D.C.
Some cables are also at the U.S. Air Force Historical Research Center,
Maxwell Air Force Base, Alabama. Copies provided to the author by
George Menzel.

USMM official letter of reprimand to First Lieutenant Myron L. King from
Major General John R. Deane, May 10, 1945. National Archives, Washington, DC. Copy provided to the author by Myron L. King.

Manuscript

Maslen, Vic. "401st Bombardment Group (H): The Deenethorpe Diary;
Flying Control Log Books." In the Library and Archives of the Mighty
Eighth Air Force Museum, Pooler, GA.

Letters, Diary, Telephone Conversation

Dolin, Leon, to George Menzel, letter, July 21, 1992. Copy provided for the author's use by Menzel.

Lowe, Richard I. Letters to author, Mar. 2007, Sept. 2007. Also Lowe to George Menzel, Sept. 1991. Copy of the last letter provided for the author's use by Lowe.

———. Telephone conversation with author, Nov. 5, 2007.

Reinoehl, Richard A. Letters to author, June 2007, Nov. 2007.

———. "Overseas Diary." In possession of Richard A. Reinoehl, Brazil, IN.

Interviews

King, Eleanor Goodpasture. Nashville, TN, Sept. 5, 2007.

King, Myron L. Nashville, TN, Sept. 18, 2006; Oct. 5, 2006; Oct. 19, 2006; Jan. 5, 2007; Jan. 22, 2007; Feb. 15, 2007; Apr. 30, 2007; July 9, 2007; Oct. 17, 2007; Nov. 7, 2007.

King, Ron. Nashville, TN, Feb. 8, 2007.

Newspaper Articles

Hayes, James H. "Rita Hayworth's Role in the Battle of the Bulge." *Los Angeles Times,* undated clipping. In author's possession.

Pegler, Westbrook. "As Pegler Sees It." *Savannah Morning News,* July 6, 1951.

Television Documentary

Wings of the Red Star: The Flying Tank, The Ilyushin IL-2 Stormovik. Documentary on the Military Channel, May 2, 2007.

Books

Allen, Frederick Lewis. *Since Yesterday: The Nineteen-Thirties in America, September 3, 1929, to September 3, 1939.* New York, 1961.

Ambrose, Stephen E. *Eisenhower and Berlin, 1945: The Decision to Halt at the Elbe.* New York, 1967.

Biddle, Tami Davis. *Rhetoric and Reality in Air Warfare.* Princeton, NJ, 2002.

Bailey, Thomas A. *Probing America's Past: A Critical Examination of Major Myths and Misconceptions.* 2 vols. New York, 1973.

Bissonette, Bruce. *The Wichita 4: Cessna, Moellendick, Beech, and Steerman.* Destin, FL, 1999.

Bodie, Warren M., and Jeffrey L. Ethell. *World War II War Eagles: Global War in Original Color.* Hiawassee, GA, 1998.

Bowman, Martin W. *Castles in the Air: The Story of the B-17 Flying Fortresses of the U.S. 8th Air Force*. Wellingborough, Northamptonshire, UK, 1984.

———. *Combat Legend: B-17 Flying Fortress*. Shrewsbury, UK, 2002.

Boyne, Walter J. *Clash of Wings: World War II in the Air*. New York, 1994.

Coffey, Thomas M. *Iron Eagle: The Turbulent Life of General Curtis LeMay*. New York, 1986.

Crane, Conrad C. *Bombs, Cities, and Civilians: American Air Power Strategy in World War II*. Lawrence, KS, 1993.

Craven, Wesley Frank, and James Lea Cate. *The Army Air Forces in World War II*. 5 vols. Washington, DC, 1983.   p. 140

Combs, Jerald A. *The History of American Foreign Policy*. New York, 1986.

Deane, John R. *The Strange Alliance: The Story of Our Efforts at Wartime Cooperation with Russia*. New York, 1947.   p. 141

Dear, I. C. B., ed. *The Oxford Companion to World War II*. New York, 1995.

Deutscher, Isaac. *Stalin: A Political Biography*. New York, 1960.

Doolittle, General James H. "Jimmy," with Carrol V. Glines. *I Could Never Be So Lucky Again*. New York, 1992.

Ergang, Robert. *Europe in Our Time: 1914 to the Present*. New York, 1958.

Faulkner, William. *Intruder in the Dust*. New York, 1948.

———. *Requiem for a Nun*. New York, 1951.

Ferrell, Robert H. *American Diplomacy: The Twentieth Century*. New York, 1988.

Freeman, Roger A. *The Mighty Eighth: A History of the Units, Men and Machines of the U.S. 8th Air Force*. Osceola, Wisconsin, 1991.

———. *The Mighty Eighth in Color*. Stillwater, Minnesota, 1992.

———. *The Mighty Eighth War Diary*. London, 1981.

———. *The Mighty Eighth War Manual*. London, 1984.

Friedrich, Jorg. *The Fire: The Bombing of Germany, 1940–45*. Germany, 2002. English translation, New York, 2006.

Galland, Adolph. *The First and the Last: The Rise and Fall of the German Fighter Forces, 1938–1945*. New York, 1954.

The Gatefold Book of World War II Airplanes. New York, 1995.

Gibson, Michael L. *Aviation in Northamptonshire: An Illustrated History*. Northampton, UK, 1982.

The Great Book of World War II Airplanes. New York, 1984.

Hand, Robert A., Sr. *Last Raid*. Johnson City, TN, 2006.

Infield, Glenn B. *The Poltava Affair: A Russian Warning; An American Tragedy*. New York, 1973.

Jablonski, Edward. *Air War: An Illustrated History of Air Power in the Second World War*. 2 vols. New York, 1971.

———. *Flying Fortress: The Illustrated Biography of the B-17s and the Men Who Flew Them*. New York, 1965.

Jones, Howard. *The Course of American Diplomacy: From the Revolution to the Present.* Chicago, 1988.

Keegan, John. *The Second World War.* New York, 1989.

Levine, Louis D., ed. *Lives Remembered: A Shtetl Through a Photographer's Eye.* New York, 2002.

Lovell, Mary S. *The Sound of Wings: The Life of Amelia Earhart.* New York, 1989.

Lyons, Michael J. *World War II: A Short History.* Englewood Cliffs, NJ, 1994.

Maslen, Vic. *614th Bombardment Squadron (H) Squadron History, 401st Bombardment Group(H).* Privately printed, n.d. Copy in the Library and Archives of the Mighty Eighth Air Force Museum, Pooler, GA.

McDonough, James Lee, and Richard S. Gardner. *Sky Riders: History of the 327/401 Glider Infantry.* Nashville, 1980.

McFarland, Stephen L., and Wesley P. Newton. *To Command the Sky: The Battle for Air Superiority over Germany, 1942–1944.* Washington, DC, 1991.

Menzel, George H. *Portrait of a Flying Lady: The Stories of Those She Flew With in Battle.* Paducah, KY, 1994.

Miller, Donald L. *Masters of the Air: America's Bomber Boys Who Fought the Air War Against Nazi Germany.* New York, 2006.

Moolman, Valerie. *Women Aloft.* The Epic of Flight. Alexandria, VA, 1981.

Morris, Robert B., ed. *Encyclopedia of American History.* New York, 1961.

Munson, Kenneth. *German War Birds: From World War I to NATO Ally.* Dorset, UK, 1986.

Parrish, Thomas, ed. *Simon and Schuster Encyclopedia of World War II.* New York, 1978.

Patterson, Dan, and Paul Perkins. *The Lady: Boeing B-17 Flying Fortress.* Charlottesville, VA, 1993.

Richardson, Stewart, ed. *The Secret History of World War II: The Ultra-Secret Wartime Cables of Roosevelt, Stalin and Churchill.* New York, 1986.

Ryan, Cornelius. *The Last Battle.* New York, 1966.

Schaffer, Ronald. *Wings of Judgment: American Bombing in World War II.* New York, 1985.

Schiller, Bill, ed. *401st Bomb Group: "The Best Damn Outfit in the USAAF."* Paducah, KY, 2000.

Seaton, Albert. *The Russo-German War, 1941–1945.* New York, 1971.

Sherry, Michael S. *The Rise of American Air Power: The Creation of Armageddon.* New Haven, CT, 1987.

Shirer, William L. *The Rise and Fall of the Third Reich.* New York, 1960.

Smith, John N. *Deenethorpe.* Airfield Focus No. 37. Peterborough, UK, 1998.

Smith, Starr. *Jimmy Stewart: Bomber Pilot.* St. Paul, MN, 2005.

Stokesbury, James L. *A Short History of World War II.* New York, 1980.

Taylor, A. J. P. *The Second World War: An Illustrated History.* New York, 1975.

Thaden, Louise McPhetridge. *High, Wide, and Frightened*. 1938. Reprint, Fayetteville, AR, 2004.

Toland, John. *The Last 100 Days*. New York, 1965.

Weinberg, Gerhard L. *A World At Arms: A Global History of World War II*. New ⌐ρ. 159 York, 1994.

Wohl, Robert. *The Spectacle of Flight: Aviation and the Western Imagination, 1920–1950*. New Haven, CT, 2005.

Wood, Tony, and Bill Gunston. *Hitler's Luftwaffe: A Pictorial History and Technical Encyclopedia of Hitler's Air Power in World War II*. New York, n.d.

Yenne, Bill. *The Pictorial History of American Aircraft*. New York, 1988.

Index